Communicating Personally

A THEORY OF INTERPERSONAL COMMUNICATION AND HUMAN
RELATIONSHIPS

THE BOBBS-MERRILL SERIES IN *Speech Communication*

RUSSEL R. WINDES, *Editor*

Queens College of the City University of New York

CHARLES M. ROSSITER, JR.
W. BARNETT PEARCE

Communicating Personally

A THEORY OF INTERPERSONAL COMMUNICATION AND HUMAN
RELATIONSHIPS

The Bobbs-Merrill Company, Inc.
INDIANAPOLIS AND NEW YORK

To all those persons who will communicate with our daughters. . . . **Erika, Tasha,** and **Kris.** . . . may they all be honest and validating

The quotations by Gerard Egan on pages 73 and 77–78 are from **Encounter: Group Processes for Interpersonal Growth.** Copyright © 1970 by Wadsworth Publishing Company, Inc. Reprinted by permission of the publisher, Brooks/Cole Publishing Company, Monterey, California.

The rating scales on pages 66, 102, and 107 are adapted from **Helping and Human Relations: A Primer for Lay and Professional Helpers, Volume I: Selection and Training** by Robert Carkhuff. Copyright © 1969 by Holt, Rinehart and Winston, Inc. Adapted and reprinted by permission of Holt, Rinehart and Winston, Inc.

The excerpt on pages 62–63 is from C. S. Forester's **The Captain from Connecticut.** Copyright © 1941 by C. S. Forester. Copyright renewed 1969. Reprinted by permission of Little, Brown and Company and of Harold Matson Company, Inc.

The Bobbs-Merrill Company, Inc.
4300 West 62nd Street
Indianapolis, Indiana 46268

First Edition
First Printing 1975

Library of Congress Cataloging in Publication Data

Rossiter, Charles M. Jr.
  Communicating personally.

  (Speech communication series)
  Bibliography: p.
  Includes index.
    1. Communication—Psychological aspects. I. Pearce, W. Barnett, joint author. II. Title.
BF637.C45R67   155'.2   74–23546
ISBN 0–672–61352–2 (pbk.)

Editor's Foreword

With remarkable industry and minimal reticence, scholars are contributing to our understanding of interpersonal communication. They have described a variety of starting points for analyzing the subject. Research into the process of interpersonal communication has become sophisticated and useful. And, directly to the point, the concept of interpersonal communication has deeply influenced textbooks in speech-communication.

As a broad generalization, the new texts are a first generation effort to argue for the importance of interpersonal communication and to attach the concept to an array of new topics ("communication processes," "communication models," "self-disclosure") and old topics ("group discussion," "public communication"). As we advance beyond these first generation texts, improvements in conceptualization and presentation can be expected.

First, authors will become more discerning, defining the unique areas of concentration in the subject, rather than assaying to encompass every communication situation. Second, the structures appropriate to the study of interpersonal communication will more clearly emerge. Third, the skills essential to effective interpersonal communication will be lucidly described, and means for their improvement suggested. **Communicating Personally** meets these criteria for a second generation text in interpersonal communication.

This book presents an original theory of interpersonal communication. Professors Rossiter and Pearce have perceived a convergence of various writers, especially humanistic psychologists such as Maslow, Rogers, and Jourard, on similar concepts. This observation led them to conclude that **honesty** and **validation** are key concepts which can be used to distinguish forms of interpersonal communication. Since the first report of their work at the Speech Communication Association convention in 1971, they have developed the implications of their basic observation that it is important to view interpersonal communication along a continuum ranging from highly impersonal (minimal honesty and validation) to highly personal (maximum honesty and validation).* This continuum is the basis for the special area of concentration in the text, personal communication.

Communicating Personally represents a second advance in communication textbooks in its unity and coherence. Since the book presents a description and explication of a theory, major terms are defined early and used consistently. There is throughout a logical progression of ideas. In order to facilitate the reader's understanding, the authors emphasize the interrelationships of the chapters.

The third advance represented by this book is the integration of theory and application to the improvement of skills. One of the most important outcomes of the theory of personal communicating is the discovery that different skills are needed to communicate personally than are necessary to communicate impersonally. Throughout the text, exercises, discussion questions, and assignments are suggested which structure the reader's experience in such a way as to facilitate his understanding of the text and to assess and develop interpersonal skills which influence the degree of personalness in his communication.

A theory can often be a belief, and a belief can be the foundation for rigid prescriptions of behavior. The aim of **Communicating Personally** is not, however, to mandate personal communication. The authors have not decreed that one must always communicate in highly personal ways, that self-disclosure is **always** beneficial, or

---

*Pearce, W. Barnett, and Charles M. Rossiter, Jr., "Viewing Communication Along a Personal-Impersonal Continuum," paper presented at the annual conference of the Speech Communication Association, San Francisco, December, 1971.

that one should become more trusting of **all** people. On the contrary, their explicit goal is to increase the reader's awareness of his choices and the choices of others in the process of communication. The merits of communicating with various degrees of personalness are examined and the reader is encouraged to come to an informed decision as to the extent to which he should modify his interpersonal communication behavior.

Russel R. Windes

Contents

ix

Appendices

Author's Foreword

Books about communication are usually categorized as "theory" or "skills" oriented, then used as if they were totally one or the other. We believe that **Communicating Personally** transcends this artificial dichotomy. It is a "theory" book in that we suggest relationships among a set of carefully defined concepts, and it is a "skills" book in that we have not neglected the practical implementation of the behaviors described in the theory.

As we wrote, we envisioned the book being used by a college or university class. We believe that this material and these activities will be a useful supplement in any study of what persons do to and with each other, particularly in courses designed to sensitize or train students to relate to other persons effectively. We have used portions of this material while teaching public speakers, interpersonal and small group communicators, business administrators, nurses, speech therapists, psychological and vocational counselors, and more. Our experience with these students from varied backgrounds and with different interests convinced us that the material in **Communicating Personally** is fundamental to interpersonal relations despite the specific circumstances and that this book may be profitably used in a wide variety of academic disciplines.

Communicating Personally consists of three sections, each of which is "harder" than the preceeding one. This feature of the book makes it useful for introductory as well as advanced classes. The first section describes our understanding of communicating personally and is interspersed with suggested activities for assessing and improving communication skills. The second section is narrower in scope but treats each topic in greater detail. The appendices comprise the third section, and provide reviews of several relevant literatures.

Introductory courses in communication skills might use the first section as assigned readings, spending considerable time with supervised performances or discussions of the suggested activities. Section Two and the appendices would provide resource material for these classes.

Advanced courses in communication might use the first section as a nontechnical overview of the concepts and relationships among concepts which occur in communicating personally, then turn to Section Two and the appendices as starting points for intensive exploration of these topics.

Writing this book has been a more formidable task than we thought it would be. Some parts of the process—such as reading everything we could find on a new topic, or making sense out of a mass of material which was contradictory and incomplete—were much more enjoyable than others. If not for encouragement and support from many people we probably would not have persisted.

We are particularly grateful to the following colleagues, students, and friends: Forrest Conklin; Joe Dwyer; Denamae Fox; Helen Franzwa; Joe Krajcik; Mary Ellen Munley; Carl Weaver; and Ken Williams. Mary Jorgenson and Bill Straub deserve thanks for an outstanding job with various mundane tasks associated with final preparation of the manuscript.

In a tradition for coauthored books which we learned from John Thibaut and Harold Kelley, we each accuse the other for any mistakes of fact or judgment and for any prose more opaque than the rest in Chapters 1, 2, and 3. Although we collaborated on these as well, Barnett must accept primary blame for problems in Chapters 4, 5, 6, and in Appendices A and B. Charles is primarily responsible for Chapters 7, 8, and 9, and Appendices C and D.

CR
WBP

PART I

A Theory of Interpersonal Communication

A theory is a set of statements which systematically describe the relationships among a set of well-defined concepts. Our first five chapters are devoted to an explication of the concepts and statements which make up our theory of interpersonal communication in human relationships. After placing our theory in the context of other ideas about communication we systematically define and explain its basic elements.

ONE

An introduction to our perspective

. . . we noticed a discrepancy between some of our communication experiences and those which we read about . . .

This book is about interpersonal communication and the role it plays in the development and maintenance of human relationships. The way we feel about ourselves, about others, and about life itself depends largely on the relationships we are able to establish with other persons. When we experience warm, close, friendly relationships, our lives are fuller, more meaningful, and more satisfying. When we do not, we feel alone, unloved, and empty.

Satisfying relationships with other persons are established through communication, and our ability to communicate well is important. As you know, sometimes communication seems to "work" and sometimes it does not. When it's working we feel very comfortable, we know what we want to say, we feel that others understand us, and we sense that they know we feel understood. We feel at peace with ourselves and with others. Frustrations and troubles seem less threatening and are more easily resolved.

Communication is not always this way, however. Perhaps you have felt, as we sometimes have, that you were at the bottom of a rock-walled well calling for help and getting no reply. These are the times when we exchange messages with others but our meanings do not touch. We do not feel comfortable and we talk about things that do not really matter, hiding behind a barricade of trivia and deception. At these times our experience affirms the lyrics of the Midnight Cowboy theme: "Everybody's talking at me; Can't hear a word they're saying; Only the echoes of my mind" (Neil, 1967).

We believe that the differences between communication events which foster satisfying human relationships and those which do not depend on the ways the participants in those relationships behave. Some people are skilled at persuading others to believe as they do or at portraying themselves as superior or highly credible while some are better able to invite others to share their experiences and to feel better about themselves. We believe that it is useful to describe these communication behaviors by locating them along a continuum ranging from "highly personal" to "highly impersonal," and that these behaviors structure different types of interpersonal relationships.

A person is **communicating personally** to the extent that he is both honest and validates the person with whom he is interacting. In being honest, an individual accurately describes his awareness of his experience at a given moment and invites the other to share that experience with him. In validating the other, he expresses his understanding and acceptance of the other person as he is at the moment, allowing him to feel worthy and that his experience is worthwhile.

Impersonal communicating occurs to the extent that an individual is not honest and/or not validating. To the extent that he does not reflect how he is at a given moment or attempts to exclude the other from his experience, his communicating is dishonest. Similarly, to the extent that an individual does not express an understanding and acceptance of the other, he is communicating impersonally.

In our opinion, most people communicate impersonally most of the time and find their interpersonal relationships more often unsatisfactory than not. Incomplete frustrating communication is "the rule rather than the exception . . . people often conclude conversations feeling more inadequate, more misunderstood, and more alienated than when they started."[1]

[1]Barnlund, 1968, p. 3.

It is important to communicate personally with some people at some times, but do not misunderstand us. We do **not** advise you always to communicate in highly personal ways and establish close relationships with everyone you meet. Not only would this be impossible, it would be unwise. There are times when it is best for all concerned to exchange information and to carry out assignments in a relatively impersonal manner. Rather than urging you to communicate personally all of the time, our purpose is to increase your awareness of personal and impersonal communicating and to give you some suggestions about how you can communicate personally when you choose to. We believe the best communicator is one who is capable of assessing situations and responding appropriately. By becoming more aware of how you and others communicate, you will be more able to evaluate your communicating and make the changes you deem desirable.

This is not as simple a procedure as it may first appear. Communicating, you see, belongs to that class of behaviors which we "overlearn." We overlearn when we develop the ability to perform a very complex series of acts while losing the ability to describe what we are doing. We have forgotten that we had to learn each individual act and can no longer distinguish each element in the more complex behavior. Walking and eating are examples of overlearned behaviors. Because they are overlearned almost none of us ever stops to think of all the specific things we must do to put one foot in front of the other or to get food from our plates to our stomachs.

Awareness of the intricacies of overlearned behaviors can be beneficial. Your podiatrist may force you to become more conscious of your walking because you have overlearned a technique which is harmful to your feet and those with whom you eat may strongly recommend that you examine your overlearned dining techniques if you eat your peas with a knife, slurp your coffee, or hunch over your plate. The point is this: we frequently overlearn ways of doing things that are less than optimal. Through gaining awareness of these overlearned behavior patterns and of alternative behavior styles we can change our ways of doing things in directions we think are desirable.

We believe that most people could benefit from an increased awareness of overlearned communication behaviors, and moreover we are convinced that the kinds of awarenesses you gain are important in determining the kinds of changes you can make in your communication behaviors. We consider the personal-impersonal dimension of interpersonal communication to be a uniquely important one and therefore our primary purpose is to heighten your awareness of the degree of personalness in your communicating and the effects that this might be having in your interactions, your relationships, and your life.

The rest of this book presents our thinking about communicating personally and its effect in interpersonal relationships. We think it will be helpful to you in understanding our perspectives if you know something more about the context in which we see this book and our motives for writing it. Because it is published in the United States in the 1970s, this book comes into existence during a century which has experienced greater technological advancement than occurred in the entire previous history of mankind. Many of these technological advances directly affect a communicator's capacities to exchange messages with various audiences. Today's speaker can use amplifiers so powerful his voice can be heard by more than a million people; he can transmit his message via radio and TV relays through satellites so that people in every part of the world can hear him simultaneously; and because we can record messages on tape, film, and wax, speakers' messages can live on long after they are dead so that years from now, unborn generations will be able to hear the same recordings we hear of Franklin Roosevelt's fireside chats, Martin Luther King's "I Have a Dream" speech, or Janis Joplin's "Pearl" album.

Still, despite these technological advances which make it possible to exchange messages with anybody anywhere in the world, we still find ourselves up against many of the same old problems: After we make physical contact, what should we say? How can we be understood? How can we better understand the other? How can we let one another know we understand each other when we do? How can we find out we don't understand one another when we don't? How do we determine the kind of relationship we want with the other, and after we decide, how do we invite him to share that kind of relationship with us? These are not technical issues, they are human issues and they are the kinds of issues we believe people living in our times should think about and learn about. This belief is an important part of our motivation for writing this book.

As a textbook, a second context is important—the academic tradition of the study of communication. Another important part of our motivation for writing this book is that we think it does something which other scholarly materials do not. The study of communication has a long and honored tradition and the social and personal value of effective communication has long been widely acknowledged, leaving a legacy of artifacts and anecdotes. For example, the oldest essay of which fragments still remain—written about 5,000 years ago for sons of the Egyptian Pharaohs—contains advice about effective speaking (McCroskey, 1972). One of the major portions of our heritage from the Greeks and Romans is the result of their preoccupation with "rhetoric" (from the Greek noun meaning "public speaker" and from which we get the word "orator"). Plato, Aristotle, Isocrates, Cicero, Quintillian, and others wrote treatises on speaking which are still being studied although they are over 2,000 years old. Some of mankind's oldest stories, frequently involving communication, are contained in the Judeo-Christian scriptures. One of Adam's first chores was to name animals, at least partly so that he could communicate about them more easily (some have said that the invention of naming, even more than the wheel, deserves credit as history's greatest labor-saving device). The story of the Tower of Babel is based on the assumption that cooperative enterprise is significantly more effective if the participants communicate, while without communication the most human aspirations of individuals and groups parch into shriveled monuments to what might have been. Current enthusiasm for good communication approaches "fad" proportions: no self-respecting politician would be without a stable of speech writers; governmental agencies have studied the effects of mass communication media on society; and thousands of people have participated in "sensitivity" or "encounter" groups in attempts to improve their abilities to relate meaningfully with others.

But the fact that communication is important or that its study is a part of a long academic tradition is not the primary reasons why we wrote this book. We wrote this book because we noticed a discrepancy between some of our communication experiences and those which we read about in the textbooks and articles in our professional literature. With few exceptions (Johannesen, 1971; Matson and Montague, 1967) the communication literature seemed to describe only impersonal communication or did not distinguish between more and less personal communication. We found no shortage of texts and articles dealing with nonverbal communication, mass communication, persuasive communication, public speaking, small group dynamics, and dozens of other specific topics, and we found these things useful when we wished to communicate in ways that would persuade, inform, amuse, or incite others to action. We did not, however, find them useful when we wanted to know how to go about trying to establish mutually supportive interaction with another person. In short, we found no dearth of materials to help us change others' attitudes or to obtain an understanding of abstract verbal messages, but we found few books or articles which helped us to create understanding between ourselves and others as persons.

After we noticed this imbalance in our textbooks, our behavior and attitudes as teachers were affected. For years we had been confronted with students who expressed considerable interest in improving their ability to communicate but who did not seem particularly enthusiastic about the subject matter they read in their texts or that we covered in class. Finally we came to understand that what we were offering and what they were asking for were two different types of communication. We offered good advice about techniques to use when asking someone to pass the salt or when explaining the Monroe Doctrine. We had emphasized such things as organization, delivery, fluency, language, credibility, even wit and charm—but our students were more interested in learning how to say "I love you" or "Thanks, friend." The need we saw for a greater emphasis on the role on interpersonal communication in the establishment and maintenance of human relationships provided the major source of our motivation for writing this book.

A very general outline of our message

The major themes of our thought about communicating personally may be expressed as eight statements. In a real sense, the rest of the book is an amplification of these themes.

1. The "relational level" of communication tells others how we see ourselves and them and sometimes proposes changes in this relationship. This is at least as important as the "informa-

tional level" of communication which conveys the abstract content of our messages.

2. Personal communicating is a very important kind of relational communication which tells the other person that we perceive him as legitimate and worthy and are willing to let him know us better.

3. When we communicate personally with others, we let them know we care for them as persons and invite them to share themselves with us.

4. The degree of personalness in our communicating is a major factor in the establishment and maintenance of significant human relationships such as friendship and love.

5. Relationships in which we communicate personally are perceived as uniquely significant and are characterized by closeness and caring.

6. Trust is necessary but not sufficient for personal communicating. Persons who trust each other may or may not communicate personally, but if they do not trust, they cannot communicate personally.

7. If we do not communicate personally for a long period of time, we run the risk of loneliness and alienation.

8. Conversely, on a long-term basis, if we do communicate in highly personal ways to at least some other people, we are likely to come to a greater knowledge and acceptance of ourselves and those others and to be more satisfied with the way we are living our lives.

Studying about communicating personally

Now that you have a general idea about the subject matter we will be dealing with, we'd like to give you a few suggestions for studying personal communicating. We think these recommendations will enhance the chances that you will be successful in your studies of personal communicating by becoming more able to analyze your communication behavior and to change in the directions you feel are desirable. Our two basic suggestions are these: "Read and think more than you are required to"; and "Try it out."

Both in the text and at the end of the various chapters we will be making suggestions of things you can do or think about and things you can read to gain a better understanding of personal communicating. To get the most from this book we advise you to take at least some of our suggestions, even if your instructor does not make them a required part of your course. The exercises we have suggested are those which we have used in our classes and which we and our students have found useful for applying concepts and ideas from the text. The suggested readings are some of the books and articles which we read as part of our own studies as we were formulating our ideas about personal communicating. While we have tried to provide you with an understandable presentation of our ideas, we know that you will learn more if you also read some of the things that we read as well as our summaries and interpretations of them. So our first suggestion to you is—read and think a little more than you are required to.

Our second suggestion is—try it out. Reading and thinking about personal communicating will enable you to evaluate your communication behavior, but the only way you will **change** your behavior is to experiment with new ways of communicating as you interact with others and to see what happens. It is sometimes fairly easy to decide that a particular way of communicating with others is better than some other way, but it is sometimes difficult to "take the plunge" when the opportunity finally presents itself. Even though we realize it may be difficult and may sometimes cause you to feel a bit strange or uneasy, we still advocate that whatever the change you think you want to make in your communicating behavior, you **try it out.**

To this general suggestion we might add some cautionary notes: try out new behaviors sensitively, and don't be afraid to tell others you are exploring new ways of communicating. It is advisable that you be sensitive to the persons with whom you are interacting because they will bring certain expectations to their interactions with you. Too drastic a change may offend or embarrass your companions or cause them to be suspicious of you—outcomes which are usually undesirable. So try out new behaviors while being sensitive to others.

Another way to enhance the benefits you might get from trying things out is to tell others what you are doing. An important way to learn about ourselves and our communication is by getting feedback from others. If you decide to try things out, don't be afraid to tell others that you are attempting to interact in new and different ways and to solicit their feedback about how they feel about you when you are doing so.

An overview

This chapter has been primarily introductory. Chapters 2 through 5, which comprise the rest of Part I, present a systematic outline of the characteristics of personal communicating. Chapter 2 discusses communication behavior in general and is designed to provide a broader conceptual context for the discussion of personal communicating. In Chapter 3 we discuss types of communication, and elaborate further on our "personal-impersonal" typology and outline some general characteristics of communication that is highly personal. Chapters 4 and 5 provide elaborate and specific discussions of **honesty** and **validation,** the two criterial attributes of personal communicating which we have already mentioned.

Part II contains four chapters, each of which describes a topic closely related to communicating personally. These are: trust, alienation, and psychological health, plus some of the research in these areas.

Where appropriate we have included suggested activities and materials which will enable you to assess your skills at communicating personally and references for further study. The appendices are primarily addressed to advanced students and our colleagues. They provide succinct statements on relevant topics and are designed to spur research as well as to locate our thinking within the context of relevant literature.

References

Barnlund, Dean. 1968. **Interpersonal Communication.** Boston: Houghton Mifflin.

Johannesen, Richard L. 1971. "The Emerging Concept of Communication as Dialogue," **The Quarterly Journal of Speech,** 57:373–82.

Matson, Floyd W., and Ashley Montague. 1967. "Introduction: The Unfinished Revolution," in **The Human Dialogue.** New York: Free Press. Floyd Matson and Ashley Montagu, eds.

McCroskey, James C. 1972. **An Introduction to Rhetorical Communication.** Englewood Cliffs, New Jersey: Prentice-Hall.

Neil, Fred. 1967. "Everybody's Talking," Coconut Grove Music Company and Third Story Music Company.

Communication behavior

... sometimes the most competent communicator is the one who walks away ...

This chapter presents an outline of how we think communication behavior occurs. We first define communication behavior and discuss **meanings** and **messages,** the basic elements involved in communicating. We then focus specifically on those messages and meanings which are involved in the relationship level of communication, discuss communication processes that go on in human transactions, and finally relate all of this to the central concern of this book, communicating personally.

As we remarked in the first chapter, communicating only seems simple because it is overlearned. Here we begin the process of helping you to examine your overlearning of communication skills. We could accomplish this in one of two ways. One way would be to trace the development of communication skills and to show you some of the things which you now know but have forgotten that you once learned. For example, it is easy and natural for you to be able to string words together in combinations which any other person who speaks the English language fluently can recognize as legitimate sentences even though he has never before encountered that particular combination of words. Rather than emphasizing your acquisition of language and communication skills, we prefer to assume that you have developed at least an average level of adult competency in communication and focus our efforts on helping you identify and understand some aspects of your communication behavior which occur out of your awareness or nonconsciously.

A definition of communicating

"Communication" is a difficult concept to deal with. In part, this is because the term refers simultaneously to that which one person does (communication **behavior**) and to something that two or more persons create cooperatively (communication **process**). We distinguish between these two perspectives by using the gerund **communicating** to refer to behavior, and the noun **communication** to designate the process.

In this book we are primarily concerned with behavior (communicating), making the assumption that the way people communicate significantly affects the communication processes which develop. At the most general level, communicating consists of behaviors for coping with messages. These two behaviors are: making meanings from messages, and making messages from meaning. A useful, though somewhat crude, model of communication behavior is shown in Figure 1. The wavy lines in the model represent messages, which are defined as disturbances in the environment which impinge on the senses (such as light and sound waves). The stick figure denotes the person who is communicating, and the curved lines designate messages which originate inside the person. Meaning is the significance which the communicator assigns to the objects, persons, and events in his environment. Although this description of communicating rather neatly identifies the kinds of behaviors we will be considering, it also neatly obscures many of the less obvious characteristics of communication. In succeeding sections, we will describe some of these less obvious characteristics of communicating while elaborating on the major concepts in our definition, **meanings** and **message**.

Meaning. Meaning is the significance we attach to things in our environment. This is one way of saying that things are not what they are for us, they are what they mean for us. A common error in this regard is the tendency to forget that things have different mean-

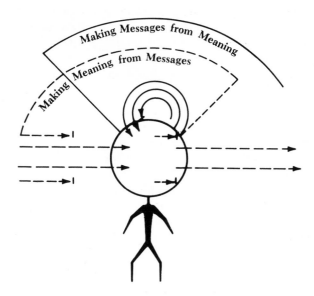

Figure 1. A model of communication behavior (The authors acknowl-edge the contribution of Dr. Forrest Conklin, who responded to preliminary versions of this model.)

ings for different people. When we are dealing with situations in which we are using words that have concrete referents such as physical objects, it is fairly easy to catch ourselves making this mistake. If a three-hundred-pound football player were to tell us it was all right to pick up a box because it is "light," we would not have too much trouble remembering that what is "light" to him will probably not be light to us. It is more difficult when discussing more abstract things, however, to remember that the words we use do not mean the same things to the other person that they do to us.

When we forget that meanings are in people and not in messages, we commit what Berlo (1960) called the "I told them so" fallacy. This occurs when we assume that the meaning we **intended** to express in a message we generated is the same as the meaning recipients of that message attach to it. Some messages encourage commission of the "I told them so" fallacy. Whenever words with which an unusual amount of meaning is associated ("holy words") are used, there is a good chance that different people will understand them quite differently.

Consider the word "library": for some the library is the spiritual and intellectual center of an academic institution and the word connotes shelves of neatly catalogued books, quiet contemplation of great truths, accumulated knowledge, a veritable storehouse of wisdom from which grateful students frequently make withdrawals. Assume that Professor McGillahay, who has this concept of a library, encounters one of his students on campus.

PROFESSOR McGILLAHAY. Hello there, Ellswood. You appear to be in somewhat of a hurry. Where are you off to?

ELLSWOOD. Hi, Prof. I'm heading for the library. Gotta get there before it closes.

PROF. M. The library, eh. I knew you were a good student, Ellswood. I've always had a fondness for the library.

E. Me, too. I've found the hunting better there than anywhere else on campus.

PROF. M. Hunting? Oh, I see. Yes, the card catalogue and reference works are helpful.

E. They surely are. All the chicks come by there sooner or later. And when I'm there, it's usually sooner.

PROF. M. Chicks? You mean girls? Ellswood, you are going to the library to study, aren't you?

E. Sure, Prof. I'm going to study selected forms of courtship behavior among American coeds. In fact, I'm going to do some participant observation!

PROF. M. In the library? Ellswood, I'm deeply disappointed in you. (Walks away)

E. Gee, what's with him today?

Among his other problems, Professor McGillahay assumed that his special meanings for the library were shared by Ellswood. They were not. For Ellswood, the library was neutral turf, a place to meet congenial young people. McGillahay was unable to grant the legitimacy of Ellswood's meanings, and this made him unable to communicate well.

The "I told them so" fallacy has a devastating effect on communication: if the recipient does not **behave** as the message source expected, the speaker generally assumes that the other has made the **meaning** he intended and that the unusual response indicates that there is something wrong with him. This inference does a number of unfortunate things, among them reducing the probability that these persons will be able to communicate effectively. Good communicators are continually aware that we never have access to other people's meaning nor they to ours, and that any understanding of another person is mediated by "translation" processes between messages and meaning. We can only know our **perceptions** of other people's meanings, and these perceptions may differ considerably from what the other person meant.

Because meanings are in people, if someone chooses to misunderstand what we mean by a particular message, there is no way we can prevent it. We can give additional messages better designed (so we assume) to create in his mind the meaning we intended or we can articulate the message more slowly, distinctly, or loudly to ensure that he is able to detect it in undistorted form. But we cannot force the other person to change the way he chooses to understand us. Sometimes the most competent communicator is the one who walks away, realizing that the other is not going to change the meanings which he associates with the message no matter what the speaker might do.

Can you remember instances in which another person was determined to understand you in a certain way and persisted in misunderstanding you despite all your efforts? Have you ever assumed that another person acted in accordance with selfish motives, or intended a comment as a "put-down," or had a particular meaning for a message, and would not allow him to change your mind regardless of what he said? How can you, as a speaker, help your listeners be more open to the meanings which you have for messages? How can you lay aside your own meanings and be receptive to other speakers, trying to understand the meanings they have for messages?

Granted that the meanings we make are sometimes quite different from the meanings intended by the speaker or those made by other listeners to the same message, the question is why these differences occur. The most important reason is that we do not make meanings from a message based only on the information

contained within the message. We continually go "beyond the information given." Remember now those curved lines in the diagram
of the communication process in Figure 1. These lines represent
information which originates **inside** the person and which is added
to the message to complete the meaning. For example, if a used car
salesman told you that the '57 Ford 500 custom convertible on his
lot was in superb condition, you probably would not accept the
message at face value. You would add to the message information
"from your head" about used cars, used car salesmen, and the
situation, probably concluding that you had better check the car
yourself.

The important point is that we frequently are not aware of the
extent to which the meanings we make depend on information from
internal sources. Messages are usually perceived as a whole in
which both forms of information are mixed, often beyond our abilities to separate and identify. This is why listeners tend to confuse
their own meanings for messages with those intended by the
speakers: they assume that all the information they have comes
from the message and that none was already in their minds.

---

*A famous man once said that there should be a revolution every twenty
years. Not only your agreement with the statement but its meaning for
you depends on whom you believe was its author. Consider this call for
periodic revolution if it were made by (1) Che Gueverra, (2) Thomas
Jefferson, (3) Karl Marx, (4) Albert Einstein, (5) Dr. Spock, or (6) John
Kennedy. Write a brief description of how you understand the statement as attributed to each of these men. Now compare what you have
written. The differences are due to the information which you supply
about the people to whom the message is attributed.*

Messages. Messages are defined as disturbances in the environment which impinge on the senses. Since this book is concerned
with human communication, we will disregard messages generated
by nonhuman sources and focus only on those which are generated
by persons.

Our dual task as communicators is the generation of messages
which will enable others to understand us and the assignment of

meanings to messages from others that will allow us to understand them. This is no simple matter because whenever human beings communicate, there are always many messages being generated at any one time by both parties. These messages may be characterized as:

1. Those which refer to meanings the source intended to communicate.
2. Those which refer to meanings the source did not intend to communicate.
3. Those which refer to meanings the source intended not to communicate.

The first type is straightforward: these are the words, symbols, etc., which he deliberately chose in an attempt to convey that which he wants the other to understand. The second and third kinds of messages are less obvious but in some ways the most important. Often while concentrating on meanings which we intend to communicate we produce unintended cues which serve as messages to others and to which they assign meaning. These messages may allow the other to understand things which we did not intend to communicate, such as when shakiness in the voice tells others we are anxious. The second and third types of messages differ as a function of the speaker's intentions. If a nervous speaker generates cues which reveal his anxiety even though he is not thinking about it, these are "type two" messages. The third type occurs when his anxiety shows despite his conscious intention to conceal it.

It is difficult to say which of these three types of messages is most important. Probably we should take the safest route by asserting that it depends on the goal of communication at any given time and on the situation. Later in this chapter and in the rest of this book you will find that we place a great deal of emphasis on the second and third kinds of messages. These are often nonverbal messages and refer to our emotional states or to our feelings about other persons. Though we used "anxiety" as an example here, you might consider that the same ideas hold true for "love." Sometimes we intentionally generate messages in an attempt to let others know of our love for them. Other times we communicate our love without consciously thinking about it, and sometimes we try to hide our love but generate love messages anyway.

An example of the difficulty in avoiding cues intended not to be

communicated provided one of the comedy spots in the TV program, "All in The Family." Sammy Davis, Jr., was (improbably) to
visit the Bunker residence and Archie feared that Edith would comment about Davis's artificial eye. Before Mr. Davis arrived, Archie
repeatedly told Edith to avoid making any references to eyes. Edith
did not, but Archie quickly handed Sammy a drink with the old
proverb, "Here's mud in your . . . eye."

Misunderstandings often occur when the receiver interprets an
unintended cue as if it were intended. A particularly difficult situation arises when the receiver fastens onto a cue intended not to be
communicated and refuses to attend to intended cues. These
breakdowns in communication are generally frustrating for the
message generator.

To compound the complexities of communicating even further
we not only send multiple messages but we also perceive messages
from others selectively. Look again at Figure 1, and note that there
are more messages (represented by wavy lines) than are perceived.
Some of these messages are not intense enough to be perceived.
These are called subliminal and are below our thresholds of perception. Messages of this sort are like those spoken loudly enough for
us to hear so that we know someone is talking, but too softly to be
understood. Beyond this, there are usually more messages available and sufficiently distinct than we can cope with at any given
time. The number of items of information which humans can handle at any given point in time is limited.[2] Confronted with more
messages than we can handle, we respond by selectively attending
to only some of them while letting others go by unnoticed. This
process goes on all the time without our consciously trying to direct
it but this does not mean that there is no consistency to our selec-
tions of messages for attending. Weaver (1972) has pointed out
that we usually select and attend to those messages which are
consistent with our biases, beliefs, and attitudes. A specific example of this has been provided by Erlichman **et al.** (1957). In their
research Erlichman and his colleagues wanted to see how persons
reduced their feelings of discomfort which preceded making important decisions. To do this, they studied the information intake
habits of persons who had recently purchased automobiles. They

[2]Miller, 1956.

found that after buying their new cars these persons were more likely than usual to read advertisements **for the brand of car they had just purchased.** They interpreted this to mean that the persons were seeking information which reassured them that they had made a wise decision, and they sought this information consistently.

The implication of these selective processes is that we do not make meaning from all of the information in all of the messages available to us. Inevitably we select and avoid messages or aspects of messages in a somewhat systematic way.

Besides specific tendencies for approaching communicating like having just bought a car or seeking information which supports our biases and beliefs, we also tend to have broad general tendencies which we follow in communicating. These tendencies are outgrowths of our personalities and our general attitudes toward ourselves and others. For example, people who are highly "ego-involved" with a topic are more likely than those who are not to misperceive messages about that topic. They exaggerate the similarity between themselves and others when the message is somewhat close to their own position (assimilation effects) and exaggerate the difference when the message deviates from their own position (contrast effects).[3] People with unresolved guilt feelings and unfilled needs evidence them in their communication behavior: depending on the strength of the stress they tend to either "fixate" on the topic or to engage in systematic avoidance of it.

People who are open-minded, self-actualizing, tolerant, and trusting of others are most likely to display well-developed skills at communicating. Conversely, those who are disturbed psychologically are generally ineffective at communicating. In later chapters we will explore these ideas in more detail.

The relationship level of communication

An important form of communication which frequently occurs out of awareness (through unintended messages and messages intended not to be transmitted) involves the relationship between the generator and the receiver of the message. Intended messages

[3]Sherif, Sherif, and Nebergall, 1965.

usually involve the content of messages: the temperature and humidity, if we are talking about the weather; scores and team standings, if we are concerned with sports; or who did what with or to whom, if we are discussing the current neighborhood gossip. But in addition to talking about content, messages reflect what the speaker thinks about himself and the person to whom the message is addressed and, by implication, the kind of relationship he perceives as existing or would like to create between them. We call this the relational level of language.

Sometimes messages make the relationship overt and obvious. For example, the use of honorifics such as "sir," Dr.," "your honor" or formally polite phrases such as "if you would be so kind" clearly indicate the way in which the speaker thinks (or wishes to be thought to think) about the person to whom he is speaking. In organizations in which status differences have been institutionalized—the military, the university, a business organization—messages such as these are insisted on as a means of reinforcing hierarchy. In other situations, however, the relationship we feel

---

The different ways in which you can express content create different relational meanings. Consider the relational messages in these statements:

1. The door is open.

2. Were you raised in a barn?

3. Do you mind closing the door?

4. Please close the door.

5. Do you think we might be more comfortable with the door closed?

6. Shut the door, stupid.

By the same token, responses to these messages might be quite different because of the relational cues:

1. I'd rather there were less noise in here.

2. Would you mind being more quiet?

3. Shut up!

What does each of these messages say about the speaker's concept about himself? About the person being spoken to? About the situation in which they are communicating?

---

between ourselves and the person with whom we are talking is expressed through rather subtle messages. For example, whether the speaker feels included or excluded from the listener's group is reflected in his choice of pronouns, while selection of modifiers denotes the amount of ambiguity in the relationship.[4] Even though all messages contain relational information, this aspect of the message may be more or less important in specific instances. Sometimes the content of a conversation serves only as a pretext for saying something about the relations between the participants, but at other times the relational messages are redundant or irrelevant. When one person tells another that there is fire in the building where they are working, little thought is given to the relational meaning of the message. On the other hand, two men in a corner bar arguing about Babe Ruth's lifetime batting average are probably less interested in accurate statistics than in which will be acknowledged by the other as the baseball expert.

Relational meanings are usually less important in stable relationships—those which have existed for some time with no significant changes—and most important in the formative stages of a relationship or after a major event has occurred to one or both of the persons. When a new person joins an established group, much of the early interaction is purely relational: the newcomer and the group must mutually decide where to "rank" him. A new man on the job in a construction crew might—not accidently—find himself forced to demonstrate his strength, skill, or courage while all of the old hands watch carefully to see how he will measure up to their standards. A new tennis player in town will find that his skills have been critically evaluated by people whom he has never met. After a few matches, he will be tacitly offered a ranking and his opportunities to compete with players of comparable abilities depends on his accepting and defending this standing.

To demonstrate how relational messages in communication function, we invented this dialogue:

BILL. Hey! How about this snow!

PETE. Yes, there must be four inches of new snow.

BILL. No, most of it is drift. I'd say that only one or two inches fell.

PETE. Well, it certainly is pretty.

BILL. Right.

[4]Wiener and Mahrabian, 1968.

—and they walk away from each other. A naïve reading might lead someone to think that this conversation was about snow. Unquestionably, the **content** of the messages refers to comparative estimates of snow depth, but—unless Bill and Pete are quite different from the way we imagined them—the content served only as a pretext for them to discuss their **relationship.** In our interpretation, Bill initiated the exchange of messages, in so doing telling Pete that Bill acknowledges Pete as a human being. This is what Berne (1964) calls a "stroke": like a mother caressing her baby, it expresses acknowledgment of identity and involvement. And these strokes are nice things to receive: Berne says that without sufficient stroking your spinal cord will shrivel up! When Pete makes an observation about the depth of the snow, he is returning the stroke, following Bill's lead by talking about a mutually relevant but not very important topic. So far the exchange has gone quite well: each has given and received one stroke.

But Bill's second statement changes the sequence drastically. He disagrees with Pete (a mild social offense in this type of banter which usually has a norm that both shall be agreeable) about the snowfall (which, remember, is only a pretext for the discussion of relationships). Since neither is really interested in the snow, this statement indicates that Bill is rejecting what he perceives as Pete's attempt to define himself as equally or more expert than Bill in meteorological judgments. His statement is a direct challenge to Pete for the role of dominance in this discussion. He disagrees bluntly ("No"), poses himself as a rival ("I'd say . . .") and offers an alternative suggestion ("most of it is drift"). He is saying, in effect, "I want to be acknowledged as the dominant person in this relationship. I see myself as superior, you as inferior."

Unfortunately, in written transcripts of dialogue, we lose the nonverbal cues which may contain important relational cues. Mentally reconstruct some of the ways Bill might have disagreed with Pete's estimate of snow depth. If he spoke mildly, matter-of-factly, he is saying, "Not only do I see myself as the superior in the relationship between us, but I see this as a natural relationship, not subject to change." On the other hand, if the statement was made shrilly, sharply, loudly, it functions as a challenge. Delivered in this way it says, "I see myself as superior to you and I will fight to prove it."

Now notice Pete's response. He immediately drops the question of snow depth and makes another judgment (pretty). This tells Bill that he (Pete) is not going to fight for or insist on the dominant role, but neither is he going to be servile (as he would have been if he had said, "Yes, yes. You are right, of course"). By switching from snow depth to aesthetic value, he submits to Bill's demand for dominance, but with some dignity.

Finally, Bill says, "Right," which functions as an acknowledgment that he has insisted on and been granted the dominant role in the relationship and dismisses Pete. Obviously, this conversation could be prolonged and complicated if Pete chose to contest Bill's position as the better judge of snow depth.

Both speakers and listeners are usually unaware of the presence and significance of the relational component of messages. It is very possible that when Pete stumbled away from his encounter with Bill he was raging, plotting retribution and ready to heap verbal or physical abuse on the next person he encountered. Yet, if you had asked him what was bothering him, he probably would not be able to identify the source of his agitation, and if he could identify it, would probably be unable to articulate it. And without the ability to be aware of and handle symbolically the problems of relationships in communication, Pete is unable to alter his behavior, doomed to repeat in subsequent days—in which rain, grass growing, wind, or sun replace snow as the **content** of messages—the same destructive and frustrating **relational** messages with Bill.

Although relational messages may take a wide variety of forms, there are only a limited number of relational meanings. According to Carson's (1969) summary of research, people perceive interpersonal relations primarily in terms of two factors: dominance-submission and friendliness-hostility. These factors can be expressed as a two-dimensional, intersecting matrix (see Figure 2).

The way each person is perceived may be identified as the point at which his friendliness intersects with his dominance. For example, person A in this figure is hostile-dominant; C is very friendly, slightly dominant, and D is very friendly, slightly submissive. According to Carson, each person's behavior communicates how he perceives himself (e.g., B sees himself as hostile and submissive) and how he wants the other to behave (e.g., B wants or expects others to be hostile and dominant). When one person (perhaps

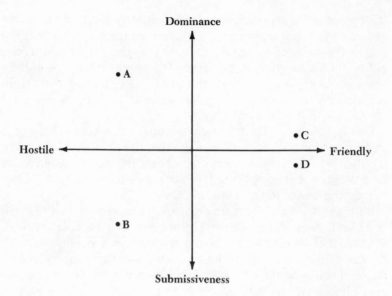

Figure 2. A model of interpersonal relationships (Adapted from Carson, 1969)

through unintended relational cues) asks another to accept a particular form of behavior, the other may agree or refuse to accept the relationship as defined by the other on either or both of the dimensions. Communication between A and B, and between C and D, can assume mutually agreed-upon definitions of the relationship, but some form of adjustment must occur if A or B were to communicate with C or D.

Many problems in communication involve the relational level of language. Messages proposing unacceptable relationships may provoke fights between the communicators which are particularly difficult to deal with because they involve unintended cues which neither person can identify as the cause of the problem. Good communicators have the ability to bring into awareness and articulate those aspects of communication which usually occur on a nonconscious level, such as "negotiations" for a mutually acceptable definition of the relationships.

"Rules" and "contracts" in interpersonal communication

Scholars who have studied various aspects of communication have discovered that there are regularities in behavior which can best be understood by assuming that the participants know and are following rules. Sapir (1966) noted that people both generate and respond to nonverbal cues in systematic ways although they cannot articulate the meanings which they associate with particular nonverbal messages and, indeed, are often unaware of the nonverbal cues to which they respond. He described the phenomenon as indicating the existence of a secret system of rules "known by none but understood by all."

Rules are developed by the participants in a communication process which "govern and guide" them as they translate between messages and meaning. Constraints (or limits) are placed on the range of permissible meanings by rules which reduce the possibility of error in understanding what each is saying or might say. Other rules eliminate some ambiguity in messages by specifying more precisely than usual relationships between particular message elements and certain meanings (Cushman and Whiting, 1972). For example, the word "run" may mean many things: a score in baseball; a group of people demanding their money at a bank; a tear in a woman's hose; a sequence of similar values in an array of scores; a small stream of water; a process of moving quickly, and more. But if you and someone else "agree" that you are talking about investments and monetary policy, and you mention the dangers of a run, the other person will know which of the many meanings you wish him to attach to the word.

A dialogue from the Marx brothers' movie "Horsefeathers" bases its claim to humor on just this function of rules. In successive lines, the speakers "agree" on a rule limiting the possible range of meaning for their words, then violate the rule and agree on the new rule. The scene takes place at the door of a Prohibition-era Speakeasy, where Baravelli (Chico) is the doorman and Wagstaff (Groucho) is trying to get in.

(Wagstaff knocks on the door. Baravelli answers through a peephole.)

BARAVELLI. Who are you?

WAGSTAFF. I'm fine, thanks. Who are you?

BARAVELLI. I'm fine, too, but you can't come in unless you give the password.

WAGSTAFF. Well, what is the password?

BARAVELLI. Oh, no, you gotta tell me. Hey, I tell you what I do. I give you three guesses. It's the name of a fish.

WAGSTAFF. Is it Mary?

BARAVELLI. (Laughs) 'At's no fish.

WAGSTAFF. She isn't? Well, she drinks like one. Let me see, is it sturgeon?

BARAVELLI. Hey, you crazy? Sturgeon's a doctor cuts you open when you're sick. Now, I give you one more chance.

WAGSTAFF. I got it! Haddock.

BARAVELLI. 'At's funny, I gotta haddock, too.

WAGSTAFF. Well, what do you take for a haddock?

BARAVELLI. Well, sometimes I take-a aspirin, sometimes I take-a calomel.

WAGSTAFF. Say, I'd walk a mile for a calomel.

BARAVELLI. You mean chocolate calomel? I like that, too, but you no guess it. Hey, what's-a matter? You no understand English? You can't come in here unless you say swordfish. Now, I give you one more guess.

WAGSTAFF. Swordfish, swordfish. I think I got it. Is it swordfish?

BARAVELLI. Heh! That's it. You guess it.

WAGSTAFF. Pretty good, eh?

BARAVELLI. Fine, you guess it. All right.[5]

A deliberate violation of the rules which "govern and guide" permissible meanings provides the humor in this Groucho Marx line:

MAN: Sir, you try my patience!

GROUCHO: Thank you. You must try mine sometime.

But rules apply to more than just meanings. They govern and guide the development of relationships between communicators and specify who has the right to say what to whom. For example, the statement, "The light is green now—or didn't you notice?" (Pearce, 1973a) clearly implies that the speaker considers the driver of the car to be less than adequately attentive. But the driver's response to the statement will depend on the nature of his

---

[5]Anobile, Richard J. **Why a Duck?** 1972.

relationship to the speaker. If the message emerges out of the shadows of the back seat, the driver is likely to become irritated and snap back with a spirited rejoinder. He is likely to accept the criticism meekly, however, if the speaker is a driving instructor or the examining officer during a driving test.

Societies develop rules for patterns of communication and specific types of relationships between persons with various statuses. A person is socialized when he learns the rules of the groups of people with whom he interacts. Usually these rules or norms are so basic to his understanding of himself and his society that he not aware that he has learned them, but successful functioning within any group requires that a communicator adopt a wide variety of conventions, mannerisms, attitudes, and taboos as his own. If he does not acquire his society's norms, he bears the stigma of being a deviate and finds his opportunities to communicate severely limited. If he is successfully socialized, he may suffer "culture shock" if and when he is immersed in a society with different norms —a painful phenomenon which frequently occurs when young adults leave home for college, military service, or work, or marry and establish their own homes.

Good communication requires that all participants understand what is expected of them and what to expect from others. In certain formal situations, these expectations are generated by making the rules explicit, for example, by following "Rules of Order" in parliamentary discussions. In informal, unstructured situations, socially shared norms of communication behavior provide a set of rules which communicators can use as guidelines for interacting with others.

Consider an informal discussion between two people: one important task is to regulate turn-taking. Usually it is handled easily: messages do not overlap or bump into each other as much as would be expected by chance. Duncan (1972) found that there are highly complex rules for both verbal and nonverbal behavior which people use without being aware of them to signal that they are ready to say something, that they have finished speaking, or that they would not like to be interrupted. When two strangers meet, they may rely on social norms common to both to enable them to avoid bumping into each other's messages. But as these persons continue to interact with each other, they will probably develop better rules for turn-taking which are based on each person's knowledge of the idiosyncracies of the other and are unique to the relationship between these specific persons. Most people signal that they are not ready to be interrupted by looking away from the person to whom they are speaking. But it is possible that two individuals may develop a tacit agreement that eye-direction is not a good turn-taking cue for them. When they are talking with each other, it may be quite appropriate to interrupt when the speaker is not looking at the listener.

We call these sets of rules which people develop to regulate their relationships with specific others **implicit contracts.** Such contracts are usually out-of-consciousness and are unique to specific relationships. The rules of an implicit contract replace more generally accepted norms and depend on mutual acceptance by both persons. Like norms, they have moral force: the violator of a rule feels guilty and the other feels that he has a legitimate reason to feel angry, to inflict punishment or to demand forgiveness.

Implicit contracts may contain a great many rules or only a few. Some rules which are important for communication involve the participant's decisions about the distribution of dominance in the relationship, how friendly they will be, how much each person will tell the other about himself, and whether they will act trustworthily toward each other.

In the absence of both appropriate norms and contractual rules, much communication behavior functions **primarily** to reach mutually acceptable definitions of the relationship. The two drunks in the bar discussing Babe Ruth's batting average probably **think** they are talking about baseball, but they are really trying to decide whose opinions will dominate the other's. The student who continually challenges his teacher's pronouncements about math may really be asking to be acknowledged as a potential peer whose thoughts are at least worth being considered. A blistering criticism of her date's manners and morals may tell a discerning roommate that the couple has not yet been successful in reaching a mutually satisfying decision about the amount of friendliness which will exist in their relationship.

As these examples show, attempts to communicate about specific matters of content may be thwarted by disagreements or misunderstandings at the relationship level of language. Particularly if neither communicator is able to deal with relational cues consciously, acceptable implicit contracts will be developed only with difficulty.

Communication is easiest and most efficient—and most likely to be satisfying to the participants—when it occurs between persons who have developed a strong implicit contract. In the context of the contract, the relational cues in messages reinforce the shared definition of the relationship and do not interfere with communication about content. Further, each person understands what is expected of him and has a well-developed set of expectations about the other. This enables each to surprise the other for the sake of humor, effect, or play without fear of being misunderstood. This is what Parry (1967) meant when he cautioned that

> . . . we must not assume that the whole purpose of communication is to ensure full understanding by every hearer. Such an ideal would entail the banishment of wit and vivacity from human discourse and the anaesthetization of keener instincts by laborious explanation. In these matters, the speaker must at times take calculated risks; sometimes his remarks will fall on strong ground and he will have lost the gamble.

In the context of a strong contract, each communicator may better calculate the risks of misunderstanding on the basis of his expectations for the other and the other's expectations for him.

Implicit contracts may be rigid or flexible. A rigid contract might specify that Bill is always to be dominant and Pete to be submissive and that both will be very friendly. A flexible contract includes several patterns of relationships with well-understood "switching cues" signaling which is appropriate at any point in time. Consider a man returning home after a day at work. His wife greets him at the door and their first messages—if they have developed a flexible contract—consist of switching cues indicating which aspect of their relationship is to be invoked. Shall they be lovers, disciplinarians of their children, colleagues in the management of their home, or conspirators in accomplishing some shared objective? He may say, "I'm beat! What a hard day!", which asks his wife to play the friendly dominant maternal role of comforter and helper. If she understands the cue and is willing to accept this role for the time, she may respond with "Oh, you poor dear. Let me get your slippers." After dinner, however, she may tire of this role and say, "The lawn needs mowing." This is a switching cue which the husband interprets as asking him to take the role of strong, able, man-about-the-house (friendly dominant).

When both communicators are sensitive and responsive to the switching cues in a highly flexible contract, satisfactory relationships and communication may occur. A disagreement about the nature or flexibility of the rules or misunderstood switching cues, however, can lead to particularly difficult communication problems.

People-watching is a profitable pastime, particularly when one of the people you watch is yourself. Spend some time observing your own relationships with other people. Do you always insist on the same type of relationship or do you form different relationships with different people? Is there any relationship in which you are usually dominant? Usually submissive? Do you maintain some mutually profitable relationships with people whom you do not like very much or must all your relationships be very friendly? What are some of the "subcontracts" in your relationship with your best friend? Your husband or wife? Your parents or children? Do some of these subcontracts please you more than they do the other person? What switching cues do you use to indicate your desire to terminate one subcontract and start another? Do you and the other person understand all the switching cues to mean the same thing? Have you ever missed or misunderstood switching cues? Are your contracts rigid or flexible?

Here is a brief dialogue. Read it and look beyond the words to the meanings which are expressed. Can you describe the relationship meaning of each message (using the descriptors in Figure 2)? What type of contract do these people have? Is it flexible or rigid? What switching cues can you identify? Did either of these people miss or misunderstand the switching cues? Does it make any difference to your interpretation if you assume that "he" and "she" are married or unmarried?

HE. *Hi.*

SHE. *How did it go today?*

HE. *Terrible. I guess I just can't make it. I'm just not good enough for this job.*

SHE. *It can't be that bad. Come see what I made today!*

HE. *It was that bad.*

SHE. *Yes, I've been thinking about that. You just haven't got what it takes.*

HE. *Oh, why don't you go back to your mother!*
SHE. *You know better than that. You are just tired.*
HE. *Yes, I guess you're right. What did you make today?*
(A hint: if you are having trouble, look at each instance where the word "that" appears. To what does it refer in each case?)

Approaches to the study of the communication process

There are three primary ways in which the study of communication processes have been approached. In order of complexity they are: linear, interactive, and transactive. The most naïve understandings of communication come from the linear model. This model views communication as something that occurs when Person A says B to Person C with effect D. Conceptually such an interpretation assumes that the person making the message (A) is an active communicator and that Person C is a passive recipient whose only function is to be affected by A. An appropriate analogy is that of a cue ball and the eight ball in pool. Assume that the eight ball is standing still: based on Newton's laws of physics, we know that it will remain at rest until acted on by an outside force. Further, assuming the cue ball is moving toward the eight ball with a specified speed and angle, a competent physicist can describe exactly how fast and in what direction the eight ball will be impelled by its collision with the cue ball. This approach to communication assumes that the effects of a message are attributable to the content of a message, thus allowing a competent communication analyst to predict the persuasiveness or clarity of messages based on an analysis of message content. But a considerable bulk of research has shown that such predictions are not very accurate. The way people behave when others talk to them is not well represented by a stationary eight ball. (Somehow that seems reassurring.) Other limitations of this approach are its emphasis on the immediate effects of communication. This emphasis is based on the unwarranted assumption that these immediate effects are enduring and that only Person C, the person spoken to, but not Person A, the person speaking, is affected by what goes on.

The notion of communication as an interaction is a bit more sophisticated than the linear approach. The idea here is that each participant brings his own personal characteristics to the communication encounter and the result is a combination of all involved. The analogy of a pool table is useful again, only this time both the cue ball and the eight ball are in motion, and each is affected by the properties of the other. A good Newtonian physicist, however, could examine the speed and direction of both balls before they hit and predict how each would respond: the interaction is determined by the characteristics of each individually.

While this approach has some advantages over the basic linear approach, it still is limited in some important ways. Although the interaction view is willing to acknowledge that both parties in a communication situation are affected by one another, it tends to approach this in exactly the same way that the linear model does. While the linear model emphasizes the activity of Person A saying B to Person C with effect D, the interaction approach points out that thereafter Person C may respond with message E to Person A with effect F. The interaction approach is arrived at by adding together the basic units of interaction viewed in the linear model. All of the assumptions of the linear model are retained, as are most of its limitations. The interaction approach is a bit more sophisticated in that it acknowledges that in most communication situations we are rarely **only** sources or **only** recipients of messages.

The greatest limitation of the linear and interactive approaches is their inability to deal adequately with communication as a process. Arundale (1973) has pointed out that if one is to view communication as a process, certain characteristics of the phenomenon must be considered. Every communicative interaction has a history, a present, and a future (continuity), involves multiple messages simultaneously generated (complexity), has effects which are impossible to erase (irreversibility), has effects which cannot be attributed to single causes (multicausality), and occurs over time.

The third and most sophisticated approach to the study of communication, the transactive, does a much better job of considering the attributes of communication viewed as a process (Dewey and Bentley, 1949; Pearce, 1973b; Wilmot and Wenburg, 1973). Rather than focusing on the generating of messages that attempt to influence, the transactive approach is perception-based. Communication is seen as an attempt to get meaning rather than as an attempt to send messages which influence others. From this vantage point, all participants are viewed as active communicators to the extent that they seek meaning in the world around them. The process nature of communication is acknowledged by viewing communicative transactions as open systems having a past and a future as well as a present. The unending stream of behavior, the constant meaning-making of the participants is acknowledged, and each communicative transaction is seen as occurring in a spatial and temporal context. From this viewpoint, causes and effects are more difficult to determine since the complexity of communication is more fully acknowledged, and there is a realization that at any time all participants are simultaneously generating and perceiving multiple messages in a spatial and temporal context with multiple influences on all present. This approach is more holistic. It recognizes that multiple messages are generated and that those messages generally have more than one effect. Finally, the transactive approach places more emphasis on the relationship of the participants. Communication is viewed as a way of establishing and maintaining relationships as well as a medium of information exchange and cognitive influence. The relationships among participants are viewed as yet another aspect of the context within which communication behavior occurs.

Our approach

Our approach is basically transactive. As noted earlier, we are primarily concerned with the role of interpersonal communication in human relationships and prefer the meaning-centered approach to communication rather than the message-generating-influence model. In addition we prefer to view communication as holistically as we can and to acknowledge the full complexity of what goes on when one person talks with another.

Unfortunately, just as there are advantages to adopting the transactive approach, there are also some important limitations. The idea of viewing communication as transaction is a fairly new one for communication scholars. Therefore, despite the fact that it seems to be a good way to approach the study of communication, very little research has been done from the transactive approach.

This situation does not exist because communication scholars are irresponsible and lazy, preferring the simplest way to do research. It merely reflects a fairly common situation in the development of theory in the social sciences. Quite often theory is developed ahead of research. In this case the theoretical notion of approaching communication as transaction has just recently been developed and there has not yet been much work at attempting to modify and invent research methodologies so that research can be carried out on a large scale from the transactive approach. Therefore, you will find that we rarely draw much support from single research studies. This is because single studies rarely approach the subject matter in which we are interested. Usually it has been necessary for us to combine various theoretical and research ideas in developing our ideas and in finding support for them. By synthesizing these theoretical statements and research studies, often created out of the linear and interactive approaches, we have endeavored as best we could to present you with a view of interpersonal communication that is transactive in nature.

References

Anobile, Richard J. 1972. **Why a Duck?** New York: Avon Books.

Arundale, Robert B. 1973. "Dissecting the 'Idea of Process': Some Implications for Theory and Research on Communication," paper presented to the annual conference of the International Communication Association, Montreal, Canada.

Berlo, David. 1960. **The Process of Communication.** New York: Holt, Rinehart and Winston.

Berne, Eric. 1964. **Games People Play.** New York: Grove Press.

Carson, Robert. 1969. **Interaction Concepts of Personality.** Chicago: Aldine.

Cushman, Donald C., and Gordon C. Whiting. 1972. "An Approach to Communication Theory: Toward Consensus on Rules," **Journal of Communication,** 22:217–38.

Dewey, John, and Arthur R. Bentley. 1949. **Knowing and the Known.** Boston: Beacon.

Duncan, Starkey. 1972. "Some Signals and Rules for Speaking Turns in Conversations," **Journal of Personality and Social Psychology,** 23:283–92.

Erlichman, D. 1957. "Post-decision Exposure to Relevant Information," **Journal of Abnormal and Social Psychology,** 54:98–102.

Miller, George A. 1956. "The Magical Number Seven, Plus or Minus Two: Some Limits on Our Capacity for Processing Information," **Psychological Review,** 63:81–97.

Parry, John. 1967. **The Psychology of Human Communication.** London: University of London Press.

Pearce, W. Barnett. 1973a. "Consensual Rules in Interpersonal Communication: A Reply to Cushman and Whiting," **Journal of Communication,** 23:160–68.

———. 1973b. "Interpersonal Communication Behavior and Communication Process: An Analysis of Perspectives and Concepts," paper presented to the annual conference of the Western Speech Communication Association, Albuquerque, New Mexico.

Sapir, Edward. 1966. **Language and Personality: Selected Essays.** Berkeley, California: Univ. of California Press.

Sherif, Carolyn, Muzafer Sherif, and Roger Nebergall. 1965. **Attitude and Attitude Change.** Philadelphia: W. B. Saunders.

Weaver, Carl. 1972. **Human Listening.** Indianapolis, Indiana: Bobbs-Merrill.

Wiener, Morton, and Albert Mahrabian. 1968. **Language Within Language: Immediacy, a Channel in Verbal Communication.** New York: Appleton-Century-Crofts.

THREE

Communicating personally: a description

. . . you cannot communicate personally without caring . . .

Most people who study communication decide, sooner or later, that it is necessary to differentiate among "types" or "levels" of communicating. All of the behavior which is sometimes lumped under the label "communicating" and could be represented by the model in Figure 2 is not alike, and a "conceptual slippage" occurs when they are described by the same terms. This is a problem for the builders of theory (Thayer, 1963; Dance, 1970).

More important for our concerns, the differences between types of communicating pose a problem for you as a communicator. The skills required for effective performance—and the whole concept of what constitutes "good" or "effective" communicating—is not the same in various types of communicating.

Most attempts to identify the differences between types of communicating focus on "structural" variables, such as the number of people involved (intrapersonal, interpersonal, public, mass), the purpose or effect of the messages (informative, persuasive, entertaining, deliberative, ceremonial), the nature of the medium used to transmit the message (nonverbal, speech, print, broadcast), or even the mode of delivery (impromptu, extemporaneous, manuscript). While these distinctions are useful for some purposes, they are not for ours. The types which we are concerned with differentiating involve the **meaning** rather than the modality or structure of the communication behavior. We chose this option because the alternative simply does not work: communication behaviors which are structurally identical may differ in important ways.

Consider these three statements:

1. Pass the salt.
2. Put out that fire!
3. I need someone to talk to.

The sentences look alike, have similar grammatical structure, and each asks the other to do something for the speaker. But they are extracted from the context of quite different communication events.

When we request a salt shaker to be passed, we are asking the other person to act on a tangible, nonpersonal object of little significance; that he do what is considered an act of elementary courtesy; and that he do something which we would surely do for ourselves if the salt were closer or our arm longer. When the person addressed has complied with this request, a brusque "thanks" and vigorous use of the shaker is sufficient acknowledgment, and if the person refuses our request, we suspect that there is something wrong with him. Finally, we are asking the other to do something which we would expect practically anyone in that spatial and temporal location to do for us.

A command to extinguish a fire is very similar to a request for salt, differing primarily in the urgency and importance of the act. Still, the requested behavior involves an object rather than a person, is something which we would ask any appropriately located individual to do, or do ourselves if we were more strategically deployed. Refusal to comply with the request implies that something is wrong with the other.

But the statement "I need someone to talk to" is quite different. In this instance, it is the speaker rather than some inanimate object with which the other is requested to become involved; it is a request for something which the speaker cannot do for himself in any circumstance; it is a request which would be directed only to specific others, not to whoever happens to be near by. The speaker is proposing that the listener engage in behavior which will not shortly terminate, but that he become part of an ongoing relationship which may exert frequent and important demands on his time and energies. If the other refuses, the speaker is likely to feel that there is something wrong with himself rather than the other.

The differences between these communication behaviors come from their meanings (that is, the significance associated with them) rather than their structure. But how can these best be described? Various persons have answered this question in different ways.

Martin Buber[1] identified three types of communication which may occur when two or more people exchange messages. The first of these resembles the example given above of asking for a friend, the other two the examples of fire-fighting or asking for salt. In **genuine dialogue,** "each of the participants really has in mind the other or others in their present and particular being and turns to them with the intention of establishing a living mutual relation between himself and them." Buber remarks that genuine dialogue is rare, usually replaced by what he called technical dialogue or monologue disguised as dialogue. **Technical dialogue** is "prompted solely by the need for objective understanding," and the relationship between the communicators is either unimportant or considered intrusive. There are several types of **monologue disguised as dialogue** in which persons "speak each with himself in strangely tortuous and circuitous ways." For example, "debates" consist of thoughts which are not presented as they exist in the mind but as adapted for maximum impact-value and function to confirm the participants' self-confidence by making impressions on other people. In "friendly chats" each regards himself as absolute and legitimate; the other is accepted only if he agrees with the speaker or conforms to expectations. There is no intent to confront the other as a person; rather, the other is rejected or the chat stopped if the other does not "play along." Finally, Buber somewhat cynically described a "lover's talk" as a process "in which both partners alike enjoy their own glorious soul and their precious experience."

Dean Barnlund (1962) differentiated coercive, exploitative, and facilitative communication behavior in terms of what the speaker tries to do to the meanings of the listener:

[1]1955, pp. 19–20.

Meaning, in my opinion, is a private preserve and trespassers always run a risk. To speak of personal integrity at all is to acknowledge this. Any exchange of words is an invasion of the privacy of the listener which is aimed at preventing, restricting, or stimulating the cultivation of meaning. Briefly, three types of interference may be distinguished. First, there are messages whose intent is to **coerce.** Meaning is controlled by choosing symbols that so threaten the interpreter that he becomes incapable of, and blind to, alternative meanings; second, there are messages of an **exploitative** sort in which words are arranged to filter the information, narrow the choices, obscure the consequences, so that only one meaning becomes attractive or appropriate; third, there is **facilitative** communication in which words are used to inform, to enlarge perspective, to deepen sensitivity, to remove external threat, to encourage independence of meaning. The values of the listener are, in the first case, ignored, in the second, subverted, in the third, respected.[2]

In a more recent paper, Barnlund[3] was concerned with the effects of communication. **Destructive** interpersonal communications "leave participants more vulnerable than before to the strains of future interactions," **neutral** communication experiences may give the person additional information but do not affect him otherwise, and **therapeutic** interpersonal communications "provoke personal insight or reorientation, and . . . enable persons to participate in more satisfying ways in future social encounters."

Richard Johannesen (1971) characterized the essential characteristics of **dialogue** as "genuineness," "accurate empathic understanding," "unconditional positive regard," "presentness," "a spirit of mutual equality" and "a supportive psychological climate." The opposite of dialogue is monologue, and Johannesen believes that monologue and dialogue represent "extremes on a continuum" by which the differences between communication events may be described.

What we call personal communicating is similar to what Johannesen called "dialogue," Buber "genuine dialogue," and Barnlund "facilitative" or "therapeutic" communication. Those forms of communication which Barnlund called "exploitative," "coercive" or "destructive," Buber "technical dialogue" or "disguised mono-

[2]1962, p. 204.
[3]1968, p. 614.

logue," and Johannesen "monologue" are similar to our concept of communicating impersonally.

But we are not satisfied just to acknowledge that these differences in communication behavior occur or even that the distinction we have drawn is similar to that made by other people. Our concern is with communication behavior. Rather than merely describing examples of personal and impersonal communicating, it is our intention to analyze what people do when they communicate in these ways. It is this emphasis—not our preference for the terms personal and impersonal—which is unique to our analysis.

Remember that there are two forms of communication behavior: making meaning from messages and messages from meaning. These behaviors are what people do when they communicate whether that communicating is personal or impersonal. But individuals make meaning and make messages in a particular way when they are communicating personally that they do not when they are communicating impersonally.

Criterial attributes of communicating personally

When a person makes a message, he may try to match the message to the meaning he has "in his head," he may distort that meaning, or he may edit it, letting only selected portions of it be expressed by the message. While communicating personally, a speaker is **honest:** he deliberately attempts to describe his present experience as he is aware of it as an invitation for the other person to share his awareness of his experience. Messages which omit portions of the speaker's awareness which he considers important or which distort or falsify his awareness are less honest.

When a person makes meaning from a message, he may interpret the message as confirming, denying, or irrelevant to his concept of himself. While communicating personally, an individual interprets messages as **validating:** he understands the message as affirming his worth as a person and the legitimacy of his experience. When he interprets messages as irrelevant to or challenging his worth as a person or questioning or denying the legitimacy of his experience, he is communicating less personally.

Communicating personally may be defined as occurring when a person interprets messages as validating him and makes messages which are honest. Obviously, more needs to be said about honesty and validation as the criterial characteristics of personal communicating, and the next two chapters do just that.

But before examining the nature of personal communicating in greater detail, remember that we have talked about a **continuum** between highly personal and highly impersonal. Despite the seemingly discrete categories of "types" of communication offered by Buber and others, communication behavior is best described as "more or less" personal rather than "either/or." Messages may be highly honest, slightly honest, slightly dishonest, or highly dishonest. Messages may be interpreted as highly validating or highly invalidating. When we refer to personal or impersonal communicating, understand us to be describing extreme points on a continuum rather than discrete categories.

Other characteristics of communicating personally

We believe that honesty and validation are the criterial attributes of highly personal communicating, but we are impressed by the differences in the ways various persons communicate personally. When expressing shared grief with a bereaved friend, one person might speak volumes, another wail in despair, and a third quietly sit in social silence—yet all may be equally personal. In casual moments of companionship, one may joke where another will be contemplative or serious. In fact, the communicators' feeling that they are free to act as themselves rather than as they think they should or as others expect them to is what makes these forms of communicating personal.

Any attempt to impose a yoke of consistency or similarity on people communicating personally must be suspect. However, some characteristics seem common to many or most instances of personal communicating, and it is these characteristics with which we are presently concerned.

Let us state our position clearly: the attributes described in this section do not define nor do they specify "necessary or sufficient conditions" of personal communicating. Rather, they are what we have come to expect to find when we communicate personally. We include them here because they help us express our understanding of this form of communication and because they demonstrate the way in which personal communicating is related to the topics which we will address in Part Two of this book: interpersonal trust, alienation, and psychological health.

Usually occurs in face-to-face situations. Several factors make face-to-face encounters the most likely environment for personal communicating. One reason involves the "risks" of being honest. There are people who will take any opportunity to embarrass or exploit those who are honest. In communicating with one person, it is possible to make a reasonable assessment of the risk involved in being honest; with a crowd it is more difficult.

As there is some risk involved in being honest, so interpreting messages addressed to you as validating involves a chance of error. There are times when apparently validating messages are phony and other times when apparently invalidating messages should be understood as not meaning what they seem to say. It is easier to know what a person means by what he says when the message is private, not circulated for public consumption.

Personal communicating develops most naturally when all participants share the responsibility for redefining the relationship as more personal. These symmetrical redefinitions are more likely when only two people are involved: each additional person increases the probabilities of a coalition between some of the members against others or of including a person unwilling to communicate personally.

Finally, communicating personally requires considerable amounts of specific information about the other and the ability to coordinate behaviors. These conditions are not always available in large groups. A public speaker has considerable difficulty learning and reacting to the specific characteristics of his audiences. Even though good speakers carefully analyze their audiences before and during their speech, unless the audience is unusually homogeneous, speakers cannot address all members of the audience simultaneously and usually wind up talking to no one in particular. A common technique is to "average" the audience characteristics and to interact with this construct rather than with any individual.

The problem confronting a person using mass communication media such as radio, television, or film is even greater. These media interpose between the message source and the receiver, making it impossible for the performer or the director to know just who comprises his audience or to observe their responses to the message in time to make any needed adjustments while it is being produced.

The characteristics of public and mass communication pose obstacles to personal communicating, but some individuals seem able to be much more personal than others using these forms of communication. Some public speakers seem impossibly remote and impersonal: think here of an overdressed, perspiring, nervously moving man reading word-for-word in a monotone from a conspicuous sheaf of pages. Others seem warm, close, and personal. Some public speakers and some television personalities seem to be personal friends of the viewers.

Verbal messages less important. An important characteristic of communication is that it proceeds by means of messages which are both complex and ambiguous. Verbal messages have at least three kinds of meanings: denotative (that which the words "point at" or stand for); connotative (the evaluational aspect of the things described); and relational (the way the speaker thinks about himself and the other).

Consider the following statements:

1. Please close the door. ˙
2. Shut the door.
3. Any civilized person would have closed the door.
4. Shut the damn door!
5. Where were you raised, fellow? In a barn?

The sense of all of these is the same: the speaker would like the door closed with the listener as the agency by which it happens. The words chosen to express these meanings, however, convey considerably more information than that.

If this were not confusing enough, the voice adds a whole new set of cues which express many sorts of meanings. We use our voices to snarl at or caress other people or to warn them of the degree of urgency (or the lack thereof) we feel toward what we are talking about. Reversing the usual interpretation of the relationship between verbal and vocal messages, Norman Markel once said that the verbal messages frequently serve as a "carrier wave" for voice sounds: we sometimes say words just as an excuse for making noises at each other. Obviously, this is the situation when a mother talks to her infant or two lovers whisper "sweet nothings" to each other. Further, vocal inflections serve as metacommunication ("messages about messages") which instruct the recipient about how the verbal message is to be interpreted. This phrase:

light house keeper

has three meanings depending on which word is vocally emphasized, and this sentence:

if you think our waitresses are rude, you should see the

manager

has two, depending on whether "waitresses" or "rude" is stressed. Try it.

Messages are complex because all these different types of cues are floating about simultaneously. They are ambiguous because few cues have less than two possible meanings and several cues may well contradict each other.

When communicators know each other well, have given and received pledges of honesty, and have cooperatively developed a stable pattern of interaction—that is, when they usually communicate personally—each is willing and able to look beyond the words that are said and to identify the other's meaning, his state of mind, and the total context of cues. They are prepared to make tentative rather than rigid interpretations and to allow the other to mean what he chooses rather than to "force" the other to mean what they expect him to mean. Those who communicate impersonally, on the other hand, tend to focus on the precise semantic and syntactic meanings of the words that are spoken.

Perhaps the feeling of the difference between these two can be best expressed by comparing the statement, "I understand **you**" with the statement, "I understand what you are **saying**."

Research reported by Watzlawick, Beavin, and Jackson[4] demonstrates the different interpretations of messages made by those who attend primarily to verbal cues as opposed to those who can place all the cues in a message into context. Typed manuscripts of conversations between three husband-wife dyads were given to a group of second- and third-year psychiatric residents doing their intern training. The first two couples had been previously diagnosed as "clinically disturbed" while the third was "clinically normal." The psychiatric residents, however, rated the third couple as

[4]1967, p. 117.

much "sicker" than the other two. One of the reasons cited for this erroneous interpretation was that their judgment "was based on content rather than on the interaction." The authors concluded that "content fades in importance as communication patterns emerge."

A similar line of research was conducted by Basil Bernstein,[5] who noted that various groups of English-speaking people use the language differently, and distinguished "elaborated" and "restricted" codes. Elaborated codes exploit the potential of the verbal language to describe exact relationships and to make precise denotations, while restricted codes rely on nonverbal cues, previously shared meanings, and active, aggressive listening by the message recipient. Impersonal communicating is usually at its best using an elaborated code, such as the precise terminology of a business contract between buyer and seller or the well-chosen words of a journalist's account of a news event. Personal communicating, on the other hand, may best use restricted codes which are packed with meaning for the communicators but unintelligible to an outsider.

Erving Goffman[6] described the difficult communication situation created at a banquet when the seating arrangements create a group of three persons, two of whom know each other well enough to communicate personally but neither of whom knows the other well enough to invite him into such intimacy. Their options are to exclude the third party—a serious offense at a social function—or to limit their conversation to forms in which he can participate. Goffman observed that the two friends will probably feel dissatisfied with this latter sort of conversation, at least in part because the elaborated code is so much less efficient than a restricted code. The ultimate in competent communication in such situations is for one person to make messages in both codes simultaneously: his friend will interpret what he says in terms of the restricted code and make one meaning from it while the new acquaintance will interpret the same message in terms of the elaborated code and make quite a different meaning.

One of the most attractive aspects of personal communicating

[5] 1964, pp. 55–69.
[6] 1971, pp. 4–5.

is the ability to speak freely, without worrying about nuances of messages being misinterpreted or having to find the most precise way to articulate meanings. While it is good to be able to use the elaborated code at times—a lifestyle in which the most articulate statement is "like man, you know, that's heavy, a real groovy experience, he's got his thing together, he's not uptight" seems a most recondite and reiterative existence—sometimes it's refreshing to use simple words from the restricted code which you know will be understood.

More person-oriented. Bales and Slater[7] differentiated between socio-emotive leaders and task leaders in groups. Task leaders are primarily concerned with getting the job done, expressing themselves by orders, suggestions, criticisms, exhortations, and the like, while socio-emotive leaders are primarily concerned with maintaining good morale and seeing that all group members are productively participating in interactions with each other. Both types of leadership are usually required for effective group performance.

When a person is task-oriented, for him it is performance that counts. But when socio-emotive factors are considered important, feelings are involved as well. Personal communicating gives a prominent place to the expression of emotions. When persons who customarily communicate with each other personally discover bad feelings or misunderstandings, they may engage in a "drill" of matching perceptions like this:

BILL. Hey, wait a minute, Pete. Let's talk a bit before we continue. I feel threatened and defensive right now.

PETE. Really? I don't see myself as saying threatening things. What is bothering you?

BILL. You keep saying "everybody knows" and then stating opinions I don't agree with. It sounds like you are denying my right to hold my opinion.

PETE. Oh. I don't mean to do that, of course. I thought that we agreed on these issues, but I guess I was mistaken. Let's see if I can do better. I believe . . .

BILL. (Interrupting) Yes, that's better.

The difference between "everybody knows" and "I believe" is really not great, but it was bothering Bill. A good task leader would be

[7]1955, pp. 259–306.

impatient with the delay in getting on with the job, but a socio-emotive leader would be delighted that the potential difficulties between Bill and Pete were so quickly resolved.

Some people are task-oriented as a lifestyle and find themselves irritated and frustrated with personal communicating by those around them. They feel that it is "messy," unimportant, and ineffi-cient. In some instances, we agree. There are situations in which personal communicating is the inappropriate form of behavior. In fact, when members' needs for communicating personally are ade-quately met in other relationships, a work environment in which getting the job done is the most important consideration may be very attractive and rewarding. On the other hand, members of an organization who have persistently unmet needs for personal com-municating will find the task-orientation of deadlines dehumanizing and frustrating.

Facilitative. Dean Barnlund (1962) described facilitative mes-sages as those which inform, enlarge the perspective, and deepen the sensitivity of the other so that he may develop as a person. The important point is that the direction in which the other develops is not decreed by the content of facilitative messages; rather, they help the person become what he chooses. Messages in personal communicating are freeing rather than restricting.

It is frequently argued that all communication is persuasion be-cause messages affect those who perceive them. But responses to messages may take many forms, and these are better differenti-ated than simply lumped together. We prefer to reserve the term "persuasion" for messages consciously crafted to elicit a pre-determined response from the other. If a speaker tries to limit the responses available to the other, he is persuasive and, as we see it, communicating impersonally. In extreme instances of demagogu-ery, the persuader lets himself be known only to the extent that it will make him more effective, and the individuality of the other is not important. As long as he is elected, the persuader does not care who casts the votes; as long as products are bought, he does not care who purchases them. Even when the persuader is well intentioned toward the other, persuasive attempts are still imper-sonal. Parents usually work very hard to develop certain types of behavior in their children, behavior which they think will benefit the children as they mature. But when parents insist that their children eat their spinach and make this a "nonnegotiable demand," it is best understood as an instance of impersonal communicating.

But let us again remind you that persuasion and other forms of impersonal communication are sometimes necessary, sometimes optimal, and that communicating personally is in some situations a poor choice of what to do. Consider a person who needs a bit of information or who is doing something which you have reason to believe will have disastrous results. Should you simply state your feelings about the matter and leave it to the other to decide or should you employ all of the available means of persuasion? The point may be best made by an analogy. Carl Rogers attempts to be "nondirective" in counseling by avoiding behaviors like arguing, ordering, lecturing, prescribing remedies, etc. Some "Rogerians" have perfected this technique to a fault. So committed to the ideal of nondirective interpersonal relationships, they lose the ability to be impersonal when they should be. The surely hypothetical story is told of a man who burst into a convention of Rogerian therapists and rather desperately asked for directions to the nearest men's restroom. Using good nondirective responses, and with the tacit support of his colleagues, one therapist replied:

"I perceive you as telling me that you need to go to the rest-room."

and the conversation went like this:

"Yes. Would you please tell me where to find it?"

"I see. You want me to take the responsibility for deciding where you should go."

"Of course. Could you hurry, please?"

"But I can't make decisions for you. Each of us must take the responsibility for his own decisions."

"What the hell is the matter with you, anyway?"

"I perceive you as getting hostile now."

Assume that the rather simple-minded therapist in this ludicrous story was really trying to help the other person and that he was attempting to initiate an interaction which would lead to personal communicating between them. What he failed to do was to recognize that the situation was not right for personal communication. What the other person most needed to hear in that instance was:

"Down the hall to your right, third door on the left."

Involves caring. When we play roles with each other, such as teacher-student or customer-salesman, impersonal communicating is appropriate because each is reserving his own unique identity and is concerned only with the other's role. When the other leaves the role, he is of no continued importance. When we use other people for our own gains, impersonal communicating is appropriate because the relationship is asymmetrical, that is, we see ourselves but not the other as worthy, and our continued relationship is contingent on utilitarian value. But when one person accepts the identity of the other as a value to be enhanced and appreciated, accepts the well-being of the other as his concern and responsibility, then personal communicating is likely to occur.

Rollo May[8] wrote an analysis of love and will, in which he concluded that a combination of love and will can best be described as caring. Caring, he writes, "is a state composed of recognition of another, a fellow human being like one's self; of identification of one's self with the pain or joy of the other; of guilt, pity and the awareness that we all stand on the base of a common humanity from which we all stem." To care for another person is to make what happens to that person, whether for good or ill, matter to you; it is to involve yourself as a person—not as a role such as friend or counselor or husband or wife—with the experience of the other; it is to establish a commitment beyond pretense and without specified terms to the other.

The opposite of care is apathy. You can care for those of whom you disapprove, for those you do not like as well as for those whom you love. But you cannot communicate personally without caring.

When we know people quite well and then are separated from them for a considerable amount of time, we are able to resume the relationship with some more easily than with others. One possible explanation for this is that those friendships which are more easily renewed are with persons with whom we have related in personal ways. Others may be those with whom we have discussed only relatively trivial matters, external to ourselves. Since the environment has changed and we no longer have activities which we share with the other, there is little in common and nothing to talk about except the remembered good times. What do you think of this explanation? How do you see the role of communicat-

---

[8]**Love and Will**, p. 289.

ing personally in long term relationships? Are there always some relationships which we can resume after a long separation or must all relationships inevitably deteriorate with the passage of time and the absence of contact?

Think back over the last ten years or so since you have been relatively mature and aware of your relationships with others and try to determine the one person who understood you better than anyone else did. It is not necessary that the person understand you today or that he understood you for a long period of time. It is only necessary that you feel that for some period of time this individual understood you better than anyone else has. Try to determine what it was about yourself, the other person, the situation, or any combination of these that made this understanding take place. Now try to figure out how personal communicating played a part in your feeling understood. Did the other person communicate personally with you? Was he honest and validating? How did you communicate with him? How did his or her communication behavior influence you? How did yours influence him or her? Does your experience support what we have said so far about communicating personally?

References

Bales, Robert F., and P. E. Slater. 1955. "Role Differentiation in Small Decision-Making Groups," in **Family Socialization and Interaction Process.** Glencoe, Illinois: Free Press. Talcot Parsons and Robert Bales, eds., 259–306.

Barnlund, Dean. 1962. "Toward a Meaning-Centered Philosophy of Communication," **Journal of Communication,** 12:197–211.

———. 1968. **Interpersonal Communication: Survey and Studies.** Boston: Houghton Mifflin.

Bernstein, Basil. 1964. "Elaborated and Restricted Codes: The Social Origins and Some Consequences," **American Anthropologist,** 66: 55–69.

Buber, Martin. 1955. **Between Man and Man.** Boston: Beacon Press.

Dance, Frank E. X. 1970. "The Concept of Communication," **Journal of Communication,** 20:201–10.

Goffman, Erving. 1971. **Relations in Public: Microstudies of the Public Order.** New York: Basic Books.

Johannesen, Richard L. 1971. "The Emerging Concept of Communication as Dialogue," **The Quarterly Journal of Speech,** 57:373–82.

May, Rollo. 1969. **Love and Will.** New York: Norton.

Thayer, Lee O. 1963. "On Theory-Building in Communication: Some Conceptual Problems," **Journal of Communication,** 13:217–35.

Watzlawick, Paul, Janet H. Beavin, and Don D. Jackson. 1967. **Pragmatics of Human Communication: A Study of Interactional Processes, Pathologies, and Paradoxes.** New York: Norton.

FOUR

Communicating personally: honesty

... to cry when you are sad, laugh when you are happy ... these are honest behaviors ...

One of the two forms of communication behavior is that of making messages from meaning. Descriptions of this behavior assume that there is some information "inside" the communicator which is at least potentially expressable and that the communicator is at least partly able to control the extent to which his messages express this information. A person communicates honestly to the extent that his messages accurately express his awareness of his experience and invite the listener to share in that experience. Let us put this statement into context.

Individuals are usually not aware of much of their experience. This is easily demonstrated: you **can** but usually **do not** detect small changes in room temperature, lighting, or ambient noise levels unless your attention is called to them. Here is a common experience: someone addresses a question to you while you are not listening. Your first awareness is only that you are expected to answer some question: you respond by asking for the question to be repeated ("Oh, I'm sorry. What did you say?") and then suddenly

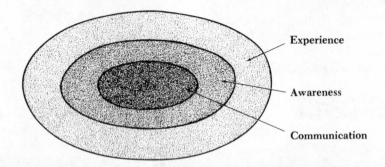

Figure 3. Relations between experience, awareness and communication (adapted from Rogers, 1961)

"remember" what the question was. Without perceptible pause you make the appropriate response. Or consider your attitude toward another person: perhaps you have felt a vague discomfort toward one of your acquaintances or professors and suddenly you become aware that you have disliked him all along. These examples clearly show that your experience is greater than your awareness of it. In fact, the physiology and psychology of perception is such that awareness probably **cannot** fully match experience (Forgus, 1966; Neisser, 1967).

But a further observation is that individuals usually do not communicate all of the experience of which they are aware. If you are bored, you may try to avoid letting your hostess know. If a celebrity appears at a meeting and you like him, you will probably clap or cheer, but if you dislike him, you will probably remain quiet rather than boo and hiss. If you are not convinced that what you are saying is the truth, you may or may not include a message which indicates this part of your awareness.

These relations between experience, awareness, and communication are diagrammed in Figure 3. To the extent that an individual's communicating in a particular instance approximates his awareness and invites the other to share it, he is communicating personally.

Note that honesty has no necessary relationship with truth. People are often unaware of their "true" motivations for important behaviors, but if the communicator expresses what he believes is his motivation, he is being honest. While Ambassador to the United Nations during the early 1960s, Adlai Stevenson claimed that the United States was not involved in the "Bay of Pigs" invasion of Cuba. He was soon shown to have been in error, but not to have been dishonest since he had not been informed of U.S. participation. Carl Rogers (1961) observed that if an individual's experiences were totally within his awareness and his awareness was totally represented within his communication, he could never make a statement of "external fact" because he only knows what he perceives, not facts themselves. Instead of saying, "He is stupid," he would say, "I perceive him as stupid"; instead of "That's good," "I perceive that to be good." The point is that communicators who are being honest add to all their statements the implicit or explicit true statement that "this is my awareness of what I am talking about."

One attempt to characterize "openness" or honesty was made by MacDaniels and his colleagues (1971). An adapted form of their "Theoretic Profile" appearing in Figure 4 shows three characteristics which distinguish open and nonopen expressions and gives examples of each. While there is no standard format for messages in honest communicating, these messages are usually characterized by immediacy, by expressing ownership of feelings

	Very Open	Neither Very Open Nor Very Closed	Very Closed
Immediacy:	"I feel . . ." . . . (Here and Now)	"I used to feel . . ." . . . "In some situations I feel . . ." (Here, Not Now; Now, Not Here)	"Once I felt . . ." (Not Here, Not Now)
Ownership of Feeling:	"I feel . . ." "Some of us feel . . ."		"Some people feel . . ." "Society feels . . ."
Source of Feeling:	"Toward you I feel . . ." "Some people make me feel . . ."		"In general, I feel . . ."

Figure 4. A Profile of "Open" Expression

Adapted from Joseph MacDaniels, Elaine Yarbrough, C. L. Kaszmaul and Kim Giffin, "Openness: Personalized Expression in Interpersonal Communication," paper presented to the International Communication Association, Phoenix, Arizona, 1971.

and by indicating that the messages reflect the speaker's perception rather than "external facts."

Let us conclude this description of honesty by considering some examples of honest and dishonest communicating. When you are in a group and someone tells a story which everyone **but you** seems to think is funny, pretending to be amused by laughing along with the crowd is dishonest. If someone says something which you interpret as critical of you, the honest response is to tell the other that you feel "put down." To cry when you are sad, laugh when you are happy, sleep when you are tired, eat when you are hungry, and quit when you are not—these are honest behaviors because they match messages to your awareness of your experience.

The ability to communicate honestly

Most people most of the time do not communicate honestly. Further, many people are incapable of communicating honestly about some important areas of their experience. Later in this chapter we will discuss some reasons why people choose not to communicate honestly much of the time; this section describes **inability** to communicate honestly.

Honesty involves a matching of awareness and messages. Some people are incapable of communicating honestly about a number of significant experiences because they are unaware of them. Since Sigmund Freud first described the function of the subconscious, psychologists have been well aware of repression or selective forgetting.[1] One way of coping with unpleasant experiences is simply to forget about them. Sometimes this technique is only partially successful: the guilt, anxiety, or hatred caused by a traumatic event remains even though the person has completely forgotten the event. He finds (usually negative) feelings associated in his mind with persons or things which do not merit such abuse, but cannot explain why. A person who has repressed a considerable amount of experience can communicate honestly only about that of which he is aware: he has a limited ability to be honest.

More important than repressed past experiences, however, is the

[1]See Freud, 1966.

limited awareness many people have about their current feelings and thoughts as they communicate with each other. At least some studies have shown that people differ in their awareness of hunger: some people eat when and until they are no longer hungry but others eat because it is mealtime and because the food is there. (The latter tend to be overweight.) Similarly, some people grow angry and behave angrily without knowing that they are mad: perhaps because their self-concept cannot tolerate them, they pay "selective inattention" to their feelings. R. D. Laing described the desiccation of experience which he believes characterizes "normal man":

> . . . as men of the world, we hardly know of the existence of the inner world . . . as for our bodies, we retain just sufficient proprioceptive sensations to coordinate our movements and to ensure the minimal requirements for biosocial survival . . . an intensive discipline of unlearning is necessary for **anyone** before one can begin to experience the world afresh, with innocence, truth and love . . . This state of affairs represents an almost unbelievable devastation of our experience. Then there is empty chatter about maturity, love, joy, peace.[2]

We have known people who moped around for months and finally overheard someone describe them as depressed. Their reaction was one of initial incredulity ("What do you mean, depressed? I'm not . . .") which slowly changed to doubt ("Well, maybe . . .") and suddenly to recognition ("Of course! That's what's wrong with me! Why haven't I been aware of it?"). The person who grows angry and, on being requested to stop shouting, replies in full voice "I'm **not** shouting!" has become a stereotype in television and movie comedies. We have known people who started—or stopped—loving a person, who decided that the material in a book or in an academic discipline was not worth knowing, who judged another person as mad, bad, or sick **without being aware** of making such important decisions. These people, some of whom were and still are our friends, are not a uniquely neurotic aggregation: "The average, normal, well-adjusted person often has not the slightest idea of what he is, of what he wants, of what his own opinions are."[3]

[2] 1967, pp. 26–27.
[3] Maslow, 1970, p. 159.

But to the extent that people are not aware of significant portions of their experience, they are incapable of communicating honestly about it.

Here are some techniques you can use to increase awareness of your experience. We suggest that you try all of them briefly, but devote a considerable effort to one or two techniques.

1. Practice catching yourself engaging in selective inattention while doing familiar things in familiar places. Stop what you are doing and take note of many of the things which you were experiencing but were not aware of. How many different noises can you hear? Do your clothes fit you badly somewhere? Are you tired from being in one position too long? Can you smell anything? Try this while talking with friends. Is there something about the way they look that you haven't noticed before? Listen to their voices: are they low-pitched or high-pitched? Do they speak with dialects or mispronounce certain words? How far apart do you stand or sit when you are talking? Do you lean toward or away from each other? What color are their eyes and hair? Are their hands neatly manicured? Do you smile when you talk to them? Do you look at or away from them? What do they do which bothers you?

2. Assemble a group and train all of the members to identify statements which do not (1) pertain to the "here and now"; (2) express ownership of feelings; and (3) indicate that the statement represents the speaker's perception rather than "external facts." As a group, discuss some topic of mutual interest, such as a moral issue or how you should feel about some political policy. But establish this as a ground rule: no one may make a statement which does not meet the criteria of immediacy, ownership of feelings, and personal perception. Any statement lacking in any or all of these must be restated or retracted. You will be surprised at what you learn about yourself and your normal mode of communicating.

3. Practice identifying your motives as you speak by using the literary device of adding "he said" plus an adjective after making a statement. For example, rather than saying just "hello," say, "hello, he said affectionately." Instead of saying, "Will you go to the party with me" say, "Will you go to the party with me, he said hopefully." Instead of "stop that" say, "Stop that, he said angrily."

Yes, your friends will think you strange. But tell them, apologetically, that you read this book by two weird fellows and they said, seriously, that this was a good thing to do. At least sometimes.

This technique does two things for you. First, it makes you see yourself at least in part as others see you: you find yourself describing yourself as he or she. Second, it forces you to match adjectives describing yourself (your experience) to your act of making a message. Sometimes this will force you to discover something you did not know about your experience; sometimes it will force you to learn new adjectives which describe a subtler shading of meaning.

The second reason for an incapacity to be honest is that many people develop personality traits or overlearn patterns of interpersonal interaction to such an extent that they are unable to invite others to share their experience. They are defensive and aggressive, seeking to protect themselves and to find ways to best or exploit the other.

Rapoport (1960; 1964) described two orientations toward interpersonal interactions. One is strategic gamesmanship or combat in which the primary question is: "In a conflict, how can I gain the advantage?" In the other orientation, based on conscience, the relevant question is: "If I gain an advantage, what sort of person will I become?" Rapoport noted that the most potent "weapons" prized by the strategist are voluntarily surrendered by the conscience-oriented person. In large measure, the difference between these styles of interaction involves a willingness to invite the other to share one's own experience.

But we are presently considering inability to communicate honestly. Even if a strategic orientation precludes honesty, this does not imply inability to communicate honestly **if** individuals can deliberately switch between strategic and conscience orientations. However, Rapoport sadly concludes that these are "ultimately incompatible" modes of thought and behavior, and there is some evidence to support his judgment. Individuals who have developed an "authoritarian personality" (Adorno **et al.,** 1950) or a "closed mind" (Rokeach, 1960) tend to view the world as threatening and tend to avoid behaviors such as honesty which would make them more vulnerable and expose their beliefs and attitudes to disconfirmation. These personality characteristics, which seem to be the basis for a strategic orientation, are somewhat stable: a person usually does not behave "openly" one day and "closed" the next. Similarly, some individuals are characteristically Machiavellian (Christie and Geis, 1970) or display a "Neanderthal mentality" (Osgood, 1962). To the extent that these are consistent behaviors —personality traits—the individual is not likely to switch between strategic and conscience orientations and is not able to communicate honestly.

Novelist C. S. Forester's most popular works involve strong, aggressive men. In **The Captain from Connecticut,** Forester's protagonist is an American naval captain who has just committed a colossal faux pas: not recognizing the flag of the French monarchy because he did not know that Napoleon had been removed as Emperor of France, he fired at what he thought was an unidentified ship. At the time, the United States was locked in the devastating War of 1812 with England, the city of Washington had just been burned and woe to the navy captain who might earn France as his country's enemy. Like all of Forester's men, Captain Josiah Peabody was most content when on his quarterdeck facing the enemy with blazing guns; most ill at ease when performing the social graces or, perish the thought, communicating personally. Forester describes the scene like this:[4]

> "And now, sir," said Dupont, "would you have the goodness to explain why your ship fired upon me?"
> "Why didn't you show your colors?" riposted Peabody. He was in no mood for a passive defensive.
> Dupont's bushy brows came together angrily.
> "We showed them, sir. We still show them."
> He gesticulated towards the peak, where the white flag fluttered. Peabody noticed for the first time a gleam of gold on the white, and felt a moment's misgiving which he was determined not to show.
> "Where are your national colors?" he asked.
> "Those are they. The flag of His Most Christian Majesty."
> "His Most Christian Majesty?"
> "His Most Christian Majesty Louis, by the grace of God King of France and Navarre."
>
> Peabody began to see the light, and at the same time worse misgivings than ever began to assail him.
> "Napoleon has fallen?" he said.

[4]1941, pp. 79–81.

"The usurper Bonaparte has fallen," said Dupont solemnly. "Louis the Eighteenth sits on his rightful throne."

. . . Peabody knew immediate qualms at the thought that he had fired upon the flag of what was presumably a neutral country. He saw the need for prompt apology, unreserved apology. . . . He had thought for the moment of laughing at the whole affair, turning on his heel and quitting the **Tigresse,** leaving the politicians to disentangle the business as best they could; but he put aside the insidious temptation to reckless arrogance. It was his duty to humble himself. He swallowed twice as he collected the words together in his mind.

"Sir," he said slowly, "I hope you will allow me to apologize for this —this unfortunate thing that has happened. I am very sorry, sir."

It was not the words of the apology which mollified Dupont as much as the tremendous reluctance with which the words came. A lion could hardly have given back a lamb to its mother more unreadily. An apology from a man so totally unaccustomed to apologizing was doubly sweet to the fat little captain, and his face cleared.

"Let us say no more about it, sir," said Dupont.

Captain Peabody was a strategist, and subsequently proved his ability to be cunning, deceitful, and determined in the conduct of his duties, but he was not skilled in communicating personally. His Puritan heritage made it almost impossible for him to abandon the pretense of emotionless competence, and his strategic orientation made him defensive. He would be honest only when honesty gave him a tactical advantage.

The point is that some people are virtually incapable of communicating honestly because they are unaware of much of their experience or because they have developed personality traits or habitual patterns of interpersonal behavior which cause them to treat other people strategically. Many more people are severely limited in their ability to communicate honestly: we believe that communicating honestly is difficult and that the ability is developed through practice and conscious effort. Few people are secure enough in their self-esteem and committed enough to conscience-based interactions with others to be highly honest most of the time.

Do you often communicate honestly? Here are two measuring devices which you can use to assess the extent to which your communication behavior is honest.

1. This is a questionnaire used in studying "self-disclosure" taken from Jourard (1971). As discussed in Appendix A, self-disclosure refers to any communication behavior in which the speaker tells the listener something about himself. This includes both "honesty" and several other types of communicating which we describe later in this chapter as "inappropriate" self-disclosure. However, the self-disclosure questionnaire is useful in discovering how you communicate with particular other people. Interpret the results like this: if you have "disclosed," you may or may not have been honest; but if you have not disclosed, you certainly have not been honest.

The questionnaire consists of a list of topics. To complete the questionnaire, indicate the extent to which you have talked about each topic to another person.

First, make a list from 1 to 21. Second, draw several vertical lines so that you make a series of columns. At the top of the columns, write the names of your best same-sex friend, best opposite-sex friend, parents, employer or colleagues. Finally, indicate the extent to which you have disclosed to the designated persons by inserting one of the following numbers in each row, where:

0= I haven't talked about this at all, or have lied or distorted information about this;

1= I have talked only in general terms about this;

2= I have disclosed quite a bit about this, but not completely;

3= I have disclosed fully and completely about this.

Scoring: The items are of different levels of intimacy. Score the questionnaire by adding the numbers you selected for items 1, 4, 7, 11, 13, 18, and 19 (these are low intimacy items); 2, 5, 8, 12, 14, 17, and 20 (moderate intimacy); and 3, 6, 9, 10, 15, 16, and 21 (high intimacy). This will give you three scores for disclosure.

Some Topics of Conversation:

1. Your views on the ways a husband and wife should live their marriage.

2. Your usual ways of dealing with depression, anxiety, and anger.

3. The actions which you have most regretted doing and why you regret them.

4. Your personal religious views and the nature of the religious participation, if any.

5. The ways in which you feel most maladjusted or immature.

6. Your guiltiest secrets.

7. Your personal views on politics, the presidency, foreign and domestic policy.

8. Your habits and reactions which currently bother you.

9. *The sources of strain and dissatisfaction in your marriage (or your relationships with members of the opposite sex).*
10. *Your favorite forms of erotic play and sexual lovemaking.*
11. *Your hobbies, how you best like to spend your spare time.*
12. *The occasions in your life in which you were the happiest.*
13. *The aspects of your daily work which satisfy and bother you.*
14. *Your personal characteristics which give you cause for pride and satisfaction.*
15. *The persons in your life whom you most resent and the reason for your resentment.*
16. *The identities of the people with whom you have been sexually intimate and the circumstances of your relationship with each.*
17. *The unhappiest moments in your life and why they were unhappy.*
18. *Your preferences and dislikes in music.*
19. *Your personal goals for the next ten years or so.*
20. *The circumstances under which you become depressed and your feelings are hurt.*
21. *Your most common sexual fantasies and reveries.*

An interesting thing to do is to complete the questionnaire in terms of your disclosure to another person, and have that person describe his disclosure to you. Then compare notes. You will be surprised at the differences you will sometimes find. Another interesting use for this questionnaire is to complete it in terms of (1) how much you have disclosed to the other; (2) how much you think the other has disclosed to you; and (3) how much you would be willing to disclose if the other initiates conversation about the topic. Comparing these scores may indicate some important things about your communication patterns.

2. Clinical psychologists have been much concerned about communication skills. For example, Rogers (1961) claimed that the whole purpose of psychological counseling is to establish good communication with a patient and help him become able to communicate well in his dealings with other people. Studies of the interaction between counselors and patients indicate that patients will not communicate better than their counselors, so trainers of counselors have devoted considerable effort to assessing and improving communication skills. Robert Carkhuff (1969) developed a series of rating scales which he uses to describe several characteristics of communication behavior. One of these measures "genuineness" in terms of five levels: level 1 describes an absolute minimum, level 5 a maximum of genuineness. The scale is used by a person who observes another communicating: the rater is to describe the speaker as, for example, a level two when talking about negative feel-

ings (dislike, hostility) and a level four when talking about positive feelings.

Tape-record a conversation (or series of conversations) in which you are one of the participants. Later, listen to the tape and rate yourself (and perhaps the other persons) on this scale. Then let a friend rate you. Compare scores. If there is a discrepancy, replay the tape and discuss why you assigned different ratings to your behavior.

Genuineness

Level 1. The speaker's verbalizations are clearly unrelated to what he appears to be feeling at the moment, or his only genuine responses are negative, critical ones. By word choice, voice quality, body movement or facial expression, the speaker displays defensiveness, not relying on his experience as a basis for developing the relationship. There is evidence of a considerable discrepancy between the speaker's inner experiencing and his current verbalizations.

Level 2. The speaker's verbalizations are slightly related to what he appears otherwise to be feeling at the moment, or when his responses are genuine they are negative in regard to the other person. The speaker does not appear able to employ his negative reactions constructively as a basis for developing the relationship. The speaker seems to be playing a role, to be rehearsed rather than spontaneous.

Level 3. The speaker gives no indication of a discrepancy between what he says and what he appears otherwise to be experiencing, but he does not provide any information about what he is actually experiencing. While the speaker does not seem insincere, neither does he seem involved in the relationship. He seems distant, cool, detached.

Level 4. The speaker presents some cues which indicate what he is feeling. Although he is clearly expressing what he really feels, he is somewhat hesitant to reveal them fully. The speaker is able to employ his feelings as a basis for developing the relationship.

Level 5. The speaker freely and deeply presents himself in a nonexploitative relationship with the other. He is spontaneous and open to experiences of all types, both pleasant and hurtful. The speaker is clearly being himself and employing his own experience constructively in the relationship.

The development of honesty

When people first meet, they usually do not communicate very honestly. They either play roles or engage in relatively uninvolving rituals. Some communication processes never get beyond these impersonal forms no matter how often they are repeated, but others develop relatively high levels of honesty. This section discusses the way in which honesty usually develops.

Let us begin by considering an example of relatively impersonal communicating. An important social skill in our society is that of filling time with words without really saying anything. There are times when not to speak at all is unacceptable, but the speaker is unwilling to say anything that is honest or significant. For these occasions, our culture has invented communication rituals which can be expanded or contracted to fill the time available in which people may participate without really being involved as persons, without revealing or inviting each other to share in their experience.

Consider this situation: each day at about the same time and place, you walk past a friend of one of your friends, to whom you have been introduced but know only by name. If he were a complete stranger, you might pretend to be a contemplating the distant skyline with such supreme fascination that you did not notice him or you might wrinkle your brow in obvious preoccupation and quickly stride past. But because he is a "second-hand" friend and because such a deceptive tactic becomes transparently ridiculous after a number of repetitions, you have to say something to him to avoid offending him. As well-socialized individuals, you probably have little difficulty. Your heritage includes prepared patterns of interaction for these situations. Your conversation with this friend-of-your-friend might go something like this:

You. Hi!
He. Hi! How are you?
You. Fine. And you?
He. Very well.
You. Good. Well, take it easy.
He. Sure thing, you too.
You. Right.

Now, if your timing is correct, your last statement will be given just as the two of you pass each other so that there will be no uncomfortable silence while you are still facing each other and neither will have to slow down or have to make an awkward over-the-shoulder reply.

Despite being purely hypothetical, this conversation is structurally identical to the most common forms of communication. The length is optional and is usually adjusted by the coordinated team-work of both participants to fill the available time. Those who walk toward each other quickly and/or speak slowly are likely to abbrevi-ate the exchange to a perfunctory "Good morning"-"Good morn-ing." Those who walk slowly and/or speak quickly (or find them-selves walking in the same direction, or sitting together on a bus, or sharing a meal or an unexpected waiting period) can lengthen the exchange by almost any amount by embedding stock patterns of comments. For example, there are near-obligatory comments (purporting to be funny) which follow the "take it easy" line which serve only to fill another 15 or 20 seconds of time. The "I can't complain"-"Well, it wouldn't do any good if you did" sequence may be substituted early in the exchange to signal the speakers' willing-ness to prolong their mutual celebration of the ritual. And one or the other may mention the weather, describe the good attributes of your mutual friend, attempt to specify when you last met, and so on until the available time (or one of the speakers) is exhausted.

In all of these greeting rituals, neither person is expected to say anything about himself except by demonstrating that he knows and is willing to perform the appropriate cultural rites. This is obviously a case of impersonal communicating because neither has com-municated honestly. Not all of our conversations are so vacuous or sterile, however. Most of us have some people before whom we need neither pretend nor hide who we are, with whom we can be ourselves. But it was not always so: most of our relationships started with impersonal greeting rituals and some, but not all, changed. How do these changes from "Hi-how-are-you" to "This-is-how-I-see-our-relationship" occur?

We believe that the development of honest communicating can be characterized as **incremental, symmetrical,** and **reciprocal.** Consider again the "Hi-how-are-you" dialogue. For any of several reasons, one of the participants may be interested in communicat-ing more honestly. In terms of Carkhuff's rating scale for "genuine-ness," he is presently communicating at a low level: at best a level 3. He might suddenly switch to a level 5, but if he does, he risks rebuff. He would probably feel uncomfortable and the other person would similarly feel that the conversation has taken an unnatural turn. Consider:

ELLSWOOD. Hi! How are you?

PATRICK. Fine, and you?

ELLSWOOD. Well, really I'm a bit bored with these types of greeting rituals. I feel that we pass each other each morning without really meeting and it becomes a bit ridiculous after a while.

Ellswood has suddenly jumped several levels of genuineness. This functions as a sort of ultimatum to Patrick: accept a radically changed form of communicating or else. Patrick is likely to be offended and withdraw. On the other hand, Ellswood may escalate his honesty by a small amount—from a 3.0 to 3.5 in the Carkhuff scale—and see if Patrick is willing to communicate honestly in return. Relationships in which very high levels of honesty occur are usually achieved by **a series of small increments** in honest communicating.

Further, highly honest communicating develops symmetrically. It is unusual to find a relationship in which one person communicates at a much higher level of honesty than the other. Again referring to Carkhuff's scale for rating genuineness, participants in most relationships would have about the same rating, whether it is low (1 and 1) or high (5 and 5). This principle of symmetricity has important implications for therapeutic effectiveness in psychological counseling. If one person is able to be more honest than the other, and **skilled** enough in communicating to be just slightly more honest than the other, then he can lead the other to be more honest by a series of successive redefinitions of the relationship as more honest. Because persons generally feel safe, comfortable, and natural when they **match** without exceeding the other's level of honesty, they will frequently communicate more honestly to persons who are themselves honest. Rogers (1961) made this principle the basis of "A Tentative Statement of a General Law" and Jourard (1971) described it as the "dyadic effect," perhaps the best-documented phenomenon in the self-disclosure literature.

One of the ways in which communicating between friends differs from that in psychological counseling involves reciprocity. Most studies of honest communicating have been conducted in counseling contexts in which one person, the therapist, assumes primary if not full responsibility for escalating the amount of honesty. In nonclinical relationships, each person is expected to share the initiative in redefining the level of their communication behavior.

Neither communicator is likely to continue escalating his honesty unless the other sometimes reciprocates.

Based on the principles of incrementalism, symmetricity, and reciprocity, this picture of the development of honesty is formed: each communicator at times proposes a redefinition of the relationship by escalating the level of honesty in his communicating by a relatively small amount. The other communicator matches the new level of honesty in his own behavior and at times proposes another escalation of the level of honesty. Note that either of the communicators can refuse to increase the amount of honesty, and if they do, this stops—at least temporarily—the development of honesty in the relationship. In some instances, under stress, guilt or grief, for example, one or both may propose a redefinition of the level of honesty downward: this can, of course, be very unsettling to a person who suddenly feels shut off from his accustomed sharing of the other's experience.

Here are a few brief excerpts of dialogue. In each, (1) identify whether either is proposing a redefinition of their level of honesty and if so, in what direction; (2) determine if the proposed redefinition was accepted or rejected; and (3) continue the dialogue by writing what each might have said next until some stopping place is reached. Remember as you become a scriptwriter to respect the principles of incrementalism, symmetricity, and reciprocity. Write several conversations in which some of these principles are followed and in some of which they are violated. What types of situations does violating these principles create? (You might find it useful to analyze these conversations by rating each statement using Carkhuff's "genuineness" scale.) Pat and Mike are good friends. Mike walks up with red, bleary eyes, a pale complexion and a nervous trembling in his hands:

1.

PAT. *You look down. What's wrong?*
MIKE. *Oh, nothing.*
PAT. *Something must be the matter. You look awful.*

2.

PAT. *You look down. What's wrong?*
MIKE. *Oh, nothing.*
PAT. *Good, glad to hear that.*

3.

PAT. *You look down. What's the matter?*
MIKE. *Down? What do you mean? I feel great!*
PAT. *You don't look well.*

4.

PAT. *You look down. What's the matter?*
MIKE. *Down? What do you mean? I feel great!*
PAT. *Good, glad to hear it.*

5.

PAT. *You look down. What's the matter?*
MIKE. *Yes. But everybody gets depressed once in a while.*
PAT. *But how about you. Are you depressed?*

6.

PAT. *You look down. What's the matter?*
MIKE. *Yes. But everybody gets depressed once in a while.*
PAT. *Yes. I was depressed just today. . . .*

7.

PAT. *You look down. What's the matter?*
MIKE. *Yes. I get that way sometimes. Let me tell you about a time when I was really depressed about five years ago. . . .*

8.

PAT. *You look down. What's the matter?*
MIKE. *Yes. There are some things bothering me.*
PAT. *What are they?*

Reasons for avoiding honesty

In a previous section, we discussed the ability to be honest. But most people are usually not so honest as they are able to be. For reasons of their own they may choose not to be honest in specific situations, and these decisions may or may not be based on their best judgment. There are times when you should avoid honesty and times when you should respect another person's request that he be allowed to avoid honesty. In the concluding section of this chapter, we specify some of the conditions affecting the level of honesty appropriate in specific situations. But we need to examine first some of the pressures which tend to limit honesty. In this section, we describe four reasons why individuals sometimes avoid honesty.

Strategy. When you are interested in persuading others or in using communication strategically to accomplish certain ends, honesty is undesirable (Moustakas, 1962). In an argument, it is often necessary to hide points of vulnerability from your opponent; in persuasion, to disguise your true motives. Anything else would sacrifice any hope of success, but such dishonesty inevitably characterizes these communication behaviors as impersonal.

In a socially and economically competitive society in which common goals include acquiring status, prestige, and power, honesty is rarely the best policy. In fact, honesty in an adult is frequently considered an indication of naïveté, immaturity, and lack of social skills. Evasion, self-denial, and distortion are usually techniques employed to influence, change, or control others, and they are successful. Those who peddle soap on TV commercials do not want the audience to be thinking, "He is only saying that because he is being well paid for it." Rather, they carefully behave in ways which make them appear sincere, because sincerity in the eye of the beholder sells. A person who reveals too much is probably not an effective conversationalist because he reveals that he is sometimes bored with the other person. He is likely to be an ineffective persuader because he does not appear sincere when he is not. He is a consistent loser at the popular party game of "oneupsmanship" because he discloses his vulnerable points and allows the other to "score." He does poorly in fights with city hall, insurance claims representatives, and rivals for his position at work, in love or in social groups.

When success according to these criteria is the objective, honesty is likely to be undesired and the speaker will avoid it by all the available means.

Safety. Jourard (1967) believes that honesty occurs only when we feel that it is safe and that vital values will be lost if we do not. The problem is that most people feel that it is seldom safe to be honest. Normal man, according to Laing (1967), has been "trained" to be dishonest by the responses of others. When we reveal our experience and others criticize, laugh, or—the unkindest cut of all—they tell **us** that **we** really do not believe or feel the things which we say, we soon get the point. We deny or hide our experience when it differs too much from that of others or that which others expect from us.

Since we so frequently find that others exploit people who are honest, our society has developed a norm which identifies privacy as a value (that is, something to be achieved for its own sake rather than instrumental to other objectives). There seem to be two ideas associated with the development of this norm. First, disclosure is felt to be a result of weakness and they who disclose are thus felt to be weak. Second, a person who is sick, mad, or bad in one area of his experience and who discloses it, may be assumed to be sick, mad, or bad in other areas as well.

Egan describes the way in which we have built a mythology of strength in quietness.

> The person who exhibits strength by suffering in silence has become a cultural stereotype in our society. "Little boys don't cry" is an early version of the masculine ideal, and the woman who, in the fiction of radio, TV, or the novel, confesses that "I simply have to talk to someone" is thought to be really confessing, not a deep human need, but her own weakness, even though such weakness might be understandable and even excused in a woman. If self-disclosure is not weakness, then it is seen as exhibitionism, and, as such, a sign of illness rather than a desire for human communication. Very often, the adolescent, in his discovery of himself and the "other", engages in a good deal of self-disclosure. But this drive to exchange intimacies . . . is often considered adolescent behavior; naive and immature . . . when the adult finds it necessary to communicate himself to a friend, he often feels that he needs an excuse for such action.[5]

Desire to avoid responsibilities. Another reason for avoiding honesty is a hesitancy to develop intimate, personal relationships with other people. Assuming that it is safe to reveal our experience and we have no ulterior motives about exploiting the other, we may simply not be prepared to assume the responsibilities of a personal relationship. To be honest is (usually) a proposed redefinition of the relationship as more personal, and obligates us to allow the other to reciprocate and to react to him honestly. Sometimes we

[5]Egan, 1970, p. 200.

are not prepared to allow the relation to move in this direction. Here are some reasons why not.

In a personal relationship, the other becomes vulnerable to us and to some extent dependent on us. Usually these responsibilities are not oppressive and are assumed spontaneously. But if the other person "forces" us into a relation more personal than we want, we are likely to find the responsibilities chafing. Because we can anticipate undesirable consequences, we avoid disclosure as a means of avoiding personal relationships.

We can manage only a finite number of personal relationships at any one point in time. If we feel overtaxed with our own or our friends' problems, and another person offers to establish a personal relationship, we may avoid it with all of the techniques we know how to use. We may not be willing to structure another personal relationship or able to share another person's experience.

We are not always able to be both honest and supportive of the other person. If we are aware that our honesty would be very threatening to another person, we may avoid a relationship in which honesty will be demanded. In a case like this, silence or distance is often preferable to either lying or invalidating the other.

Desire to avoid self. Many of our most important memories and experiences are not always available to us. For any of several reasons, including a failure to be adequately honest in our relationships with others, we can become alienated from our own experience and desensitized to our interaction with the world. Crucial memories may be repressed beyond recall. To achieve personal well-being, psychologists such as Jourard (1971) urge people to be honest to appropriate others as a means to recapture an awareness of self and to integrate the personality. Honesty may function in psychotherapy as a means of self-exploration.

But we do not always want to find out more about ourselves. Self-exploration may uncover things which would cause us to feel inferior, weak, or worthless. One reason for avoiding honesty is a desire to avoid confronting ourselves.

Most of us find it painful to acknowledge our weaknesses and faults. It is important for us to maintain a relatively high self-esteem if we are to function effectively in social interaction, and this esteem is frequently achieved by selective inattention to various memories or experiences which threaten it. But there are other forms of self-knowledge, less obvious than this, which we avoid no less intensely.

We avoid information about ourselves which pertains to change. We often find that we have made a pledge of sameness, a commitment to what we are at one point in time. And we usually have more help than we need to make such commitments. When we contract our services for any long-range project (such as repaying part of an NDEA loan by working for five years in a given occupation), we are expected to remain essentially the same person for the duration. When we pledge allegiance to an ideology (the church, the flag, and the republic for which it stands, etc.), there are strong pressures against changing our commitment at a later date. Pressures come from the animosity of former friends: no one is detested quite so heartily as a former ally who defected. But the strongest pressures not to change come from those who know us and want us to remain predictable. When we do not confirm their expectation, they are likely to punish us with various degrees of negative evaluation, ranging from a scowl to that most terrible statement of all: "but it is not like you to do that." Consider what is being said: the other (who may be a parent or close friend) is declaring that they will not recognize us as being their child or friend if we persist in this behavior. No wonder we avoid honesty as a means of ignoring or preventing change.

Jourard (1968) described how we must avoid honesty if we are to honor our pledge to sameness. When we do change, "then every time my **actually** changed being discloses itself to me, I will become threatened and repress it . . . and I will believe my own pretense to my self. Then, I shall not grow. My concept of myself will become increasingly estranged from actuality, the disclosure to me of my changed being will become more insistent. I will then have to pretend and repress much harder."

One definition of growing old is that it is a process of becoming more and more like yourself.[6] We know that (after adolescence) people disclose less as they get older (Jourard, 1961). This does not **prove** an inverse relationship between disclosure and change, but it is suggestive.

We sometimes choose not to confront ourselves in honesty be-

[6]Weaver, 1972, p. 68.

cause we often do not want to accept responsibility for our competencies. Maslow[7] noted a "kind of fear, of awe, of feelings of weakness and inadequacy" when confronted with our "best side . . . our talents . . . our finest impulses . . . our highest potentialities . . . our creativeness." To admit the best in us is to increase the gap between what we know ourselves (usually) to be and what we know we could/should be. As Maslow says, "to discover in oneself a great talent can certainly bring exhilaration, but it also brings a fear of the dangers and responsibilities and duties."

Since honesty frequently threatens to force an unwanted confrontation with ourselves, we avoid communicating our awareness of the best that we are (because acknowledging this is disturbing), the worst that we are (because this provokes guilt and shame), and the fact that we change (because this violates our pledges of sameness). Avoiding honesty in these situations may be wise: Maslow observed that "defensiveness can be as wise as daring; it depends on the particular situation in which one has to choose. The choice of safety is wise when it avoids pain that may be more than the person can bear at the moment."[8]

Techniques for avoiding honesty

Individuals who choose not to communicate honestly employ a number of techniques to signal their unwillingness to express their awareness. These techniques constitute methods for redefining relationships as less personal.

Silence. Sometimes we avoid honesty by following the adage which prescribes it better to remain silent and be thought a fool (or mad or bad) than to speak up and remove all doubt. When students have not prepared for class, they frequently sit impassively, not responding to the teacher or other students. Silence is often used when a person finds himself in a situation in which he does not know what is expected of him or what to expect from others. Rather than admit having the "wrong" experience, a new member of a group may try to avoid saying anything at all about his choice of political candidates, his respect for certain individuals or whether he enjoyed specific entertainment programs.

[7]Maslow, 1968, p. 61.
[8]1968, p. 54.

As a technique for avoiding honesty, silence means more than not talking. It also includes an attempt to strip from our behavior nonverbal cues which would express our experience. Do some people-watching and notice how some people always seem to look pleasant, others preoccupied, strong, or aggressive. Sometimes these characteristic expressions have been carefully selected or have become habitual attempts to conceal experience. Compare the facial and vocal expressions of your friends with those of a three-year-old child. When the child is happy, he shows it naturally, spontaneously, and uninhibitedly. When his emotions change, there is little question about it. But adults, being as sophisticated and well-trained as they are, have learned to try to suppress their expressions until after they have thought about them.

Although most studies of nonverbal communication show that people are not particularly successful in masking nonverbal expressions of feelings (Knapp, 1972), we sometimes desperately try to keep the anger or boredom out of our voices so that others will not detect our emotional state. When we feel threatened by a social situation, we may carefully avoid displaying confusion or uneasiness. These are all forms of silence as a means to avoid disclosure.

Camouflage. When silence (the most direct way to avoid honesty) will not suffice (perhaps because what we think people will imagine us to be, lacking evidence to the contrary, is worse than we really are), the technique of camouflage is often used. The basic nature of this technique is to distract the other sufficiently so that he will lose interest in us, shift attention, or be confused. The most insidious aspect of camouflage as a technique for avoiding honesty is that it sometimes masquerades as authentic self-disclosure. Egan differentiated between "history" and "story." "History" consists of a barrage of facts about the person which are purposively unrelated to his current awareness, and is **not** an invitation for the listener to share his experience.[9]

> [History] is actuarial and analytic, and usually has a strong "there and then" flavor. It clicks off the facts of experience and even interpretation of this experience but leaves the person of the revealer relatively untouched; he is accounted for and analyzed, but unrevealed. The person relates many facts about himself, but the person within still

[9]1970, pp. 234–36.

remains unknown. History is often a long account. It is long and often steady because it fears interruption. Interruption might mean involvement, and a person engages in history to avoid, rather than invite, involvement. History has a way of saying "Be quiet" or "Don't interrupt"; both these are dodges to keep others at bay. The steady clicking off of facts keeps the group focused on the revealer, but does not allow the members to deal with him.

In history the manner of self-revelation is usually somewhat detached. There is little ego-involvement and thus little risk. The speaker deals with himself as object rather than as subject. Intimate life details might be revealed, but their intimacy has no particular meaning. They are just more facts. On the other hand, history might be a concatenation of generalities—generalities poorly disguised by the first-person pronoun. But whether history consists of intimate details or generalities, the message is always the same: "Keep your distance." It is as if the revealer were trying to intimate to others that he is rather invulnerable: "This is not really affecting me; I don't see why it should affect you." Sometimes sheer quantity of intimate information about self is divulged because the historian implicitly realizes that if he relates enough, quickly enough, the others will not be able to react effectively to any particular part of it.

"History" is likely to be told when a person is in a situation in which honesty is appropriate, but for some reason he is unwilling to be honest. To escape, the speaker shifts attention from the way he **now is** to what he **has done.**

The nature of "history" as camouflage is made clear when it is contrasted with what Egan called "story," which is honest.

> [Story] is an attempt to reveal the person within, and more than that: it is an attempt to get him involved with his listeners. Story is an invitation for others to come in; it is an opening of the door.
>
> Story is not actuarial; it is rather selective in detail, for the revealer intuits that it is not the transmission of fact that is important but the transmission of self. It does not avoid detail, but the choice of detail is secondary to the act of communication. Story usually avoids interpretation, too: it allows experience to remain unintellectualized and thus speak for itself. The storyteller, even if he leaves out detail, is graphic and specific; he does not hide behind generalities disguised by the first-person pronoun. Facts are selected for their impact value,

for their ability to reveal the person as what he is now through what he has experienced.[10]

Another form of camouflage consists of rationalizations. To avoid honesty, we sometimes invent reasons which explain what we have done or why we did not do what we should have. Our conversation then becomes replete with appeals for understanding and approval for acts which may be repugnant even to ourselves. In fact, some people have made a fine art of this type of camouflage, particularly those with "ruined" public images such as criminals or alcoholics. In an (perhaps nonconscious) attempt to avoid honesty, they make a career of (1) flaunting their record or problem, (2) suggesting various interpretations of the reason for their deviant behavior, and (3) persuading others to accept as legitimate the reasons for their behavior. Such rationalizations are camouflage because they disclose almost everything except the most important aspect of the individual: the way he feels about how he is.

Lying. The most blatant form of avoiding honesty is that of deliberately presenting a false, misleading image of one's self. Despite its obviousness and almost universal moral disapproval, lying is a skill which almost everyone learns to employ and one which most people expect others to use in appropriate situations. For example, when asked the condition of our health, an honest answer is often socially offensive. At the end of a boring party, too extreme a devotion to honesty is sometimes disconcerting to all concerned.

Although lying to avoid honesty may be innocuous in some situations, it may be very important in others. Jourard described encounters which "mystify" as contrasted with those which "reveal." Seduction is a classic example of a type of relationship in which the person does not want to be known as he is. Rather, the Lothario "tries to mislead her as to his intentions . . . to manipulate her experience and action so that she will behave in service of **his** goals, not her own . . . he will show aspects of himself that aim at persuading or influencing the other."[11]

Signaling for distance. Sometimes those with whom we talk disclose more about themselves than we wish to hear or invite us

[10]Ibid.
[11]1968, pp. 19–21.

to be more honest than we want to be. One way of reducing the level of honesty in the relationship is simply to stop talking to the other or to say something like "Don't get so nosy." But sometimes you want to reject the other's proposed redefinition of the relationship without offending him. This can be done by giving subtle cues calling for "distance" to be maintained between you. For example, you may continually switch the subject from personal to impersonal topics. A person who is being interrogated about his drinking habits by a well-meaning neighbor may continually attempt to introduce a "safer" topic such as sports or the behavior of a third party. A desire for greater distance may be signaled by choice of vocabulary, such as using exclusive pronouns (you, them) rather than inclusive (I, we) ones.

Nonverbal behavior may also function as cues for distance. You may have noticed that there are culturally shared norms prescribing appropriate units of space between persons engaged in various types of interactions. In his book **The Hidden Dimension,** Hall (1966) identified an inverse relationship between intimacy and the distance between people. Intimate relationships (lovers snuggled in a restaurant booth) occur within 18 inches, while personal relationships (good friends talking while standing) establish a distance ranging between 1½ to 4 feet. When more than 4 feet separate the individuals, the interaction tends to be businesslike, formal, somewhat cold. You may signal for less intimacy by increasing the distance between you and the other: honesty is most appropriate for people who feel no strain being close together.

These techniques for avoiding self-disclosure may or may not work. In optimal situations, both persons are aware that one has signaled his desire not to disclose and the other honors that request. In less-than-optimal situations, the request for less honest communicating is not understood or, if understood, is ignored by the other. These conversations can develop into tragic arguments which, stripped of the specific content and trappings of civility, take the form of a desperate plea to be let alone which is repeatedly and callously rebuffed. Competence in communicating requires the ability to indicate when you want to avoid communicating more honestly and to detect when others are asking to avoid increased honesty.

Determining appropriate levels of honesty

Our insistence that communicating personally is a uniquely significant form of human experience and that one of the two defining
characteristics of communicating personally is honest may lead
you to think that we believe that all honesty is good, more is better
and dishonesty is always and inevitably bad. This is **not** the case,
however. No responsible person advises you to communicate totally honestly to every person whom you meet. It is **appropriate**
honesty that contributes to interpersonal rapport and personal
well-being. You may err by being either too honest or not honest
enough. The problem is that of determining what level of honesty
is appropriate in specific situations.

These judgments about appropriate levels of honesty are sometimes difficult, and, although most people err by not communicating honestly enough, the other type of error occurs as well. In a
study of the faculty of the University of Florida School of Nursing,
Jourard (1959) found that those who disclose **most** and **least** were
least liked. This indicates that **both** the highest and lowest discloser
erred—in opposite ways—in their judgment of the appropriate
amount of disclosure. A number of studies (Levinger and Senn,
1967; Voss, 1969) have shown that marital satisfaction is a function of openness in talking about some—but not all—topics. When
spouses are honest about such things as children and shared activities, the marriage seems to work better. But when they tell each
other that they dislike things about the other which cannot be
changed, troubles begin.

But these studies only confirm what we already knew: that there
are instances in which honesty is inappropriate. The problem is
that of specifying the conditions under which honesty is appropriate. We suggest that the appropriateness of honesty is affected by
three factors. The first involves the nature of the social situation.
There are times when the purpose of an interaction precludes
honesty. For example, the greeting rituals we described a few pages
ago serve more as social lubricants than as opportunities for the
exchange of information: "hi-how-are-you" routines allow individuals to pass each other with minimal friction and maximum economy
of effort. To answer the question "how are you" as if it were a
serious request for detailed information about your physical and

emotional status is frequently a gross misunderstanding of the nature of the social situation.

If the only type of communication you ever experienced consisted of greeting rituals, casual chats, or technical dialogues, your interpersonal relationships would be barren indeed. But this does not imply that you cannot or should not engage in impersonal communicating sometimes. In fact, we believe that the most competent communicators are able to adapt to the type of communicating appropriate for a variety of situations.

Honesty is appropriate in situations in which the sharing of experience is the purpose. A quarterback who notices that his flanker has limped back to the huddle may ask, "How do you feel?" but he is not suggesting a sharing of experience. He wants to know if the flanker can run his pass-patterns. This situation calls for impersonal communicating and does not necessarily imply that either person will suffer for it. By the same token, if the only type of communicating the flanker is ever offered is this impersonal, he may well begin to think that he is valued only for his pass-catching skills, not as a person. The same question, "How do you feel?" may be asked by the quarterback after the game in the locker room or at dinner in a very different way, this time meaning "How do you feel about your injury—are you depressed or do you feel that you can shrug it off?"

A second factor affecting whether honesty is appropriate involves the effect of what is said. There are times when the other person has no "need to know" your awareness of your experience. Although most people may exaggerate the amount of their experience which is best kept to themselves, this does not deny the fact that revealing some aspects of one's experience is deliberately hurtful, irrelevant, or unimportant.

Consider irrelevant experience: If you are working with a committee making decisions about emergency procedures designed to reduce casualties in case of accident in an industrial plant, you may be aware of a slight headache, some minor discomfort in the temperature of the conference room, and perhaps a repulsion at the physical features of one of your colleagues, but to continue interrupting the committee's deliberations to tell them all these things is inappropriate. There is little virtue in a surgeon who communicates honestly his desire to be elsewhere and revulsion at the shattered body on the operating table before he begins to try to save the patient's life: sometimes it is time to get the job done and worry about feelings later. We have known students who have been so fascinated by their own emotional reaction to an impending examination that they never got around to studying for it.

By the same token, there are times when so-called frankness or "brutal honesty" is nothing but a coverup for an opportunity to hurt someone else. When another person is overwhelmed by his own awareness, they may neither want nor be able to cope with yours. When your friend is exuberant with success, is this the time to describe your headache or encounter with a policeman which led to a traffic ticket? When your friend is grieved because of bereavement or the destruction of his ambitions, is this the time to prattle on about the trivialities of your experiences? The Biblical story of Job is a remarkable one for many reasons, not the least of which is the portrayal of a man and his friends coping with grief. After Job suffered a series of calamities which destroyed his wealth, his family, and his health, he donned sackcloth and ashes—his culture's proclamation of mourning, similar to our wearing black or posting a wreath of flowers—and his friends came to comfort him. When they arrived, they tore their clothes, threw dust on themselves, and cried with him— matching his own culturally sanctioned expression of grief—and then sat with him for a week **without saying a word** "for they saw that his grief was very great" (Job 2:13). Thus far they had done well, but after a week they opened their mouths and became a fresh torment for poor old Job. He really did not need to hear his friends' theology, which held that all of his troubles were punishments for some great, secret wickedness that he was hiding.

The third condition affecting the appropriate level of honesty is the nature of the relationship between you and the other person. Remember the principles of incrementalism, symmetricity, and reciprocity which describe the development of honesty in most relationships. A level of honesty which significantly violates one or more of these principles is inappropriate.

But there is another aspect of interpersonal relationships which affects the appropriate levels of honesty. When we discussed the "relational level of language" in Chapter 2, we demonstrated how many conversations may be best described as successful or unsuccessful attempts to achieve a mutually satisfactory definition of the relationship between the communicators. But such a mutually acceptable definition of the relationship is comprised of a series of judgments (Laing, Phillipson, and Lee, 1966). For example, each person has a concept of himself, of the other person, and of himself as seen by the other person. Misunderstandings and disagreements about the optimal state of the relationship may occur at any of several levels. The healthiest relationships seem to be those in which both persons are aware of their own and the other's perception of their relationship. Although this state of knowledge and agreement probably occurred because of a relatively high level of honesty, it does not always require continuous discussion. Persons who continually find themselves saying, "Right now I feel that you . . ." are probably in the process of developing (but have not yet developed) a relationship characterized by agreement and mutual knowledge.[12] Consider a relationship in which you like another person, and that person likes you and both of you know it. You might mention your mutual affection periodically—more importantly, your affection provides an unspoken context for much else that you do say—but something is amiss if this becomes the major and repetitive topic of conversation between you.

Like most forms of human behavior, communicating honestly requires your good judgment. There is probably no social act which is not inappropriate in some context regardless of its value and naturalness in other contexts. We suggest that your decisions about the appropriateness of honesty be based on the nature of the social situation, on the effect of honesty on yourself and the other person, and on the characteristics of your relationship with the other person.

In his analysis of "sensitivity training," which includes T-groups, encounter groups, and similar activities, Back (1972) noted that groups deliberately reverse the taboos of ordinary society: "frankness substitutes for tact, self-expression for manners, nonverbal techniques for

---

[12]The converse of this observation would state: "people who do **not** frequently match perceptions about their relationship have successfully developed healthy relationships." This statement is emphatically **not** true. The absence of such messages may indicate mutual understanding **or** mutual insensitivity, defensiveness and inability to communicate about relationships.

language, and immediacy for responsibility." The reason for such an inversion of custom is that the sensitivity-training movement is based on a belief that the individual must be changed by having an intense emotional experience in the group, and that such an experience is facilitated by adopting the "myth of the here and now" and rejecting the individual's history (his past and future), symbolism and abstractions (his intellect, his time binding, his interpretation of his experience). Here are some questions which do not have easy answers. Discuss them with some others who have (and maybe some who have not) read this chapter.

    1. What would society be like if everyone were always honest?

    2. Is it good for a person who has to live in a society in which honesty is not always the best policy to participate periodically in a group which requires almost total honesty?

    3. What functions do history, symbolism, and abstractions serve? What would be different in your own experience if you were far more oriented to the passing moment (the "here and now") and your own current awareness than you now are? How do the concepts of "delayed gratification," "rational decision-making," and "long-range planning" fit into this topic?

Here are some other sources which will help you discuss questions: Rogers (1970); Back (1972); Condon (1966); and Berger and Luckmann (1966).

Rogers and Back describe the function and particularly the effects of participating in the special society of sensitivity training or encounter groups, and they arrive at differing evaluations of the "movement." Condon explores the functions of language: when you read his book, think of which functions are best served by rules requiring or taboos forbidding "here and now" frankness, immediacy, and self-expression. Berger and Luckmann's book examines "The Foundations of Knowledge in Everyday Life" as its first section. Notice the dependence on interactions with other people—at both abstract and immediate levels —as the process by which we learn about our society and our environment as well as about ourselves.

References

Adorno, T. W., E. Frenkel-Brunswik, D. J. Levinson, and R. N. Sanford. 1950. **The Authoritarion Personality.** New York: Harper and Row.

Back, Kurt W. 1972. **Beyond Words: The Story of Sensitivity Training and the Encounter Movement.** New York: Russell Sage Foundation.

Berger, Peter L., and Thomas Luckmann. 1966. **A Treatise in the Sociology of Knowledge.** Garden City, New York: Doubleday.

Carkhuff, Robert. 1969. **Helping and Human Relations: A Primer for Lay and Professional Helpers.** New York: Holt, Rinehart and Winston, Vol. I.

Christie, Richard, and Florence L. Geis. 1970. **Studies in Machiavellianism.** New York: Academic Press.

Condon, John C., Jr. 1966. **Semantics and Communication.** New York: Macmillan.

Egan, Gerard. 1970. **Encounter: Group Processes for Interpersonal Growth.** Belmont, California: Brooks/Cole.

Forester, C. S. 1941. **The Captain from Connecticut.** Boston: Little, Brown.

Forgus, Ronald H. 1966. **Perception: the Basic Process in Cognitive Development.** New York: McGraw Hill.

Freud, Anna. 1966. **The Ego and the Mechanisms of Defense.** New York: International Universities Press, Rev. ed.

Hall, Edward. 1966. **The Hidden Dimension.** New York: Random House.

Jourard, Sidney M. 1961. "Age Trends in Self-Disclosure," **Merrill-Palmer Quarterly of Behavior and Development,** 7:191–97.

_____. 1967. "To be or not to be—Existential Psychological Perspectives on the Self," **University of Florida Monographs, Social Sciences.** Gainesville: University of Florida Press, No. 34.

_____. 1968. **Disclosing Man to Himself.** New York: Van Nostrand, Reinhold.

_____. 1969. "Self-Disclosure and Other-Cathexis," **Journal of Abnormal and Social Psychology,** 59:428–31.

_____. 1971. **Self-Disclosure: An Experimental Analysis of the Transparent Self.** New York: Wiley-Interscience.

_____. 1971. **The Transparent Self.** New York: Van Nostrand, Reinhold, Rev. ed.

Knapp, Mark L. 1972. **Nonverbal Communication in Human Interaction.** New York: Holt, Rinehart and Winston.

Laing, Ronald David. 1967. **The Politics of Experience.** New York: Ballantine Books, Inc.

―――, H. Phillipson, and A. R. Lee. 1966. **Interpersonal Perception: A Theory and a Method of Research.** New York: Springer.

Levinger, G., and D. Senn. 1967. "Disclosure of Feelings in Marriage," **Merrill-Palmer Quarterly of Behavior and Development,** 13:237–49.

MacDaniels, Joseph, Elain Yarbrough, C. L. Kaszmaul, and Kim Giffin. 1971. "Openness: Personalized Expression in Interpersonal Communication," paper presented to the annual conference of the International Communication Association, Phoenix, Arizona.

Maslow, Abraham H. 1968. **Toward a Psychology of Being.** New York: Van Nostrand, Reinhold. Sec. ed.

―――. 1970. **Motivation and Personality.** New York: Harper and Row. 2nd ed.

Moustakas, Clark. 1962. "Honesty, Idiocy and Manipulation, **Journal of Humanistic Psychology,** 2:1–15.

Neisser, Ulric. 1967. **Cognitive Psychology.** New York: Appleton-Century-Crofts.

Osgood, Charles E. 1962. **An Alternative to War or Surrender.** Urbana: University of Illinois Press.

Rapoport, Anatol. 1960. **Fights, Games and Debates.** Ann Arbor: University of Michigan Press.

―――. 1964. **Strategy and Conscience.** New York: Harper and Row.

Rogers, Carl. 1970. **Carl Rogers on Encounter Groups.** New York: Harper and Row.

―――. 1961. **On Becoming a Person.** Boston: Houghton Mifflin.

Rokeach, Milton. 1960. **The Open and Closed Mind.** New York: Basic Books.

Voss, F. 1969. **The Relationships of Disclosure to Marital Satisfaction: An Exploratory Study,** unpublished Master's thesis, University of Wisconsin-Milwaukee.

Weaver, Carl H. 1972. **Human Listening: Processes and Behavior.** Indianapolis: Bobbs-Merrill.

FIVE

Communicating personally: validation

> . . . you are known and accepted . . . free to grow or change . . . you may let the other know you as you are . . .

In Chapter 2 we identified two forms of communication behavior: making messages from meanings and making meanings from messages. When a person communicates personally, the **messages** he makes are honest, accurately describing, and inviting the listener to participate in his experience as he is aware of it, and the **meanings** he makes from messages are validating. A message is validating[1] if it is interpreted as affirming the communicator's worth as a person and confirming the legitimacy of his experience.

Messages inevitably have at least two "levels" of significance. In Chapter 2 we labeled these the "content" and "relationship" levels

---

[1]Language sometimes creates obstacles to the precise expression of ideas. Obviously, we do not mean that some messages are validating and others are not. To affirm this would negate the principle that meanings are in people, not in messages. But it is much more awkward to say "messages which an individual interprets as validating" than to say a "validating message." For the sake of semantic gracefulness, we will at times use the word "validating" as if it were an adjective and modifies messages, but when we do, please remember that this is a compromise with our language. It is **people** who interpret messages, and validation is properly used as an adjective describing only that process which people do.

of meaning, in which one aspect of the latter consists of the identity which the speaker is willing to grant the listener. At this level of meaning, each speaker says, "This is how I see myself and this is how I see you" in addition to whatever "content" is in his message. These relationship meanings may be implicit or explicit, and they may vary in their importance to the communicators. When communicators are task-oriented, intent on getting the job done, they may virtually ignore relationship meanings in their concentration on the content level of meaning. The stilted and precise phrases used by police dispatchers and airport ground control officers are constructed for maximum intelligibility and economy of expression, and communicators using these message systems are expected to disregard how the speaker thinks about himself and about those to whom he is speaking. On the other hand, relationship meanings are the most important aspect of messages when the way the communicators feel and think about each other is at issue: remember the two drunks arguing about which was to be acknowledged as the baseball expert even though they thought they were discussing Babe Ruth's batting average.

Consider a business conference in which one person is singled out as the source of most of the company's problems. If he says something like "How dare you call me incompetent?" he will likely be admonished not to "take it personally." Rather, he is expected to note the problem and take remedial action without thinking about the implications for himself as a person. This is hard to do, even if he receives a lot of help from his colleagues in the form of advice such as "Take it like a man, Ellswood" or "Stiff upper lip there, old boy." In impersonal communicating, the way the communicators feel and think about each other is either suppressed or ignored or it is "negative": the meanings made from messages indicate that the speaker does not value the listener or questions the legitimacy of the listener's experience.

There are occasions when the ability to disregard the relationship level of meaning, to attend to what the other is saying without worrying about how he thinks and feels about you, is important. But there are other situations in which a failure to communicate about relationships is grotesque and awkward. Proposals of marriage are one such situation and an inability to communicate personally in such moments has provided playwrights a theme for comedy. One scene in the TV program "Maude" depicted the heroine being proposed to by a suitor who tried to impress her with his successful storm-screen business, his house and his life insurance. "We'll have some problems," he confided, "like deciding in whose house to live." Intimately: "How's your plumbing?"[2]

We believe that communicating personally is a uniquely significant form of social behavior. One of the reasons for this opinion is that what people tell you about yourself is an important factor in the development of your concept of yourself and your ability to participate in sophisticated forms of coordinated interpersonal interaction. If you are consistently told by the people who are important to you (your "significant others" or "reference group") that you are mad, bad, or sick, you will eventually come to believe it. On the other hand, if you are frequently assured of your worth as a person and of the confidence you can place in your own judgment, you are likely to respect and trust yourself. Your ability to interpret messages as validating depends on several factors, including the types of messages other people address to you and your own self-concept. Before discussing these abilities, let us first consider the importance of people to persons.

The importance of people to persons

A popular song proclaims "people who need people" to be "the luckiest people in the world," (Merrill, 1963). If so, it is well that it is so because every person needs people.

How did you come to think and feel about yourself as you now do? Do you consider yourself handsome or ugly? tall or short? energetic or listless? intelligent or unintelligent? witty or dull? The answer is that other people have "trained" you to think as you do about yourself, either by describing to you how they think and feel about you or by providing the standards of expectations and performance against which you measure yourself. The point is easily demonstrated: in the country of the blind, the one-eyed man is, if not coronated, at least acknowledged as having superior vision; in an isolated tribe of pygmies, a man five feet six inches tall is considered a giant; and in a colony of beauty contest winners, a girl

[2]Maude (dryly): "It works."

who otherwise would be considered an extremely attractive person comes to think of herself as plain. The people whom we consider important—who may be those we spend our time with or some mystical group who only exist in our minds—are "the backboard of our personalities. How can we come to know ourselves except through gauging the reactions of others to us?" These reactions "shape the self that we come to recognize."[3]

The importance of the image of ourselves which we see reflected in the behavior of others can be seen by considering persons who rather suddenly change reference groups. Many a high school valedictorian has had to construct a new concept of himself when he enrolled in college and for the first time was an "average" student. Athletes who were standouts in college sometimes find that they are marginal at best as professionals, and the unaccustomed lack of praise may be a bitter experience. But self-concepts can be improved as well as depreciated by a new reference group. The traits of independence and analytical ability which make a poor soldier may equip the person to be a prized and respected graduate student. A widely circulated anecdote describes the experience of "a very plain girl who seemed to fit the stereotype (usually erroneous) that many have of graduate student females." A group of male students began treating her as they would if she were the most attractive girl on campus. They drew lots to set up a schedule by which they would ask her for dates and, "the loser, under pressure from the others, asked her to go out." During the dates, each man behaved as if she were stunningly attractive. The woman began to change her behavior by taking far more care in her appearance and acting with much more self-confidence. The men got their due, however: their schedule of whom was to ask her for dates when was unexpectedly upset when she refused an invitation and remarked that she was "pretty well booked up for some time in the future." It seems there were more desirable males around than those "plain" graduate students (Kinch, 1967). Even if this story is not true, and it seems suspiciously neat in the retelling, it should be. It does not take a great psychologist to realize that love given to the unlovely may help them become more lovable and that hate begets hateful and hatable people.

[3]Borden et al., 1969, p. 90.

We have portrayed persons as somewhat dependent on others for their very knowledge of themselves. Although such a description offends those "rugged individualists" who would be obliged to no one if they could help it, this is an accurate description of the human condition. Some more than others to be sure, but all persons need to be "told" periodically who they are. If a person has no social contact, for example by being isolated in a sensory deprivation environment (Zubek, 1969), or if the only type of communication he knows is impersonal and he has to pretend that he isn't aware of the relational level of meaning, he will not thrive. William James once judged that "no more fiendish punishment could be devised, even were such a thing physically possible, than that one should be turned loose in a society and remain absolutely unnoticed by all the members there of."[4] Perhaps such a punishment will be possible some day: "invisibility" is the more squeamish but not necessarily more humane punishment inflicted on social offenders in a science fiction story by Robert Silverberg (1973).

> And then they found me guilty, and then they pronounced me invisible, for a span of one year beginning on the eleventh of May in the year of Grace 2104, and they took me to a dark room beneath the courthouse to affix the mark to my forehead before turning me loose.
>
> Two municipally paid ruffians did the job. One flung me into a chair and the other lifted the brand.
>
> "This won't hurt a bit," the slab-jawed ape said, and thrust the brand against my forehead, and there was a moment of coolness, and that was all.
>
> "What happens now?" I asked.
>
> But there was no answer, and they turned away from me and left the room without a word. The door remained open. I was free to leave, or to stay and rot, as I chose. No one would speak to me, or look at me more than once, long enough to see the sign on my forehead. I was invisible.
>
> You must understand that my invisibility was strictly metaphorical. I still had corporeal solidity. People **could** see me—but they **would not** see me. . . .
>
> I was invisible.
>
> I went out. . . .

[4]Quoted by Watzlawick **et al.**, 1967, p. 86.

You will be surprised how this story ends.

To a considerable extent, people behave toward others in ways consistent with the self they know themselves to be, and they know themselves to be what they have been told or shown to be by others. Communication behavior in which relationship levels of meaning are important contribute to the development of a person's concept of who and what he is. This is one of the ways in which people are important to persons.

And there is another way. Many forms of behavior cannot be performed by one person alone: the cooperation or at least coordinated behavior of another person is necessary. Policemen owe their jobs to criminals, for there is no need for law-enforcement personnel if laws are not broken. "Good Samaritans" and charitable organizations require for their existence victims to whom to minister. If you pride yourself on the ability to excel in sports, you must have teams or individuals against whom to pit yourself. If your self-concept stresses your ability to lead, there must be followers or you simply cannot perform the behaviors important to you. A futuristic short story described how participants in feuds depend on each other: two land barons had hated each other and fought during their entire lives. Finally McDermott tired of his two hundred and thirty years of life which had left him without friends or family and plugged into a bank of machinery which did the job of his heart, lungs, liver, etc. McDermott called his archenemy Holt and asked him to disconnect the life-support apparatus so that he would die. Holt refused. "McDermott did not understand. Not cruelty, but simple selfishness, had kept him from killing the enemy lord . . . 'Once you are gone, Andrew, who will I have to hate?' "[5]

William Schutz (1966) identified three "interpersonal needs": inclusion, affection, and control. These are appropriately considered **needs** because they orient the person's behavior toward those forms of interaction which will satisfy them, and because gratification reduces the drive toward those activities, and deprivation increases it. They are **interpersonal** because each is met only when the individual and at least one other person behave toward each other in particular ways.

Consider the effects on a person's communication behavior if

[5]Silverberg, 1970.

these needs are not met for a prolonged period. An individual deprived of affection is likely to engage in communication behaviors in one of two forms: he may escalate his requests for affection from others; or, deciding that he will not get affection no matter what he does, he may behave in ways which expect and call for hostility from others as a technique for protecting himself from the pain of having requests for affection refused. Affection may be sought by begging for compliments ("You don't like me, do you?"; "Do you really think I can do this?") and using self-deprecating humor ("You'll never believe what a stupid thing I did today!"). If he decides that the probability of obtaining affection is too low, or the cost of being rejected is too high, he may become hateful, aggressive, and destructive. Harry Stack Sullivan described this latter form of behavior as a "malevolent transformation" of the need for affection. The transformation develops in this way: if a person is not given affection when he needs and asks for it, and if he cannot control his social environment by moving or changing friends, he may develop a protective maneuver which prevents subsequent rebuffs; he simply does not ask for affection. Not expecting warmth, he neither offers it to others nor is able to accept it when it is offered to him. The point is that a person who acts with hostility toward others may do so primarily because of the types of social relations he has been able and expects to establish with other people, and this behavior determines the nature of his subsequent relationship with others (see Mullahy, 1970).

Consider another example. Suppose that Ellswood is a full-fledged member of a social group: they include him in their activities and extend to him appropriate expressions of warmth and affection, and he identifies himself and the others as "we." His needs for affection and inclusion are being met, but what about his need for control? Assume that none of Ellswood's groups ever allow him to exert control and he finds this unsatisfying. If his attempts to exert some influence on the group are consistently rejected, this deprivation will begin to be a dominant factor in his behavior. Ellswood's first response is likely to be an increasing insistence that the others accept his influence by following his choice of conversation topics, accepting his judgment on relevant issues, and (if the group has a formal structure) electing him to a responsible position. He becomes more aggressive, brash, insistent. If all of this fails, something like the "malevolent transformation" may occur: he begins to avoid any social situation which looks as if he will have any influence. Feeling that others will not accept his advice, he no longer offers it. Rather than be defeated for high office, he will not run. Rather than be shown to be wrong, he takes no position and refuses to express his opinion.

To say that we have a need for control is somewhat misleading. It is more accurate to say that there is a control dimension to interpersonal needs. Some of us have a prolonged deprivation of the need to be controlled rather than to exert control. What types of situations might produce an unmet need to be controlled? How might a person with an unmet need to be controlled act? Which of your needs (to exert control or to be controlled) is most often unfulfilled? If you saw a person with an unmet need for control, how would you act toward him? What does this say about you?

These examples are of persons whose behavior is dramatically affected by severe deprivations of interpersonal needs. Most persons' needs for inclusion, affection, and control are met at least sometimes by some people. If an adult who is socially mobile finds himself in a situation in which interpersonal needs are not well met, he will terminate his current relationships and form new ones. Unfortunately, such mobility is not always possible. Children are usually forced to remain with siblings and parents even though the social environment may be disastrous for them. Adults are frequently limited in mobility by economic or institutional factors. Perhaps most seriously, a person whose self or communication skills have been stifled or warped by poor social relationships at one point in time may be unable to form the type of new relationships he needs.

This discussion of the importance of people to persons has ranged considerably beyond the focus of this chapter on validation as an aspect of communicating personally. But these larger considerations provide the context for an examination of the nature and significance of validation. If an individual is to realize his potential as a person and communicate effectively in a variety of contexts, he must believe in his worth as a person and trust his own experience. Good feelings about and confidence in one's self are developed in interaction with other people. Part of this process involves the individual's own comparison of himself against the performance and expectations of others, but another aspect occurs when various people tell the individual how they think and feel about him. Communication experiences such as these are both pleasant and important. Jurgen Ruesch (1957) described the gratification which occurs when persons feel that they are understood and reach agreements about mutually relevant issues. "If such gratification is repeated over and over again, the individual or group is likely to be well informed, adaptable and capable of withstanding frustration." Speaking to the same point, Carl Rogers explained his concern with communication this way: "The whole task of psychotherapy is the task of dealing with a failure in communication. . . . We may say then that psychotherapy is good communication, within and between men. We may also turn that statement around and it will still be true. Good communication, free communication, within or between men, is always therapeutic."[6]

We believe that an essential part of the "good," "free" communication described by Rogers consists of the participants interpreting messages addressed to them as validating.

A description of validating communication behavior

Since validation involves the meaning of messages, and since the meaning of messages is in the mind of their recipients, we cannot look at messages and by fiat classify them as validating or invalidating. We can, however, identify some of the types of meanings which are associated with validation and we can describe characteristics of messages which are interpreted as having these meanings. Messages which are interpreted as validating usually are characterized by appropriateness, clarity, and positiveness.[7]

Appropriateness. Messages which are appropriate are responsive both to the **intent** and **content** of previous messages, and indicate that the speaker understands you and is attentive to and genuinely interacting with you. To be understood implies that the

[6]1971, p. 182.
[7]See Sieburg and Larson, 1971; Dance and Larson, 1972, pp. 138–43.

other person knows not only what you have said but what you intended by the message. Frequently, the way others respond to what you say indicates that they did not understand your intent or content or both.

Consider the simple transaction which occurs when you pass an acquaintance on the way to work. If you say, "Hello, how are you?" and he replies, "Fine, and you?" you both have exchanged one stroke and may proceed about your business. But something has gone wrong if your acquaintance replies, "Well, my back is still sore from the accident last week—but you didn't hear about that, did you? Well, it started when my wife's niece. . . ." In this case, your acquaintance has responded appropriately to your **content** (you did, after all, ask about his well-being) but inappropriately to your **intent** (which was to extend a friendly acknowledgment of his presence). You were **not** well understood. A more serious form of invalidation occurs when you ask, "Hello, how are you?" and your acquaintance retorts, "It's really none of your business, you know!" Here not only your intent to communicate has been denied, but your right to include that content has been challenged.

If unacceptable responses to ritualized greetings were the only form of inappropriate messages you ever received, their effects might be troublesome but not serious. But some communication situations are far from trivial. Consider these examples of inappropriate responses cited by Kim Giffin (1970):

> Little Johnnie, age five, comes home from kindergarten and says, "I have a girl friend!" His mother does not respond at the moment, and later says, "Eat your soup, Johnnie." This constitutes a denial of Johnnie's capability of discussing girl friends. Ten years later Johnnie says, "Dad, Joe Smith is taking his folks' car to the picnic Saturday." Dad says, "Finish your homework, John." Here again is a denial of Johnnie's existence on the "family car level."

Perhaps the clearest instance of an inappropriate and invalidating message is that used by Archie Bunker, of the TV program "All in the Family," when his wife says something of which he disapproves: "Edith, stifle yourself!"

Ruesch[8] identified several ways in which messages may be inappropriate. **Quantitatively** inappropriate messages involve the mag-

[8] 1957, pp. 53–55.

nitude and timing of the response to the other. When a person responds to a statement, the response should (if it is to be validating) acknowledge that the listener understood what was said. Misunderstanding is evidenced when the response is too much or too little, too soon or too late. Poorly timed or poorly measured responses occur when the listener did not attend to the content, did not understand the content or is ridiculing the content of the other's message.

Humor is a good example of communication in which appropriately **timed** responses are important. When you tell a joke, you want laughter, but only at the appropriate place. When your audience laughs loudly—but **before** you get to the punch line—you feel that they have misunderstood the content of the joke, perhaps keying on the wrong idea or trying to be polite by guessing and responding where they think you intended them to. When your joke ends and there is a prolonged silence which finally gives way to laughter, you can assume that your audience is being polite and trying to accommodate you or—the unkindest cut of all—laughing at you for telling such a bad joke. Both of these are examples of invalidating communication because of inappropriate timing.

The appropriate **magnitude** of the response is also important in validating messages. Invalidation may occur if the response is too small or too great.

Poor Ellswood has been confronted with invalidating messages many times. Put yourself in his place in these experiences. Once he was convinced that he had broken his grandfather's car. The manual shift transmission froze in first gear. No matter how hard he tried, he could not shift into reverse or higher forward gears. Convinced that he had somehow done something terribly wrong and afraid to confront his grandfather, he drove slowly to an uncle's house for advice. The uncle laughed, reached under the hood and unjammed the gear, explaining that this happened quite often. Ellswood felt relieved to be sure, but also that he could not trust his experience with cars and never became much of a mechanic.

On another occasion Ellswood and his high school class were taking an exam. Through some combination of circumstances, all of the teachers proctoring the exam happened to be out of the room at the same time for a period of about five minutes. On returning to the examination room, one of the teachers noted that the students were unsupervised. Interrupting their test-taking, he demanded that all papers be turned in immediately, and proceeded to tear them up. In response to the outcry from the students, he explained that "you had a chance to cheat and probably did. If you did not, then you're stupid." Ellswood, who had not cheated and had not even noticed the lack of monitors, felt that this teacher attached much more importance to this situation than he did and began wondering if he were stupid for not looking for opportunities to cheat.

On yet another occasion a group of Ellswood's friends were discussing historical monuments. Ellswood expressed interest in their conversation and was presented a fanciful tale in which seventeenth-century British history and eighteenth-century American history were purposefully jumbled. Although what he heard did not fit his previous knowledge of the events being discussed, Ellswood was eager to learn and ready to be instructed. After stretching the account to a truly improbable extent, Ellswood's friends then informed him that there was more error than truth in the tale and laughed loudly at his gullibility. Years later at every gathering of the group this experience was retold and, naturally, embellished in the retelling. In addition to his chagrin, Ellswood began to doubt his ability both as a historian and as a judge of his friends.

Rudyard Kipling's (1936) poetic portrayal of the masculine mystique proclaims that "If you can keep your head when all those around you are losing theirs, . . . you'll be a Man, my son!"[9] But by being calm while others are not, you tacitly deny them the right to trust their own perceptions, to behave on the basis of their own experience. By responding with an inappropriately small amount of excitement or enthusiasm, you invalidate them.

Invalidating messages may consist of overreactions as well as underreactions to what we say or do. A person tends to value himself less and question the legitimacy of his own experience when he says something innocuous and others react as if it were profound or important. Consider our friend Ellswood, who cannot gain any power in his group. If Ellswood asks for someone to tell him the time, this sequence of responses may occur:

---

[9]The popular parody of this line reflects more sensitivity to the issue of the appropriate magnitude of responses: (If you can keep your head when all those about you are losing theirs, then perhaps you just don't understand the situation.)

"Hey, hold it! Ellswood has something important to say."

"What is it? What did he say?"

"He asked what time it is."

"He did! Good thinking, Ellswood!"

"Right! That's the way, Ellswood, we knew we could count on you to keep us straight."

"Everybody ready now? At my mark it is ten-oh-five-thirty. Less than five seconds . . . mark!"

"No, no, it's closer to ten-ten."

"What's the matter with you guys, it's ten-oh-two."

"Come on, we've got to help Ellswood. Let's take a vote. . . ." And the banter is likely to finish with:

"Hey, where did Ellswood go?" He had left, having perceived these overreactions as invalidating.

In addition to these quantitatively inappropriate messages, people may be invalidated when the other says the wrong thing. Ruesch[10] calls these **qualitatively** inappropriate messages, or **tangential responses.**

A tangential response is one which acknowledges the speaker's intent to communicate but disregards the content of his message. The response may be related to the **form** rather than the **meaning** of the message, may exaggerate the importance of the qualifications made about the message, or may reflect the emotion rather than the reasoning of the speaker. Here are some examples of tangential responses:

1. A young speaker has delivered a long, carefully prepared speech about a topic that he feels is very important. Afterward, one of the listeners shakes his hand and whispers conspiratorially, "Better look up the pronunciation of _____," (one of the words he used in the speech), then walks away with a patronizing grin.

2. A student is evaluating his performance in a course and concludes honestly, "I think that I did a pretty good job." His instructor replies, "Yes! But you think! You don't know, do you!"

3. A women's lib advocate and a self-professed male chauvinist are arguing. The woman says passionately, "You men have got to quit thinking of women only as sex objects. We are people." The

man replies, "You're cute when you get mad, your eyes just spar-kle."

In each of these examples, it is hard for the first speaker to inter-pret the reply of the second as confirming his worth as a person and the legitimacy of his experience. Ruesch described the effect of tangential responses as depriving the sender of the pleasure of being understood, and simultaneously making a bid for control of the conversation by "switching" to a different topic or emphasis.

Communicating well requires a considerable amount of skill. To under-stand another person's content and intent involves more than just recog-nizing the words he says, and to express this understanding necessitates even more expertise. Carkhuff developed a rating scale used to describe the extent to which individuals express "empathic understanding." Level one on this scale represents the least and level five the most complete expression of empathy.

1. Observe other people talking about a variety of topics and rate them on this scale. To what extent are they careful to let the other person know the extent to which he is understood? Are their responses appropriate or tangential? Are misunderstandings quickly exposed or do they derail the conversation for some time? What do they do which most impresses you as good and bad ways to express understanding of each other? Can you detect differences in satisfaction, agreement, and other criteria of effectiveness which are caused by different levels of expression of em-pathic understanding?

2. Tape-record some conversations that you have with some of your friends. Ask some other people to rate your communication behavior on this scale and compare their ratings with your own perception of your performance. Do your ratings match those by other people? Listen again to the tapes to see if you can determine what aspect of your communica-tion behavior accounted for these differences.

3. Listen again to the tape recordings you made for #2. Stop the recorder at specific places and say what you **might** *have said that would have been* **more** *and what would have been* **less** *empathic than what you actually said.*

4. Read some scenes from plays or some fiction. Rewrite the dialogue to make it better express empathic understanding. Compare your revi-sion with that of other people who rewrote the same dialogue. How do they compare? Do you find that your "style" differs from that of other people?

A Scale for Rating Expression of Empathic Understanding[11]

Level 1: *The verbal and nonverbal expressions of the speaker either do not attend to or detract significantly from the verbal and nonverbal expressions of the other. The speaker apparently is aware of less of the other's experience than the other has communicated. He appears bored, disinterested, distracted, or unable to shift from his own meanings to those of the other person.*

Level 2: *The speaker responds to only a part of the expressed feelings or meanings of the other. He acknowledges only the obvious, surface meanings expressed by the other or expresses his own meanings which are only partly congruent with those of the other person. When compared to what the other said about himself, the speaker's messages seem partial or incomplete.*

Level 3: *The speaker's responses to the meanings and feelings expressed by the other are essentially interchangeable. The speaker neither subtracts from or adds to the expressions of the other. Although he accurately understands the surface meanings and may indicate a willingness to understand the other's "deeper" meanings, he does not express an awareness of the other which exceeds what the other has told him.*

Level 4: *The speaker's responses indicate that he knows more about the other than the other has expressed to him. His statements express the meanings and feelings of the other more deeply, more precisely, more fully than the other expressed them.*

Level 5: *The speaker's responses accurately express the other's feelings and meanings much more deeply or completely than the other described them, and this enables the other to acknowledge and express these meanings and feelings. The speaker has a full awareness of who the other person is and responds to his deeper as well as his surface feelings and intentions.*

Clarity. A second characteristic of validating messages is clarity. As used in this context, clarity refers to two characteristics: (1) the message is not inconsistent; and (2) the message has a single implication for the listener. Clear messages make the listener feel that he knows what the speaker means and that he knows what is expected of him in the relationship.

[11]Adapted from Carkhuff, 1969, pp. 178–79.

Perhaps the most common cause of unclarity is dishonesty, which we discussed at length in Chapter IV. Jourard[12] described two strategies which people use in interacting with others. In "encounters that mystify," one person tries to mislead another about himself and his intentions. The example Jourard gave is seduction, in which a man strives "to manipulate her experience and action so that she will behave in the service of **his** goals, not her own." On the other hand, "encounters that reveal" are honest in that the person "aims to show his being to the other **as it is for him** . . . to show oneself in willful honesty before the other and to respond to the other with an expression of one's experience as the other has affected it."

Some people can "mystify" others with considerable adroitness, but usually, sooner or later, the truth will out. And when it does, to find that one has been "mystified" or "duped" is invalidating because the messages are not consistent, and their implication not single. Dishonesty may be revealed through ambiguous cues when the façade is incomplete or through contradictory cues when unintentional elements slip into the message. Nonverbal behaviors such as the tone of voice, micromomentary facial expressions, posture, or use of space frequently appear as unintentional cues in a message. When verbal and nonverbal cues contradict each other, most people believe the information conveyed by the nonverbal cues (Mehrabian and Wiener, 1969). But more important for our concerns, the person giving contradictory or ambiguous cues is perceived as dishonest, and this implies that there is a good deal of uncertainty about what he is really like or what he wants from the other.

Another type of unclarity comes from a particular form of messages known as the **double-bind**. Double-binds occur in relationships which are important to the participants and from which they may not withdraw. In this context, a double-bind describes the experience of a person who receives a message (or set of messages) that is paradoxical in that it implies that the listener should engage in two or more mutually exclusive behaviors simultaneously. The message may imply that he both should and should not read a certain book; or it may define a person or relationship as being healthy only if he or it is unhealthy. Such messages have

[12]1968, pp. 19–21.

multiple, contradictory implications for the individual and thus are unclear.

When formally described, double-binds seem exotic and unusual. But you probably have been on the receiving end of a good many. Harold Vetter (1969) noted that children are frequently caught in double-binds created by faulty teamwork by their parents. If a boy is told by his mother (1) always to obey his father and (2) not to get into fights, and is told by his father (1) always to obey his mother and (2) to stop letting other boys pick on him without fighting back, the young man has a real problem. No matter how he acts in the next push-and-shove situation, one of the messages from one of the parents will make him value himself less (by implying "You are bad because you have been disobedient"). Here are some examples of statements which impose double-binds:

1. "You ought to love me more than you do." If both persons understand love as something which is offered without compulsion, stating that one "ought" to love the other produces a paradox. Any subsequent expressions of affection violate the norm of spontaneity, and absence of affection reveals the person as morally deficient. There is no way to escape the double-bind: a highly invalidating situation.

2. "Do as I tell you: think for yourself!" To allow this message to influence one's behavior would be to violate the injunction about thinking for oneself.

3. "You don't really trust me; you are just trying to make me think you trust me." This is a challenge for the receiver to prove to the speaker that he (the speaker) is trusted, but it clearly expresses the kinds of responses any such attempt will encounter. No matter what the person says or does, it will be perceived as an attempt to convince the speaker of a phony confidence in him. As long as the speaker chooses to misperceive the other, he will continue to do so regardless of the other's efforts. In effect, the statement says that there is nothing the listener can do to demonstrate trust but that he should try.

4. "Why do you act so strangely? Why don't you just be yourself?" If the other had been acting honestly, this statement quickly puts him into a peculiar position. And finally:

5. "Don't be so obedient!" The multiple implications of statements such as these are a source of unclarity. The recipient not

only is unsure of how he should respond or what the speaker means, but there is no way in which he can acknowledge the whole message. Such unclarity is invalidating.

Here are some statements. Identify them as clear or unclear and, if they are unclear, describe what makes them so.
   1. Traffic sign on a highway interchange: "Disregard this sign."
   2. Sign on a construction site: "Unauthorized persons not permitted."
   3. An example of Russell's Theory of Types:

> All statements in this box are false.

   4. (Shouting:) "I am not upset!!"
   5. Instructions purportedly given British seamen on recruitment: "Do your duty as you are told and you have nothing to fear."
   6. "Toothy" used car salesman: "Tell ya' what I'm going to do, friend. It's going to cost me money, but I want to make you a good deal. . . ."
   Develop some statements which are unclear. Be able to explain why they are unclear.

Positiveness. Messages which validate the receiver are usually positive. As used here, positiveness does not necessarily imply **approving** what the other thinks, feels, or does. Rather, it denotes **accepting** the other. Laing[13] noted that even rejection is validating if it grants to the other "significance and validity."

Someone may disagree with you about a question of fact, morals, or faith without being invalidating if he expresses his feeling that you have a right to make your own decision about the matter and that your decision is legitimate. This disagreement about your **ideas** is not a rejection of the you as a **person.** On the other hand, disagreement which is invalidating implies that you are sick, mad, or bad if you do not share the other's opinion. Messages such as these are invalidatingly negative: "Only a stupid fool would think that . . ."; and "Anybody with any sense in his head would know better than that."

Just as not all disagreement is negative, some agreement is not positive. When someone agrees with you but implies that you are

[13]1962, p. 89.

only fortuitously correct or that his approval of you is contingent on your continued conformity to what he considers orthodoxy, this is not positive and you are not validated. Groups often communicate in such a way that all members understand quite well that their continued good standing in the group requires their ideological or social conformity. When the largest and strongest member of a labor union bellows, "Wouldn't none of us good fellows here want to try to break the strike lines, now would we, boys?"; an aunt at a gathering of the clan asks defiantly, "Of course, no member of this family would vote for a Democrat, would they?"; a religious group makes adherence to a doctrine of a "Triune" diety a test of fellowship; and a demagogue shouts, "All right-thinking Americans support the President's conduct of the war!" the message is clear: positive regard is contingent on continued agreement or compliance. This is not positive and not validating.

Considerations such as these led Rogers (1957) to develop the concept of unconditional positive regard as a characteristic of therapeutic communicating. Unconditional positive regard is **unconditional** because it is offered to the other regardless of what the other does or is; it is **positive** because it accepts the other as a legitimate and sufficient judge of his own behavior; and it is **regard** because it implies a commitment to a continuing relationship with the other. When one person offers another unconditional positive regard, he accepts the other as a person even though the other may now or sometime later do things of which he disapproves.

Someone once defined a friend as someone who likes you even though he knows a lot about you. This is the essence of positiveness in validation. It conveys to you the feeling that you are known and accepted by the other; that you are free to grow or change without risking rejection by the other; and that you may let the other know you as you are rather than laboriously maintaining a façade or adhering to a predetermined image in the other's perception.

Honesty is easier when messages from the other are perceived as positive because there is no fear of exposing some area of yourself which, by eliciting disagreement or disapproval, will destroy the relationship or make you subject to criticism or condemnation.

But if a person is extended unconditional positive regard, he need not edit his presentation of self to the other. Released from an ideal of consistency, he may express his changing, growing, developing self to the other and be aware of the processes of growth without fear of giving offense, losing membership in groups, or being derogated by the other.

Messages which are positive express the speakers' respect for the other. Carkhuff developed a scale which can be used in rating the expression of respect. Use this scale in the same way you did the scale for empathic understanding.

A Scale for Rating Expression of Respect[14]

Level 1. The speaker's verbal and nonverbal behavior express a clear lack of respect for the other. He indicates that the other's feelings and experiences are not worthy of consideration and that he is unable to act constructively.

Level 2. The speaker responds to the other in such a way as to communicate little respect for the feelings, experiences and potentials of the other. He may respond mechanically or passively to the other or simply ignore many of his feelings.

Level 3. The speaker expresses a minimal acknowledgment of and concern for the other's feelings, experiences and potentials. He is open to the other's experience and indicates that what happens to the other matters to him.

Level 4. The speaker clearly communicates a very deep respect and concern for the other. The speaker helps the other to feel free to be himself and to feel "prized."

Level 5. The speaker communicates the very deepest respect for the other's worth as a person and his potentials as a free individual. He expresses his commitment to enabling the other to actualize these potentials and to act freely and constructively.

Remember the examples of poor Johnnie, denied at age five the right to talk about girl friends and at age fifteen about cars. Two instances of invalidation in ten years is inconsequential; two instances per day for ten years is a different matter. When a person's social environment—or at least an important part of it—is characterized by communication which is appropriate, clear, and positive,

[14]Adapted from Robert Carkhuff, 1969, pp. 178–79

the conditions are established for the person to develop the capacity for personal communicating and, at the same time, a healthy, strong personality capable of mutually productive and satisfying relationships with other people. When he is repeatedly confronted with invalidating messages, both his personality and communication skills suffer.

The ability to communicate validatingly

Two skills are important in validation: the ability to interpret other people's messages as confirming your own sense of worth; and the ability to generate appropriate, clear, and positive messages to other people. People differ widely in the extent to which they possess each of these skills.

Consider first the ability to interpret a message as validating. Some people interpret almost any message as validating and others interpret almost any message as invalidating. What accounts for this difference?

For an answer, we must again remember the axiom (from Chapter 2) that meanings are in people, not in messages. If ambiguity is understood to describe a message which may be interpreted in two or more ways, all messages are ambiguous. No message is inherently validating or invalidating: it is the person who interprets it who determines which it will be. The reason why different people may interpret the same message differently lies in the way people perceive messages.

Given an ambiguous stimulus, people make meaning according to what they expect and/or want to perceive. This has been repeatedly demonstrated. Subjects who see pictures of two faces simultaneously—one with each eye—usually see a composite face with the most attractive features of both included (Cantril, 1957). When a picture which may be perceived either as a pretty girl or an ugly witch is shown, people generally see the face they have been told is in the picture. When they are not told which face is there, some see one and some the other (Hastorf and Polefka, 1970). Listeners to the Nixon-Kennedy debates in the 1960 presidential campaign were confronted with a number of equivocal statements. In a study which demonstrates that people interpret messages to match the meanings already in their minds, Larry

Samovar (1962) found that the supporters of each candidate perceived the equivocal statements attributed to their favorite as sensible and meaningful, but the similarly equivocal statements attributed to the candidate they planned to vote against as impossible to interpret.

Three factors affect your ability to interpret messages as validating: your concept of yourself, your habitual forms of communicating, and the distribution of "rewards" in your relationship with particular others.

If you believe that you are worthless, if you have no confidence in your own experience and judgment, or feel that others believe you to be inferior, you will tend to interpret messages as invalidating. Because you have a poor concept of yourself, you expect that others will think of you as if you were inadequate. Projecting these feelings onto other people, you interpret messages as invalidating whether they are or not because you expect others to express such meanings.

A speaker who wants a defensive, insecure listener to interpret a message as validating has a difficult task. No matter how hard he works to make his messages appropriate, clear, and positive, a person who thinks of himself as inadequate may be unable to interpret them as confirming his worth and legitimacy. On the other hand, a person who has a strong self-concept may be unable to perceive a message as invalidating. Consider an actor who has just completed a dramatic performance with which he is completely satisfied. He meets some friends and, flushed with success, asks them how they liked the show. If their reaction was more critical than his, they might respond like this:

> —I've never seen you better;
> —I just don't have words . . . ;
> —That was really it;
> —Right on, you know; or
> —Wow! I'm astonished.

All of these are definitely ambiguous. An insecure person would probably interpret them as invalidating, but the self-impressed thespian described above would bask in perceived approval and say, "Thank you, I thought so myself."

If you are accustomed either to being validated or invalidated, you are likely to interpret subsequent messages similarly. Some groups develop the habit of saying inappropriate, unclear, or negative things to each other, so much so that every message is assumed to be invalidating until proven otherwise. In this context, it is extremely difficult for a person to suddenly perceive a particular message as validating, even if it were intended as such by the speaker. Expecting an invalidating message, persons interpret the ambiguity of the message as threatening their sense of worth. Other groups develop patterns of reciprocal validation. People in these groups expect and interpret messages as validating unless confronted with overwhelming evidence to the contrary. These processes indicate the spiraling nature of personal communication: as honesty often prompts honesty from others, so a climate of validation facilitates subsequent validation, and vice versa.

The nature of the relationship also affects your ability to interpret messages as validating. One way of describing interpersonal relationships is in terms of the "rewards" and "costs" each inflicts on the other (Gergen, 1969). The "outcome" of a relationship consists of each person's rewards minus his costs. Rewards are anything which the person does or has done for him which he values; costs are those things which he does or has done to him which he does not like.

People develop expectancies about the outcomes they should obtain in interpersonal relationships. Thibaut and Kelley (1959) called this the person's "comparison level" because it is the standard against which the outcome of any particular interaction is judged. If an outcome is below the comparison level, the person is dissatisfied with the relationship and, if acceptable alternatives are available, will try to change it. Figure 5 describes a continuum of values for outcomes ranging from $+5$ (in which rewards are greater than costs) to -5 (in which costs outweight rewards) where the comparison level is equal to 0.

People are most satisfied when their outcomes fall within a relatively narrow range just above the comparison level and when the other person's outcomes are proportional. When outcomes for each individual are disproportional, strains are imposed on the relationship. The person receiving disproportionately high outcomes feels guilty and uneasy; the person receiving disproportionately low outcomes feels angry or imposed on (Homans, 1961). Unless the individuals are remarkably **aware** of the nature of their relationship and are **able to talk about it** to each other, these strains reduce the probability that either person can interpret the other's messages as validating. The "guilty" person feels that he "ought" to incur more costs than he has and thus expects the other to inflict costs on him as a way of offsetting the imbalanced outcomes and thus stabilizing the relationship. At the same time, the "angry" person feels that he has the "right" to punish the other and expects the other to behave defensively.

This impasse can be avoided in two ways: (1) by the development of "contracts,"[15] which prevent an imbalanced distribution of costs and rewards; or (2) by unusually competent communicators who make these aspects of their relationship explicit and hence manageable by conscious choice rather than by hunch and reflex.

One of the important functions of implicit contracts is to regulate efficiently the distribution of rewards and costs in a relationship. In this way contracts facilitate personal communication both by specifying "rules" (Pearce, 1973) for honesty and mutual acceptance of the other and by stabilizing relationships in forms which are acceptable to both individuals.

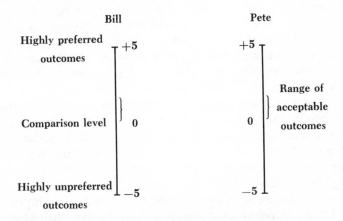

Figure 5. Range of acceptable outcomes in an interpersonal relationship

[15]Carson, 1969, pp. 172–217.

If the distribution of outcomes becomes disproportional despite or in the absence of contractual rules, the best corrective is good communication. But people differ substantially in their ability to communicate honestly and validatingly in these less-than-optimal conditions. Mindful that dishonesty and/or invalidation tend to start a cycle of increasingly impersonal communication, let us consider now the ability to encode messages which are appropriate, clear and positive.

The factors which affect your ability to interpret a message as validating—your self-concept, habitual modes of communicating, and relationship with the other—also affect your ability to encode messages which facilitate the other person's validating behavior. But in addition, your knowledge of the rules governing personal communicating is also important.

Psycholinguists (such as Slobin, 1971) have shown that we do **not** learn to speak simply by memorizing sentences we have heard others use and then repeating them in other contexts. Rather, we learn rules of sentence structure and extrapolate on the basis of these rules to create sentences in particular conversations. The sociolinguists (such as Ervin-Tripp, 1972) have shown that we learn conventions about what meanings to express in what situations and how they shall be expressed in much the same way. Our choices of how to encode messages—should we be serious or joking, direct or evasive, outspoken or demurring—depend on the rules we have learned and how we can extrapolate from them to a specific case. But few (if any) people know all of the rules of all forms of communication. If an individual has not learned the rules of behavior which should occur in personal communicating, he will make messages characteristic of impersonal communicating— such as oneupsmanship or debate as a decision-making procedure —when honesty and validation are in order. To see a person who has superior forensic and deliberative skills but who is unable to encode messages properly in personal communicating is a pitiful but not uncommon event.

Just as people need to practice skills in public speaking or argumentation, we believe that people need to develop their abilities to communicate personally. We recommend improving your skills at recognizing appropriateness, clarity, and positiveness in messages. By becoming more sensitive to these characteristics of messages, you may eliminate some of the limiting effects of your self-esteem, habits, and relationships on whether you interpret messages as validating. In addition, we recommend improving your skills in encoding messages characterized by appropriateness, clarity, and positiveness. By developing these skills, you will be better able to communicate personally when you choose to do so and to recognize personal communication behavior and its counterfeits in other people.

One way to increase your ability to detect and encode messages which are appropriate, clear, and positive is to construct some hypothetical conversations (or reconstruct some actual exchanges of messages) and "break into" them at some convenient spot. Then decide what one of the speakers **could** *say at that point which would have all, some, or none of the characteristics which would help the other to interpret the message as validating. For example, write a message which would be appropriate* **and** *clear* **and** *positive, then three messages each of which lacks* **one** *of these characteristics, and finally a message which lacks all three. Consider this conversation:*

PAT. *Hi! Where are you going?*

ELLSWOOD. *To the bookstore.*

PAT. *What for?*

ELLSWOOD. *To buy the new science fiction story by Emil McGillahay. What will Pat say now? (1) If he says, "Why do you waste your time on that trash?" Ellswood will be invalidated because he will interpret the message as negative, not accepting his judgment about reading materials as legitimate. (2) If he says, "Oh, come on! You don't expect me to believe that you would go all the way to town to buy a science fiction book! What is your real reason? Come on, be honest!" and if Ellswood really is after the book, he will be invalidated because he will perceive the message as unclear. This response poses a paradox similar to "Be yourself: do what I tell you to do." (3) If Pat says "Stay out of the pool hall," Ellswood will not be validated because he will interpret the response as inappropriate: it denies his content and his right to be interested in science fiction. (4) The following tirade is maximally invalidating because it is inappropriate, unclear, and negative: "Yes, I'll bet you are! Why do you try to give me an excuse like that? You wouldn't waste your time on that science fiction trash. What's your real reason for going? I'll bet it's to play pool. Why do you want to waste your time in these pool halls!" (5) However, if Pat says, "You've enjoyed McGillahay's*

other books, haven't you? Which was your favorite, 'The Eighth Day'?"
Ellswood will interpret the message as validation because it is appropriate, clear, and positive.

Try your hand at composing the missing messages in these conversations:

CAROL. *Are you going to the party tomorrow night?*
KENT. *Probably, I haven't thought much about it.*
CAROL. *Oh, it will probably be a lot of fun.*
KENT. *Yeah! Are you going?*
CAROL. *Well, I haven't been asked for a date yet.*
KENT. *??*

ERIKA. *Daddy, what color is thunder?*
HER FATHER. *??*

ELLSWOOD. *May I ask a favor from you?*
TASHA. *Sure, you may ask.*
ELLSWOOD. *What are you doing Saturday night?*
TASHA. *Why do you ask that? I thought you wanted to ask for a favor? Would my telling you my plans be a favor to you? Gosh! That's pretty weird.*
ELLSWOOD. *What I mean is, would you like to go to the movie with me?*
TASHA. *??*

Now write some other conversations and compose messages which will be interpreted as validating and invalidating. Work on this project in groups. If you are studying in a class, act them out and discuss the meanings of various persons in the dialogue. Doing this will help you internalize the "rules" for constructing messages appropriate for personal and impersonal communicating.

References

Borden, George A., Richard B. Gregg, and Theodore G. Grove. 1969. **Speech Behavior and Human Interaction.** Englewood Cliffs, New Jersey: Prentice-Hall.

Cantril, Hadley. 1957. "Perception and Interpersonal Relations," **American Journal of Psychiatry, 114**:119–26.

Carkhuff, Robert. 1969. **Helping and Human Relations: A Primer for Lay and Professional Helpers.** Vol. I. New York: Holt, Rinehart and Winston.

Carson, Robert. 1969. **Interaction Concepts of Personality.** Chicago: Aldine.

Ervin-Tripp, Susan. 1972. "On Sociolinguistic Rules: Alternation and Co-occurrence," in **Directions in Sociolinguistics: The Ethnography on Communication.** New York: Holt, Rinehart and Winston. John J. Gumperz and G. Hymes, eds., 213–50.

Gergen, Kenneth J. 1969. **The Psychology of Behavior Exchange.** Reading, Mass: Addison-Wesley.

Giffin, Kim. 1970. "Social Alienation by Communication Denial," **The Quarterly Journal of Speech, 56**:347–58.

Hastorf, Albert, and Judity Polefka. 1970. **Person Perception.** Reading, Mass.: Addison-Wesley.

Homans, George C. 1961. **Social Behavior: Its Elementary Forms.** New York: Harcourt, Brace.

Jourard, Sidney M. 1968. **Disclosing Man to Himself.** New York: Van Nostrand.

Kinch, J. W. 1967. "A Formalized Theory of Self-Concept," in **Symbolic Interactionism.** Boston: Allyn and Bacon. J. G. Manis and B. N. Meltzer, eds., 232–40.

Kipling, Rudyard. 1936. "If," in **The Best Loved Poems of the American People.** Garden City, New York: Garden City Publishing Co. Hazel Felleman, ed., 65–66.

Laing, Ronald D. 1962. **The Self and Others.** Chicago: Quadrangle.

Mehrabian, Albert, and Morton Wiener. 1969. "Decoding and Inconsistent Communication," **Journal of Personality and Social Psychology, 13**:37–58.

Merrill, Bob. 1963. **People.** New York: Chappell and Co.

Mullahy, Patrick. 1970. **Psychoanalysis and Interpersonal Psychiatry:**

The Contributions of Harry Stack Sullivan. New York: Science House.

Pearce, W. Barnett. 1973. "Consensual Rules in Interpersonal Communication: A Reply to Cushman and Whiting," **Journal of Communication, 23:**160–68.

Rogers, Carl. 1957. "The Necessary and Sufficient Conditions for Therapeutic Personality Change," **Journal of Consulting Psychology, 22:** 95–103.

———. 1971. "Communication: Its Blocking and Facilitation," in **Communication: Concepts and Processes.** Englewood Cliffs, New Jersey: Prentice-Hall. Joseph DeVito, ed.

Ruesch, Jurgen. 1957. **Disturbed Communication.** New York: Norton.

Samovar, Larry. 1962. "Ambiguity and Equivocation in the Kennedy-Nixon Television Debates," **The Quarterly Journal of Speech, 48:** 277–79.

Schutz, William, C. 1966. **The Interpersonal Underworld.** Palo Alto, California: Science and Behavior Books.

Sieburg, Evelyn, and Carl Larson. 1971. "Dimensions of Interpersonal Response," paper presented to the International Communication Association, Phoenix, Arizona.

Silverberg, Robert. 1970. "Neighbor," in **The Cube Root of Uncertainty.** New York: Collier.

———. 1973. "To See the Invisible Man," in **Earth's Others Shadow.** New York: New American Library, 41–52.

Slobin, Dan I. 1971. **Psycholinguistics.** Glenview, Illinois: Scott, Foresman.

Thibaut, John W., and Harold H. Kelley. 1959. **The Social Psychology of Groups.** New York: Wiley.

Vetter, Harold J. 1969. **Language Behavior and Psychopathology.** Chicago: Rand-McNally.

Watzlawick, Paul, Janet H. Beavin, and Don D. Jackson. 1967. **Pragmatics of Human Communication: A Study of Interactional Patterns, Pathologies and Paradoxes.** New York: Norton.

Zubeck, John P., ed. 1969. **Sensory Deprivation: Fifteen Years of Research.** New York: Appleton-Century-Crofts.

PART II

Cause/effects of communicating personally

If we engage in "enough" personal communicating, we tend to become psychologically healthier and more trusting of ourselves and others. On the other hand, our level of psychological health and capacity for trusting influence how often we communicate personally. Since this implies a two-way cause-effect relationship we use the term "cause/effects" to refer to the topics discussed in the next three chapters. Trust, alienation, and psychological health both influence and are influenced by personal communicating.

SIX

Trust and communicating personally

... trust cannot be forced ...

For many years Charles Schulz celebrated the advent of football season each fall with a "Peanuts" story featuring Charlie Brown's troubles with Lucy. The plot was always the same. Lucy offered to hold a football so Charlie could practice his place-kicking, but each year she jerked the ball away just as Charlie kicked through it, causing him to fall heavily to the turf. Readers of the strip knew what would happen: the only suspense involved what Lucy would do or say to overcome gullible Charlie's well-founded suspicions. For example, one year Lucy explained, "I represent an organization and I'm holding this ball as a representative of that organization." Charlie reasoned that "if she represents an organization . . . she must be sincere," and came running at full speed to kick the ball. Seconds later, as Charlie lay prone and stunned, Lucy explained: "This year's football was pulled away from you through the courtesy of women's lib!"

Most people find Charlie Brown's troubles similar to their own. And in this instance, the problem involves trust. Should Charlie trust Lucy? How could he determine before he committed himself to a lusty swing at the pigskin whether he would score a field goal or wind up on his back suffering Lucy's taunts? Few of us, alas, have to worry about girls with naturally curly hair offering to hold our footballs when we are out for a little kicking practice, but all of us have to make hard decisions about whether, and how much, and with what to trust other people.

During the early 1970s, Texaco spent many thousands of dollars for TV advertisements which proclaimed that "trust is everything." While this slogan seems a bit overstated, the importance of trust in the development of productive and satisfying interpersonal relationships is obvious. Granted its importance to human relationships generally and to communication behavior specifically, we were surprised to discover how little formal study has been made of trust. Giffin and Patton (1971) noted that trust is frequently "viewed as a somewhat mystical and intangible factor defying careful definition." We believe that it is important to do better than that; to do more than emote about the goodness of trust or pedantically document its obvious importance. Appendix B presents a review of four literatures in which trust has been studied, and this chapter contains a formal analysis of what it means to trust. After achieving an understanding of trust, we will be better able to consider its relationship to personal communicating and the problems of deciding when and whom and how much to trust and how to demonstrate to others that we deserve their trust.

The analysis of trust presented in the next few pages is, we believe, logical and intellectually rigorous. But our purposes are not served if reading this chapter is nothing but an intellectual exercise for you. The second part of the chapter deals with the way you communicate and the decisions you have to make about trust. We think you will be best prepared to read those sections if you first refresh your experience with trusting and being trusted.

Here are some activities which will help you bring to conscious attention some of your experiences with trust. We suggest that you work through each of the activities before continuing to read.

1. Name two persons in public life (politicians, entertainers, athletes, etc.), one of whom you trust and one of whom you do not. What would be your reaction if you read an article by syndicated columnist Jack Anderson charging that the person whom you trust was guilty of repeated tax evasion and flagrant child abuse? Write your feeling about the person, about tax evasion, and about child abuse. Do you believe that he/she is guilty as charged? What do you think about Jack Anderson? Now assume that you have read the same article, this time charging the person whom you distrust with the same accusations. Again write your reaction. Now compare what you have written in the two instances. What are some of the most important differences? What does this tell you about trust?

2. Remember a specific instance in which you trusted another person. Describe this experience to a friend or classmate. How did you act in this situation? What would you have done differently if you had not trusted the person? How did you feel? How do you think the person you trusted felt?

3. Remember a specific instance in which you were trusted by another person. Describe this experience to a friend or classmate. How did you act knowing that you were trusted? How did you feel? How do you think the other person felt?

The meaning of trust

The relationships which persons establish between themselves take many forms. Consider what we call "love": there are important differences between "loving" your country, hot dogs, your parents, your best friend and body-surfing. But our language glosses over these differences by describing them with the same word. In English, we differentiate these relationships primarily by degrees of intensity: love is "stronger" than like which is "stronger" than affection. The Greek language differentiates by type rather than by intensity: "eros" (sexual love) is not the same as "philia" (brotherly love), which is not the same as "agape" (altrusitic love). The point is that experience—with love as with trust—is richer and far more multifaceted than our ability to symbolize and describe it.

There are many forms of interpersonal relations to which the term trust is applied and many almost-synonyms for trust which are often used instead of trust. Consider these: hope, reliance, confidence, dependence, belief, and credibility. Securing any amount of precision in our discussion requires clearly specifying what we mean by trust, and the usefulness of this chapter depends on identifying the most significant characteristics common to all experiences of trusting.

Let us begin by considering the context of trust. Trust occurs only in interpersonal relationships, and only in relationships having certain characteristics.

Characteristics of situations in which trust occurs. Unless an interpersonal relationship is characterized by **contingency, predictability,** and **alternative options,** it is impossible to experience trust. Contingency describes situations in which the trusted person's behavior affects the outcomes of the truster in nontrivial ways. Predictability describes situations in which the truster has some degree of confidence in his expectations or predictions of the trusted person's behaviors and/or intentions. Finally, the criterion of alternative options describes situations in which the trusting person can do something other than trust, in which he has a choice whether to maintain or increase his vulnerability to the other.

In situations where one or more of these characteristics are absent, either the behavior or experience of the person may be shown to differ from what we call trust. If there is no contingency between persons, it is inappropriate to speak of trust because neither can importantly affect the other and there is no occasion for trusting behaviors as we will define them later. Without predictability, hope may be present but not trust. Consider a man carrying a large amount of money late at night through a section of a large city known for its high crime rate who hears footsteps in the shadows both in front of and behind him: he may hope for the best but he has a much different experience than if he knows who is there and can predict their behavior (i.e., by trusting them not to rob him). Lacking available alternative options, nothing that a person can do will alter what happens to him, precluding trusting behaviors. Again, he might hope for the best, perhaps even expect it, but this is quite a different experience from that in which he deliberately chooses between options which affect his own well-being.

When a person is in an interpersonal relationship in which what happens to him is contingent on the behavior of the other, in which he has some basis for predicting how the other will behave, and in which he has the option to behave in a way which will increase or limit the extent to which the other's behavior will affect him, he is in a condition in which trust may occur. Let us now turn to a consideration of trust per se. (This concept of trust is diagrammed in Figure 6.)

The cognitive state of trust. An adequate definition of trust

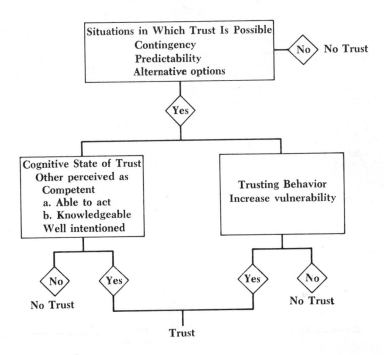

Figure 6. A diagram of the concept of trust

must specify both a range of **observable behaviors** and a **cognitive state** which provides their context. Trusting behaviors are those which **deliberately increase a person's vulnerability to another person.** The cognitive state of trust is **a belief that the other is both willing and able to conduct himself in such a way as to prevent the trusting person from receiving intolerably negative outcomes.**

People with whom you communicate can engage in any of a wide range of behaviors. But if you have some confidence in your ability to make predictions about their behavior in specific instances, you can identify some of these as more probable than others. And if what the other person does affects you, you can differentiate between those acts which are in your best interests and those which

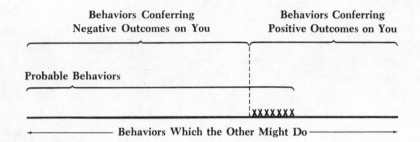

Figure 7. The cognitive state of trusting

are not. These estimates about the other's behavior are diagrammed in Figure 7. The cognitive state of trusting consists of
expecting the other's behavior to be in the overlap of his probable
behaviors and those which result in positive (or at least not
severely negative) outcomes for you. This range of behaviors is
indicated by the crossmarks (xxxx) in the diagram.

To attain the cognitive state of trust requires that the trusted
person be perceived as both competent and well intentioned.
Competence involves perceiving the other's knowledge, judgment,
and abilities as adequate. Specifically, competence involves the
other's knowledge of the nature of the relationship between you
and his ability to perform the appropriate behaviors. If you broke
one of your legs, you probably would not trust some of your friends
to set it for you even though you had no doubts about their good
intentions: questioning their competence, you might prefer to wait
for an M.D. In this sense, competence refers to ability to perform
appropriately. But competence also involves understanding the
nature of the contingency between you. Some public officials are
not trusted by certain of their constituents, not because they are
perceived as unable to perform certain actions, but because their
awareness of the effects of those programs is questioned. In addition to perceiving the other as competent, the cognitive state of
trust requires that he be perceived as well intentioned toward the
truster. If a man thrice convicted of rape offered to drive you home
from a party, your trust might not be forthcoming. While you might
have no qualms about his driving ability, his intentions toward you
might be suspect.

To summarize: the cognitive state of trusting requires the conditions of contingency, predictability, and availability of alternative options and consists of a belief that the other's behavior will prevent unacceptably negative outcomes from being conferred on you. It is based on your perception that the other is competent (both knowledgeable about the effects of his actions and able to perform them) and well intentioned toward you.

Trusting behavior. The essential characteristic of trusting behavior is that it increases or maintains your vulnerability to the other person. As such, trusting behavior may take a number of forms in different situations.

Consider ambiguous behavior. In situations characterized by contingency, predictability, and alternative options, most actions are equivocal, subject to several interpretations. When we act ambiguously, the other engages in trusting behavior when, without adequate corroborative evidence, he interprets our act as trustworthy, assuming that it will not confer an unacceptably negative outcome on him. In the movie "Winds Across the Everglades," Burl Ives played the character of a notorious poacher of egrets and blue herons. In one scene, he was in the bow of a dugout canoe, being brought to Miami to face charges by a young game warden whom he respected highly. Feeling confident that he would not be convicted in the local courts, he had agreed to accompany the warden but was not under arrest. Suddenly he dropped his oar, grabbed his shotgun, and fired it, narrowly missing the game warden's head. Interpreting this as an attack, the game warden hit Ives with his oar. Knocked from the boat and thrashing in the swamp, Ives gasped, "A snake. I thought it was a snake." Then the warden saw that there was a branch close to his head which could have been perceived as a snake dropping from a tree. But the delicate trust between the two was broken and could not be regained: every subsequent ambiguous act was interpreted as threatening and hostile.

A second form of trusting behavior consists of not evaluating, monitoring, or checking on the behavior of others in contingent situations. When what the other does affects you and you do not trust him, you will try to find out what he plans to do so you can increase your ability to predict his behavior and thereby reduce your vulnerability when necessary. Such surveillance may be conducted by deliberate spying or by demanding reports from him about what he is doing, explanations of his purposes, and estimates of the effects he believes will occur. Institutional expense account procedures provide a good example. If the administrative officer trusts the people using the account, he will ask them only to tell him how much they charged to the account. But if he does not trust them, he will insist on an itemized report. Perhaps it is significant that every expense account system of which we are aware insists not only on itemized reports but documentary evidence that large expenditures were actually made for the purposes claimed.

Trusting behavior may take yet a third form. In Chapter 3 we characterized persuasion as a form of impersonal communication. (This decision, interestingly enough, prompted many of our friends and colleagues to attempt to persuade us that we were wrong.) Our thinking about persuasion is based on our belief that communicating personally requires trust and that one manifestation of trust is in **not** trying to persuade others to do what **we** think is best for **them.** Consider this: if you believe that a person is competent (able to do what he decides is best and knowledgeable enough to know the consequences of his actions) and well intentioned toward you, why would you try to persuade him? You would not want him to change his decisions about what to do because you believe that he knows what is best and that he needs no exhortation to be kind, loyal, considerate, humble, or whatever virtue is relevant. The only time you have occasion to persuade others is when you perceive them as not knowing, not able, or not willing to do what is best (unless, for devious purposes of your own, you want them to do what is not in their best interests, such as an encyclopedia salesman trying to unload leftover copies of the now-outdated edition to a poor-but-hopeful family who does not know better). Persuasion serves as a substitute for trust.

Of course this does not imply a silly rule like "where persuasion is, there can be no trust," if that is interpreted to mean that **any** persuasion excludes **all** trust, and vice versa. As a cognitive state, it is quite appropriate to speak of greater and lesser degrees of trust. Likewise, trusting behavior usually takes a variety of forms ranging from cautious to complete trusting. In fact, it requires considerable effort for researchers to create a situation in which trusting and not trusting are dichotomous choices. The implication of all of this is that it is very possible for people to trust a little bit.

And, without equivocating from our original position, this allows us to explain that there may be both some persuasion and some trust in a relationship; however, we insist that the presence of persuasion is a symptom of an area in which trust is less than total, and that the volume of persuasion in a relationship is a reliable criterion of the amount of trust in that relationship.

Some functions of trust in interpersonal communication

There is considerable ambivalence in our society about trust. The lack of trust is frequently cited as the cause of various social problems, while being trusted is considered an estimable virtue. Every shyster lawyer, crooked politician, and greedy salesman lusts for trust; yet people who are too ready to trust them are contemptuously labeled gullible and shamelessly exploited. This seems most curious.

There is no question about the significance of trust in human affairs. In this section, we will discuss only some of the ways trust affects interpersonal relations.

Despite the generally negative tones we have taken toward persuasion, the exercise of personal influence is an important part of our society. In fact, one of the most significant forms of impersonal communication is that which achieves social coordination and accommodation. Particularly in the socialization processes of children and the policy-making deliberations of adults, techniques of nonviolent social influence are both necessary and desirable. Interestingly enough, persuasion is most effective when there is already some trust existing between the persuader and his target audience. The literature of speaker credibility clearly shows that those perceived as most competent and with the best character are believed most readily. (The willingness of speakers to engage in persuasion, by the way, has not been studied. It would be interesting to know if people aware that they are trusted are more hesitant than others to try to persuade those who trust them. This notion, of course, reflects the sentiment of the familiar disclaimer, "I would not be so bold to speak if I thought it my due to be believed.")

Another important form of highly impersonal communicating is that which occurs when individuals or groups have to make decisions. In these situations, efficiency is an important concern, and

efficiency deteriorates in the absence of trust. In formal organizations, the frequency, type, and length of messages exchanged between individuals vary as a function of trust. If two individuals trust
each other, they will not waste time trying to maintain surveillance
on each other, but will assume that each will do his job well. Their
messages will apply to the issues at hand rather than consisting of
apologies (in the technical sense of careful statements explaining
the reasons for a belief or act) or polemics. Their communication
will be relaxed and cooperative rather than tense and defensive.

Decision-making, task-oriented discussions also prize accuracy,
which suffers in the absence of trust. Mellinger (1959) studied
communication between members of a scientific research organization, some of whom trusted each other and some of whom did
not. Communication between members of the organization increased the accuracy with which they understood each other's
feelings about mutually relevant topics when they trusted, but not
when they did not trust the other. Mellinger interpreted these data
as evidencing a tendency to use communication to conceal the way
we feel from distrusted others.

Finally, certain types of interpersonal relations are precluded by
a lack of trust, including some of the most appealing and mutually
beneficial. For nations to avoid both war and ruinously expensive
arms races requires trust. The potential for military retaliation
(second strike capacity) is a persuasive device not needed if the
parties involved trust each other. Similarly, intimacy, self-disclosure, and the best types of cooperation must be preceded by trust.
Gibb (1964) believes that the capacity to be interdependent in a
group effort requires that the persons involved trust one another.
He described some characteristics of individuals and groups lacking in trust, and noted that these characteristics prevent ready
attainment of group goals. Individuals working in groups with people whom they do not trust persistently defend their public image,
attempt to change the attitudes and beliefs of others, attempt to
make decisions for others, avoid open conflict and expressions of
feelings, engage in flattery, are cynical and derogatory about the
group (particularly in private), maintain formal behavior and established control mechanisms, and deny close identification with the
group. Groups composed of people who do not trust one another
have definite characteristics as well. They insist on chains of com-

mand and status differences, rigidly preplan their agendas and define their jurisdiction, preserve social distance between members, and avoid controversy.

Genuine and counterfeit proposals for mutual trust

One of the most serious problems in interacting with others is caused by the impossibility of distinguishing counterfeit from genuine proposals for the establishment of mutual trust. Let us illustrate these situations by analyzing what Eric Berne called "games." According to Berne, a game is "an ongoing series of complementary ulterior transactions progressing to a well-defined, predictable outcome," or more colloquially, "a series of moves" with a "gimmick."[1]

Two common games are "Rapo" and "NIGYSOB" (an acronym for "Now I've Got You, You Son of a Bitch"). Each game involves deceiving the other by strategic use of the "relationship" meanings of language. The essential characteristic of each game is that one person "invites" or "asks" the other to take a particular role in their relationship, knowing that the other cannot defend his "right" to that role, then attacks him, forcing him to abandon the role. Rapo consists of movements along the friendly-hostile continuum in relationships while NIGYSOB involves the dominant-submissive continuum.

NIGYSOB begins when one person (whom we will call Gamer) expresses a feeling of inferiority or willingness to submit to the other (whom we will call Ellswood). One of the cultural norms in our society is that when one person asks to be allowed to be submissive, the other may legitimately take the dominant role (for a discussion of these behavior patterns, see Carson, 1969). Most people, like Ellswood in this instance, are only too happy to assume the proffered dominant role. The fraudulent part of the game occurs when, by a series of statements which express an increasingly submissive role, Gamer leads Ellswood to become more and more dominant. The trap is set when Ellswood assumes an indefensibly dominant position, such as by acting as if he is more expert than he really is. The game is consummated when Gamer suddenly

[1]Berne, 1964, p. 48.

reverses roles, now challenging Ellswood for the dominant position. If Gamer has been successful, Ellswood will have no alternative but to make an embarrassing switch to the submissive role. Gamer can now shout the name of the game.

Here is an example of NIGYSOB in which each behavior is labeled. Let D represent "dominant" behavior and S "submissive."

GAMER. (S) Do you know anything about chess?

ELLSWOOD. (slightly D) Well, yes. I know a little bit about the game.

GAMER. (S) Good. I've been looking at this game and I need someone to explain one of the moves to me.

ELLSWOOD. (D) Sure. Let me take a look at the board.

GAMER. (more S) What I don't understand is White's thirty-ninth move.

ELLSWOOD. (more D) The move is Knight to King's eight. This puts the Black King in check.

GAMER. (very S) Is that good?

ELLSWOOD. (very D) Of course. The whole idea of chess is to place your opponent in a check from which he cannot escape. That's called checkmate and forces. . . .

GAMER. (very D) But Knight to King's eight obviously leads to an interposition with Black's Bishop and to mate in five moves.

ELLSWOOD. (still D) Well . . . surely there is a way for White to defend himself. That still looks like a good move.

GAMER. (very D) No way! Grandmaster Petrosian called this the worst blunder he had ever seen in international play, and demonstrated that there is no way White can even prolong play.

ELLSWOOD. (S) Oh . . . Well, I guess you'll have to check with someone else. I really don't know much about the game.

GAMER. (very D) Yes, I'll have to talk with someone more knowledgeable if I'm going to finish this article for **Chess News.**

ELLSWOOD. (S) **Chess News,** huh. Well, see you around.

GAMER. (very D) Not if I see you first.

The insidious aspect of a game like NIGYSOB is that it looks just like a relationship which might develop into a healthy and mutually profitable one until Ellswood begins to exaggerate his expertise and Gamer snaps the trap. Look at Gamer's first four statements in the example above: if he really was a beginner at chess and wanted help, he would have acted in just this manner. How is poor Ellswood to know whether this is a learner who wants help or a game-player who wants to embarrass him? The answer is that there is no completely sure technique for distinguishing between them.

The game of Rapo is exactly the same as NIGYSOB except that it occurs on the friendly-hostile rather than the dominant-submissive continuum of interpersonal relationships. For example, Gamer might be an attractive woman who hints that amorous advances from Ellswood, an eligible man met at a cocktail party, would be welcomed and reciprocated. As Ellswood becomes more and more forward, each redefinition of the relationship as more friendly is matched by Gamer until Ellswood commits himself to an indefensible position, perhaps by suggesting that they retire to his apartment for some privacy and heavy breathing. Suddenly Gamer reverses roles, becoming very hostile. If the game was played correctly, Ellswood has no option but to accept an embarrassing put down.

It might amuse you to invent dialogues for other instances of these games. Or just listen to people: you will hear them play these or other games on their acquaintances. Whenever one person proposes a redefinition of the relationship in such a way that the other person is offered a positively evaluated position, he must decide whether to be trusting or to suspect the other of setting him up for a game like these.

Building trusting relationships

Having discussed the meaning of trust and its importance in interpersonal relationships, we are ready to turn our attention to the decisions you have to make about trust and communicating personally. How can you create a relationship with another person based on mutual trust? How can you differentiate between behavior which offers trust and that which is designed to set you up for a game of Rapo or NIGYSOB? How can you convince others that your behavior is genuinely based on respect or affection and is not just a "line" you are using for some ulterior purpose?

Being trusted by others. There is no universally effective way to convince others to trust you. We can summarize what usually happens in this manner: **Trusting behavior on your part sometimes produces trust in the other, but distrusting behavior almost always produces distrust.**

Consider what is involved in the other's trust of you: he must be convinced that you are competent and well intentioned toward him in this specific situation. But any information you provide him about your character or present inclinations is filtered through his perceptual processes and cognitive interpretations, and there may be wide differences between the way you perceive your own competence and intentions and the way they are perceived by him. This problem is a basic one in any analysis of communication, and may be expressed this way: if the other person wishes to misunderstand you, he will, and nothing you can do or say can change it. What can you do if a friend says, "You don't like me any more!" If you protest to the contrary, he will accuse you of maliciously lying or cowardly denying the truth; silence will be interpreted as implying consent; and a recital of acts demonstrating your devotion may be interpreted as evidence that you have deliberately tried to prove the existence of an affection not really present. Finally, unless you are unusually able to create an atmosphere in which you can discuss relationships, you may finally agree with him. Similarly, how can you prove to an accusor that you are not prejudiced toward Blacks, southerners, Birchers, communists, men, yankees, etc.? If the other is determined to see you as prejudiced, there is no way to dissuade him. Even the ultimate attempt, reporting that "some of my best friends are _____ (fill in the appropriate group)," is generally interpreted as proving that you are so prejudiced that (1) you are abnormally conscious of group distinctions, and (2) you have made "token" friends in that group just to hide your real feelings.

The fact that you cannot prevent another from misunderstanding your meanings, your intentions, or your actions has important implications for building trusting relationships. Unless the other is able and ready to trust you, there is no way in which you can develop his trust. People differ in their ability to trust—an important fact about which we shall say more later. But consider now the way in which successful attempts to produce trust occur.

Swinth (1967) described the process of developing trust as one in which each person suggests to the other that they trust each other a little more than they do at that instant. When this process is reciprocated, continuing trusting relations occur. The means by which trust is "suggested" is important: Swinth described it as performing behavior which exposes the actor to the risk of personal loss. The other "accepts" the redefinition of the relationship by not exploiting the first but, in turn, performing trusting behavior. Bennis and his colleagues (1964) noted the mutually reinforcing nature of this process: "When one person trusts enough to make himself vulnerable by exposing himself [to personal loss], trust is generated in the other." When the other reciprocates, "there is a continual build-up of trust, a growing confidence that they will not hurt each other intentionally." But when the other does not reciprocate by making himself vulnerable, he has disapproved or rejected the first's proposal for a more trusting relationship and "the relationship freezes at that point, is terminated, or testing begins anew."

We can now make with confidence three statements about the establishment of trusting relationships. (1) The development of trust requires at least one person who engages in trusting **behaviors** even though he may not have the **cognitive state** of trust. That is, he makes himself vulnerable to the other **without** a high degree of subjective probability that he will not be exploited. (2) The development of trust requires that all persons involved be **able** to trust, that is, to suspend tendencies for exploiting vulnerable others and to interpret the other's ambiguous behavior as trustworthy rather than a gambit or foolishness. (3) The development of trust occurs by an incremental process in which all concerned engage in negotiations or tests which successively redefine the relationship between the communicators, culminating in contracts or norms of trustworthiness.

Consider now some behaviors which function as requests for a change in the amount of trust in the relationship. When two people are in a situation where each person's outcomes are contingent on the decision that both make, selecting an option which makes the chooser more vulnerable to the other may be interpreted both as a statement and a question: "I would like for us to trust each other. How do you feel about it?" In studies using the Prisoner's Dilemma game, in which subjects must choose between cooperative and competitive strategies, subjects usually achieve mutual cooperation (where both choose the high risk option, simultaneously declining the opportunity to exploit each other) when they play the game many times, but not necessarily when they play only a few times (Rapoport and Chammah, 1965). This finding reflects the incremental process of the formation of trust. It takes time to construct norms which enable each to predict how he and the other will behave. Further, cooperation occurs most frequently when one person's strategy "matches" the other's rather than consisting of choices which invariably increase or decrease vulnerability to the other (Solomon, 1960; Gallo and McClintock, 1965). Subjects who are unconditionally competitive, resisting vulnerability, are perceived as not trustworthy and not trusting. On the other hand, those who are unconditionally cooperative are perceived as gullible, masochistic, or uninterested in the relationship.

When individuals or groups perceive themselves as antagonists, they sometimes plead for "more communication" as a solution to their problems. A sudden faith in communication is not necessarily well founded, however. When the problem involves a lack of trust, increasing communication may produce better relations or increase tensions and distrust. Two studies found communication producing increased cooperation. Deutsch (1958) found that an individual's motivation determines whether communication increases cooperation. A number of subjects played the Prisoner's Dilemma game (see figure 8).[2] Some were instructed to maximize the combined scores for themselves and their opponent (the "cooperative" orientation); some were told to play to score as many points as possible without regard to their opponent's score (the "individualistic" orientation). Communication was allowed for some individualistically oriented subjects, not for others. The results clearly show that communication facilitated cooperation for these subjects: individualistically oriented subjects who communicated acted as though they were cooperatively oriented; those who did not communicate as if they were competitively motivated. The subjects in Loomis' (1959) experiment perceived mutual trust when they exchanged his previously prepared notes. Further, trust

---

[2]The Prisoners' Dilemma game (see Rapoport and Chammah, 1965) consists of a two-by-two matrix in which each of the four cells contain two scores representing the "outcomes" for each player. A typical matrix is shown in Figure 8. The game is a "dilemma" because the outcomes are arranged in such a way that each player has a "high risk" and "low risk" option; the outcomes for each player depends on his own selection and that of the other; and both players lose if they both select the low risk option and both win if they both select the high risk option. The game is played in a series of trials during each of which both persons select one of the dichotomous options. They are said to be playing "cooperatively" if they select high risk options, "competitively" if they select low risk options.

Person A's	Person B's Choices			
Choices	Outcomes for:		Outcomes for:	
1				
(low risk)	Person A	Person B	Person A	Person B
	−5	+5	+10	−10
2				
(high risk)	−10	+10	+5	+5

Figure 8. The prisoners' dilemma game

increased as the notes the subjects selected included more specific information about the relationship.[3]

Other studies found that communication may be used to deceive, frustrate, or provoke a fight with the other rather than building trust (see Vinacke, 1969). Gahagan and Tedeschi (1968) found that cooperation increased when subjects exchanged promises and subsequently kept them but decreased when the promises were not kept, and Evans (1964) found a direct relation between cooperation and the constraints on the other to keep his promises. Without a way of forcing each other to act as they promised they would, however, communication in competitive situations may function, to paraphrase Clausewitz, as warfare by other means. Wallace and Rothaus (1969) concluded that communication was unrelated to the development of trust among their subjects.

But an analysis of communication which does not differentiate between types of messages is too simplistic. Messages characteristic of trusting behavior are different from those expressing a lack

[3]The subjects in these studies were placed in artificial and constraining social relationships. For example, they could communicate only by exchanging notes and in Loomis' study the content of these notes were limited. These situations may have affected the way the subjects played the game; they surely affected the way they communicated.

of trust. Gibb (1961) described "defensive" (nontrusting) and "supportive" (trusting) interpersonal relations. Persons who trust each other will exchange messages which are descriptive, problem-oriented, spontaneous, empathic, equalitarian, and provisional. Further, persons who wish to redefine their relationship as more trusting may most profitably do so by communicating in these forms—if the other reciprocates, there is a good chance that they will develop mutual trust.

Distrusting behavior has the opposite effect: it almost always provokes distrust. "Defensive" communication behavior (evaluational, control-oriented, strategic, uninvolved, superior, and dogmatic) is curiously two-sided: it "protects" the person from the other by reducing his vulnerability, and simultaneously encourages the other to defend himself by responding in kind (see Gibb, 1961). A study by Strickland (1958) showed how a person behaving defensively may develop distrust for another regardless of how that person acts. Two men were assigned to work under a supervisor who was told that he should closely monitor the work of one of them. Both men, however, were accomplices of the experimenter and performed identically, one under constant surveillance and the other without surveillance. At the end of the task, the supervisor was asked to evaluate both workers. Despite identical performance, he expressed much more confidence in the worker who was **not** watched than in the one whose work he monitored, reasoning that the unattended worker displayed trustworthiness while the other worked well only because of the surveillance. This study shows one means by which the perceiver's suspicions are projected on the other person and then perceived as the other person's untrustworthiness.

This tendency for people to "discover" reasons for their suspicions in their perceptions of others has important implications for the question of how you can convince others to trust you. The answer must be that trust cannot be forced. If the other person is determined to distrust you, he will always be able to find something on which to base his judgment. Ultimately, all you can do is to offer trusting behavior in the hope that the other person is capable of trusting and will respond with trust. But there is no guarantee that he will: when you deliberately make yourself vulnerable to the other, sometimes you create trust; sometimes you pay the price.

In specific situations, you have to decide whether you can afford the risk of behaving trustingly and whether the risk is worth the potential gains.

This discussion assumes that you must play an active role in developing trust rather than waiting for other people to take the initiative. There is some evidence that more people are willing to respond with trust to another person's trusting behavior than are willing to initiate trusting behavior. Of Swinth's (1967) subjects, 52.8 percent responded trustingly to trusting behaviors, but only 11.1 percent behaved trustingly if the other did not.

But what about those situations in which other persons behave ambiguously? How can you know when they are behaving trustingly and when they are attempting to set you up for exploitation? Unfortunately, there is no simple answer to this problem.

Deciding whether to trust. We could give you some practical tips for spotting counterfeit proposals of trust. A discrepancy between the real and asking value of a commodity should cue your suspicions: buying the Brooklyn Bridge or a legitimate treasure map for a few dollars is obviously unlikely. But to be forewarned is not necessarily to be forearmed. Sophisticated people still succumb to "get rich quick" schemes fostered by fried chicken franchise distributors. Otherwise hard-nosed consumers buy "lakefront" property in Florida and discover that their land is under six feet of water even during the dry season. Teenagers and young adults spend their money on devices promising to make them physically intimidating, socially devastating, or mentally superior.

When another person behaves trustingly toward you, particularly when your previous relationship has been characterized by distrust, there is no way for you to be sure that he is sincerely proposing a redefinition of your relationship. Rather, the question becomes that of deciding in which direction you would prefer to err —to trust when you should not or to distrust when you should trust —if you do make a mistake. Consider these lifestyles: you may decide never to be caught trusting someone who will not vindicate your faith. Confronted by ambiguous behavior by other people which may or may not signal their willingness to develop mutual trust, you may consistently assume that they are not trustworthy. By viewing others in this way, you will rarely be considered gullible; you may be respected as a shrewd and careful person; but you will err sometimes by misinterpreting genuine offers of trust. On the other hand, you may decide never to miss an opportunity for trust. Thus you interpret every ambiguous behavior as trusting and respond with trust. If you choose this lifestyle, some people will consider you warm and considerate, but others will think of you as gullible and will at times shamelessly exploit you.

Descriptions of either of these lifestyles seem grotesque and unpleasant. Fortunately, we are not committed to an either/or decision about trust for a lifetime. We may use our best judgment in each specific instance to determine whether trust or distrust is the wisest course to follow. But we do have to make such decisions and make them repeatedly. For example, like most professors, we prize books on several levels. They are at once our most useful tools, vital to our professional activities; a valuable portion of our financial estates; and the object of irrational and perhaps perverted affection. What happens when you go to one of your teachers' office and ask to borrow a book? If he limits his vulnerability by refusing to lend it to you, by making you use the book only in his office, or by requiring your signature on an incriminating document, he probably will not lose the book but he will also not develop a trusting relationship with you. On the other hand, if he increases his vulnerability by lending you the book without a means of requiring that you return it, he may well lose the book. However, if you respond both **trustworthily** (by returning the book) and **trustingly** (by increasing your vulnerability, perhaps by lending him one of your favorite books in return), then a relationship of unusual warmth and intimacy, characterized by personal communicating, might develop.

In most instances, your decision whether or not to trust will be based on emotion, habit, or hunch. But sometimes you will want to choose between trust and distrust as a result of carefully analyzing the situation. When you do, there are several factors which you should consider, including the range of your options, the probability that the other person deserves trust, your evaluation of the possible results of trusting or distrusting, and your ability to risk potentially negative outcomes.

Taking all these factors into account simultaneously gets complicated. Constructing a decision matrix is a technique which helps you think through some aspects of the situation. Let us describe this technique by presenting a hypothetical example.

Assume that you have just met a Mr. Smith, who says that he is very impressed with your intellect and personality and wants to offer you a position as vice-president of the manufacturing company which he owns. He tells you that the job is yours if you will appear at 11:00 P.M. Saturday night at an address in a high-crime section of a nearby city. How might you make a reasonable decision about whether to go or not?

To construct the decision matrix, first determine what options you have. In this example, assume that there are only two: you either show up at the specified time or you do not. (For convenience, we are eliminating options such as taking a brawny friend along or previously checking Mr. Smith's credentials.) Going to the appointed place increases your vulnerability and is appropriately considered trusting behavior; distrusting behavior consists of not going.

Next, consider Mr. Smith's behavior. Again for convenience, assume that he is either sincerely offering you a position or trying to exploit you somehow (by luring you to a deserted location where you can be mugged).

By combining your options and the motives potentially behind Mr. Smith's behavior, a two-by-two matrix can be formed like this:

		Mr. Smith's Behavior	
		Sincere	*Insincere*
Your options:	*Trusting Behavior*		
	Distrusting Behavior		

Now consider each combination of your options and Mr. Smith's motivation. Assign to each a numerical value with an algebraic sign which expresses your evaluation of each outcome. For example, if Mr. Smith is in fact sincere and you behave trustingly, you are likely to get a good job. You would evaluate this eventuality positively (it's good rather than bad) and you might quantify it as 10 (recognizing that these numbers indicate relative magnitude—greater than/less than—but not precise ratios such as 10 is twice as favorable as 5). If Mr. Smith is sincere but you respond distrustingly, assume that the loss of the job would be a −5 outcome. And so on until you have overtly expressed your evalua-

tions of all possible outcomes. The completed matrix might look like this:

		Mr. Smith's behavior	
		Sincere	Insincere
Your options:	Trusting behavior	+10	−10
	Distrusting behavior	−5	−2

A matrix like this enables you to assess the risks and potentials of each of your options. Given the evaluations specified in this matrix, trust is risky: you may acquire a very negative or a very positive outcome depending on whether Mr. Smith is sincere. No positively evaluated outcome will be produced by distrusting behavior, but neither outcome is so negative as that which will occur if you trust and Mr. Smith is insincere.

So which is the best option? That depends on factors not in the matrix —such as your willingness to accept risks and what you know about Smith's probable sincerity—but the decision matrix can facilitate your analysis of the situation.

The ability to trust

Several times in the preceding pages we have referred to your ability to trust others. We believe that every adult who lives in society has developed some ability to trust: our institutions and lifestyles demand it. But an additional phenomenon is clear: among reasonably well-socialized adults, some are more able to trust than others. We believe that these differences account for the fact that some people are more able than others to establish and maintain satisfying interpersonal relationships.

Your psychological needs and beliefs about human nature affect your ability to trust others. Marlowe (1963) found that subjects who played the Prisoner's Dilemma game cooperatively had a need for "abasement" and "deference" while those who played competitively needed "aggression" and "autonomy." Wrightsman (1966) found that subjects who believed human nature to be altruistic, trustworthy, and independent were the most trusting.

The way you feel about yourself and other people is an important factor in your ability to trust others. People who are self-confident are more able to trust than those plagued with self-doubt. Giffin and Patton (1971) explained the effect of self-confidence on interpersonal trust by invoking the concept of selective exposure and selective perception. Those who feel that they are inferior seem to be disproportionately aware of any relationships or messages which express criticism of them, to avoid situations in which they may be shown inadequate, and—perhaps most importantly—to misperceive the actions and statements of others by exaggerating the extent to which they are criticized, exploited, and rebuked. These selective processes make it highly difficult for persons with low self-confidence to initiate trusting behavior or respond to ambiguous behavior by another by interpreting it as trusting.

People who are authoritarian ("closed-minded") are both less trusting and less trustworthy than those who are not. Deutsch (1960) noted that people who scored high on a measure of antidemocratic personality traits (the "F" scale) were more likely than those who scored low to play the Prisoner's Dilemma game competitively, regardless of the other person's behavior. Other studies with the F scale found that high scorers "tend to be more authoritarian, less intellectually sophisticated, less liberal in their political views, more cynical concerning human nature, more prejudiced toward minority groups, and to have experienced and to favor stricter child rearing practices."[4] Deutsch concluded that these characteristics as well as an inability to trust others reflect differences between high and low "authoritarians" in the values which they have internalized. In the terms we have used in this chapter, "authoritarians" prefer the types of communication which Gibb (1961) described as defensive and prefer to err in the direction of trusting too little rather than too much.

You might be interested in determining your ability to trust others. One way of doing this, of course, is to think through the relationships you have formed with others, identifying those which involve mutual trust. But there are some empirical ways to assess your own trusting behavior.

To measure your general trustingness, rather than how much you

[4]Deutsch, 1960, p. 140.

*trust a specific person, there are three questionnaire-type tests which
you might take. Wrightsman's (1964) test measures your philosophy of
human nature. To the extent that you like other people and believe that
they are altruistic, trustworthy, and independent, you can conclude that
you are able to trust others. The "F Scale," found in Adorno, Frankel-
Brunswik, Levinson, and Sanford's (1950) book, measures your au-
thoritarianism. The higher you score on this scale, the less trusting you
are likely to be. Finally, Rotter's (1967) scales measure the extent to
which you believe that specific types of people will do what they promise to do. Unfortunately, Rotter includes only a few items from his test.
You might find his summary of findings (Rotter, 1971) more interesting
than his report on the development of his test.*

*We suggest that you spend some rainy Saturday afternoon at a good
library taking these tests. They may cause you to discover things about
yourself which you did not know—things which may explain why you
have difficulty establishing trusting relationships with others or—hap-
pily—why you are more successful than some at trusting and being
trusted.*

*But more important than your general ability to trust is the amount
of trust in your relationships with particular others. Since this depends
on the unique characteristics of yourself and the other, it is difficult to
devise a scale which would be universally useful. Based on our analysis
of trust and Gibb's (1961) analysis of types of communication, however,
we have developed a series of questions which may help you measure
mutual trust between yourself and your acquaintances.*

A measure of supportive and defensive communication.

> *Instructions: Think of a person with whom you are acquainted.
> Keeping this person firmly in mind, respond to
> each of the twelve items listed below by circling the answer
> which best describes the other person as you perceive him.*

*1. Does he insist that his beliefs and evaluations are correct and refuse
to consider new information?*

Always Very Frequently Frequently Seldom Very Seldom Never

2. Is he willing to interact with you as a respected partner, an equal?

Never Very Seldom Seldom Frequently Very Frequently Always

*3. Does he feel that what happens to you really does not involve or
affect him?*

Always Very Frequently Frequently Seldom Very Seldom Never

*4. Does he express what he feels spontaneously, without reserve or
careful preplanning?*

Never Very Seldom Seldom Frequently Very Frequently Always

5. Does he try to persuade you or offer advice?

Always Very Frequently Frequently Seldom Very Seldom Never

6. *Does he describe people and things without insisting that you share his evaluation of them?*

Never Very Seldom Seldom Frequently Very Frequently Always

7. *Does he criticize you or others, describing them in terms of his likes and dislikes?*

Always Very Frequently Frequently Seldom Very Seldom Never

8. *Does he share information, ideas, and experience with you without demanding special consideration for his contributions?*

Never Very Seldom Seldom Frequently Very Frequently Always

9. *Does he try to manipulate your behavior by persuasive tricks and stratagems because he has hidden motives?*

Always Very Frequently Frequently Seldom Very Seldom Never

10. *Does he make you feel that your ideas and emotions are important?*

Never Very Seldom Seldom Frequently Very Frequently Always

11. *Does he indicate that he feels superior to you?*

Always Very Frequently Frequently Seldom Very Seldom Never

12. *Does he accept new information readily and change his ideas when appropriate?*

Never Very Seldom Seldom Frequently Very Frequently Always

> **Scoring:** *Assign a numerical score of 1 to the response listed at the left side of the page, 2 to the next one and so on until you assign a 6 to the response on the extreme right. Sum the scores of all items: potential scores range from a low of 12 to a high of 72. The higher the score, the closer your relationship is to the "supportive climate" described by Gibb (1961).*

Suggestions for using this measure. *Make six copies of this questionnaire for every dyadic (two-person) relationship you wish to explore. You and your acquaintance should first describe each other; second, each of you should complete the questionnaire describing how you think you really are; and, finally, each of you should describe yourself as you think your friend did.*

Interpreting the results. *When scores on this questionnaire are compared, the higher score denotes a greater degree of supportiveness (and trust). First, compare the way you and your acquaintance described each other. If the scores are similar, you have a symmetrically balanced perception of the relationship. If one score is higher than the other, one or both persons are making perceptual errors. Now compare the way you perceive yourself, the way your acquaintance perceives you, and the way you thought your acquaintance would perceive you. Here are some possible results: If you:*

perceived yourself	were perceived by your acquaintance	thought your acquaintance would perceive you	then
high	low	low	you are aware of some difficulties in your relationship;
high	low	high	you need to become aware of some difficulties in your relationship;
low	high	low	cheer up!
low	high	high	you are successfully lying to your acquaintance;
high	high	high	congratulations.

A measure of interpersonal trust.

Instructions: Think of a person with whom you are acquainted. Keeping this person firmly in mind, answer the three items listed below. Cite specific instances which illustrate the basis for your answer.

1. *Does he understand the effects which his behavior has on you?*
2. *Is he able to do what he decides to do?*
3. *Would he do something which he knew would be harmful to you?*

A final word

As we noted in Chapter 1, there is an asymmetrical relationship between trust and personal communication. You may or may not trust those with whom you communicate impersonally, but communicating personally always requires trust.

Our concern in this chapter has been a broad one. We have tried to develop an understanding of trust suitable for both personal and impersonal communication—a decision forced on us by the nature of our topic. But at this point we wish to think specifically of personal communication.

We have noted that people differ in their ability to trust and that most people are better able to respond to the trusting behavior of others than to initiate trust into a relationship. This implies that those who most need trust are least likely to develop it. Consider two people, each wanting to trust the other but both afraid to initiate trusting behavior. At this point, these individuals with their defensive communication techniques seem very like two nations, neither of which wants war but both afraid to appear weak or indecisive to the other. Developing the capacity for trust is an important task for individuals as well as nations.

Ultimately, the decision to communicate personally is a decision to trust the other person. Trust begins (usually) with tentative, hesitating steps. It can be stifled easily. An important aspect of your ability to develop personal communication is your sensitivity to the other's willingness to trust you and your own ability to generate trusting behavior. We hope that the material in this chapter will enable you to free yourself from debilitating mistakes in trusting and being trusted.

References

Adorno, T., E. Frankel-Brunswik, D. Levinson, and R. Sanford. 1950. **The Authoritarian Personality.** N.Y.: Harper.

Bennis, W., E. Schein, D. Berlew, and F. Steele. 1964. **Interpersonal Dynamics.** Homewood, Illinois: Dorsey.

Berne, E. 1964, **Games People Play.** N.Y.: Grove.

Deutsch, M. 1958. "Trust and suspicion," **Journal of Conflict Resolution,** 2:265–79.

————. 1960. "Trust, trustworthiness and the F scale," **Journal of Abnormal and Social Psychology,** 61:138–40.

Evans, G. 1964. "Effect of unilateral promise and value of rewards upon cooperation and trust," **Journal of Abnormal and Social Psychology,** 69:587–90.

Gahagan, J., and J. Tedeschi. 1968. "Strategy and the credibility of promises in the prisoner's dilemma game," **Journal of Conflict Resolution,** 13:224–34.

Gallo, P. and C. McClintock. 1965. "Cooperative and competitive behavior in mixed-motive games," **Journal of Conflict Resolution,** 9:68–78.

Gibb, J. 1961, "Defensive communication," **Journal of Communication,** 11:141–48.

————. 1964. "Climate for trust formation," in L. Bradford, J. Gibb and K. Benne (eds.), **T-Group theory and laboratory method.** N.Y.: Wiley, 279–309.

————. 1965. "Fear and fascade: defensive management," in F. Farson (ed.), **Science and human affairs.** Palo Alto: Science and Behavior Books.

Giffin, K., and B. Patton. 1971. "Personal trust in human interaction," in K. Giffin and B. Patton (eds.), **Basic readings in interpersonal communication.** N.Y.: Harper and Row, 375–91.

Loomis, J. 1959. "Communication, the development of trust, and cooperative behavior," **Human Relations,** 12:305–16.

Marlowe, D. 1963. "Psychological needs and cooperation: competition in a two-person game," **Psychological Reports,** 13:364.

Mellinger, G. 1959. "Interpersonal trust as a factor in communication," **Journal of Abnormal and Social Psychology,** 12:305–16.

Pearce, W.B. 1973. "Trust in Interpersonal Communication," presented to the annual conference of the International Communication Association, Montreal, Canada.

Rapoport, A., and A. Chammah. 1965. **Prisoner's dilemma.** Ann Arbor: University of Michigan Press.

Rotter, J. 1967. "A new scale for the measurement of interpersonal trust," **Journal of Personality,** 35:651–65.

_____. 1971. "Generalized expectations for interpersonal trust," **American Psychologist,** 26:443–52.

Solomon, L. 1960. "The influence of some types of power relationships and game strategies upon the development of interpersonal trust," **Journal of Abnormal and Social Psychology,** 61:223–30.

Strickland, L. 1958. "Surveillance and trust," **Journal of Personality,** 26:200–15.

Swinth, R. 1967. "The establishment of the trust relationship," **Journal of Conflict Resolution,** 11:335–44.

Vinacke, W.E. 1969. "Variables in experimental games: toward a field theory," **Psychological Bulletin,** 71:293–318.

Wallace, D., and P. Rothaus. 1969. "Communication, group loyalty, and trust in the prisoner's dilemma game," **Journal of Conflict Resolution,** 13:370–80.

Wrightsman, L. 1964. "Measurement of philosophies of human nature," **Psychological Reports,** 14:743–51.

_____. 1966. "Personality and attitudinal correlates of trusting and trustworthy behaviors in a two-person game," **Journal of Personality and Social Psychology,** 4:328–32.

SEVEN

Alienation and communicating personally

An individual who is estranged . . . experiences himself as an alien . . .

Chapters 7, 8, and 9 may be considered parts of a single message. In them we will assert that psychological health may be viewed along a continuum which extends from a high degree of healthiness through normalcy to extreme self-estrangement, a form of alienation. We further assert that personal communicating stands in a cause/effect relationship to one's position on the alienation-psychological health continuum. The first part of our message asserts that if we do not get "enough" personal communication in our lives we stand a strong chance of becoming alienated and, if we are alienated, we will have difficulties communicating personally.

Unlike the topics of trust and self-disclosure, there is very little research about alienation that is pertinent to our theme. In fact, many who have written about alienation have used the term so loosely that they have confused their discussions and rendered the term nearly useless. This being the case, our first task will be to clarify the concept of alienation and to discuss the closely related concept of dehumanization. Following this the relationship of these concepts to communicating personally will be explored, research about the relationship of alienation to communication will be examined, and some areas of investigation for communication research will be suggested.

Alienation has been referred to by sociologists, psychologists, and many others as the central problem of man in contemporary society. Unfortunately, professionals are not very cautious with their use of the term "alienation" and have used it to refer to many different psychosocial states of individuals. Among the things that alienation has been used to refer to are: "loss of self, anxiety states, anomie, despair, depersonalization, rootlessness, apathy, social disorganization, loneliness, atomization, powerlessness, meaninglessness, isolation, pessimism, and the loss of beliefs or values."[1] In a wide variety of articles and books almost every member of society has at one time or another been considered alienated in some way or another. Among groups referred to as alienated have been: "women, industrial workers, white-collar workers, migrant workers, artists, suicides, the mentally disturbed, addicts, the aged, the young generation as a whole, juvenile delinquents in particular, voters, non-voters, consumers, audiences of mass media, sex deviates, victims of prejudice and discrimination, the prejudiced, bureaucrats, political radicals, the physically handicapped, immigrants, exiles, vagabonds, and recluses."[2]

One problem with assigning the same label to so many different people is that it makes the label relatively useless. If all of mankind is alienated, to label one person as such does nothing to distinguish him.

Popular usage of the term has been no better. In our classes students speak of being alienated from their families because they have difficulties relating to their parents or of being alienated from some group in which they feel uncomfortable. Others naïvely equate alienation with loneliness; speak of being alienated when they are unable to communicate successfully with some individual or group; and identify disagreement with an individual or group as a cause of alienation. Since rather precise definitions of the term have been developed we believe that such imprecise usage is un-

[1]Josephson, 1962, pp. 12–13.
[2]Ibid., p. 13.

necessary. Before discussing specific aspects of alienation, however, we might first present a brief explanation of some of the things alienation is not.

Loneliness was distinguished from alienation by Clark Moustakas (1961). In his excellent book, **Loneliness,** Moustakas claimed that "existential loneliness" is an inevitable part of human experience in which we become fully aware that our life and experiences are uniquely our own and that each of us must make for ourselves the important decisions in our lives and live with the consequences. Though others may try to help us and to share our experiences, ultimately we alone confront our own unique experience. Moustakas contrasted existential loneliness with the feeling of self-estrangement which he said, is not really loneliness but rather a "vague and disturbing anxiety." Existential loneliness is not the same as alienation. Like Moustakas, we believe that a person experiencing existential loneliness is likely to be very much in touch with himself and less estranged from himself than when he feels no existential loneliness.

Another state which might be confused with alienation is that of aloneness. To be alone is to be without the company of others. Those who are alone may or may not experience existential loneliness and may or may not experience some form of alienation. While aloneness may accompany either of the other two states, it need not necessarily do so. The alienated individual may or may not be alone.

Dimensions of alienation

The writings on alienation do not all focus on the same aspects of the phenomenon. In attempting to bring some order to the information about alienation, Seeman (1959) proposed five major dimensions of alienation and suggested that the writings on alienation generally could be found to discuss one or more of these five dimensions. While some of the research has found several of these dimensions occurring simultaneously in some individuals, the interrelationships of the dimensions have not been explored to any great extent. Most authors refer to individuals as alienated if they manifest any one of the traits discussed by Seeman.

Powerlessness. Seeman defines powerlessness as "the expectancy or probability held by the individual that his own behavior cannot determine the occurrence of the outcomes or reinforcements he seeks."[3] This concept of alienation grew out of the writings of Karl Marx, who was concerned with the powerlessness of workers in newly industrialized societies. Marx believed that workers were alienated because they were powerless to make decisions about their work. Rather than being involved in decision processes and being considered human elements in the industrial setting, they were merely treated as another aspect of the machinery of industrialization. Since Marx, the application of the concept of powerlessness as alienation has been expanded. Seeman proposes that the concept be applied to individuals who feel they have no power over the social or political systems in which they live. Though sociologists like Seeman are primarily concerned with powerlessness as it applies to the relationship of the individual to the larger society, the concept also applies to interpersonal relationships. It is just as important that individuals feel that they make some sort of impact on other individuals with whom they interact as it is that they have power to have an impact on society and social institutions. Individuals who feel that their presence is not felt in interpersonal settings should also be considered among the alienated.

Meaninglessness. A person sees events as meaningless to the extent that he has a "low expectancy that satisfactory predictions about future outcomes of behavior can be made." A person who views life as meaningless is unclear about what to believe in and about his own purpose in life. He lacks understanding of the events in which he is engaged. He sees no pattern in what goes on around him. While powerlessness is related to the ability to control outcomes, meaninglessness is related to the ability merely to predict outcomes or to understand why things happen. Seeman observed that intellectuals often experience the peculiar combination of high feelings of powerlessness combined with an **absence** of meaninglessness. That is, as the intellectual learns more and more about the workings of society he may become very able to see patterns and to predict future outcomes of various decisions made by political and economic leaders but at the same time he is powerless to influence these predicted outcomes since he is sometimes far

---

[3]1959, p. 784.

removed from those making the decisions. In such a situation, the individual cannot control what he can very clearly foresee. He is powerless but does not experience things as meaningless.

For an interesting analysis of one kind of behavior of individuals who experience meaninglessness, we suggest you pick up a copy of Eric Hoffer's book, **The True Believer** (1951). In this book Hoffer discussed the appeal of mass movements. He postulated that a great source of the appeal of these mass movements is that they provide meaning in life for individuals who do not have it otherwise. Hoffer argues that involvement in an important crusade to make the world a better place can suddenly give an empty life a meaning for existence.

Normlessness. A state of normlessness exists when norms regulating individual conduct have broken down and have become ineffective as rules for behavior. This is closely related to the concept of "anomie" first explicated by Durkheim (1951). A state of anomie is a state of normlessness in society. Sociologists have been concerned with normlessness as it relates to deviant behavior. Defining normlessness in terms of expectancies, Seeman called it a state in which there is "high expectancy that socially unapproved behaviors are required to achieve given societal goals." When the general norms of society have broken down, there is a tendency for individuals to develop instrumental, manipulative attitudes and to look out for themselves without regard for social norms of any sort.

This kind of condition of normlessness can exist when an individual is some sort of "man-in-the-middle." That is, he is normless because his old norms do not serve him and he has not fashioned or adopted a new set of norms to govern his behavior. An example of this might be a person who has suddenly risen several social classes through education and who has not adopted the mores of his new class. "Second generation" immigrants also have this kind of problem. The children of immigrants often are torn between adherence to norms of the "old country" to which their parents may cling and those of the new country which are embraced by their peers.

The rapid changes going on in society can also create a general state of normlessness when old norms do not seem to be adequate to the new situation that changes have created but when new norms have not yet been created. A similar condition can arise when new norms are developing, but individuals have not completely given up the old.

The changing of norms in society is not the only way an individual can find himself caught between two sets of norms. It is also possible that individuals who are going through changes in their lives will find themselves in this same position because their own personal norms are in a period of transition. For instance if you, like many other college students, find yourself undecided about whether you wish to continue to follow the moral-ethical norms of the religion in which you were raised or if you wish to abandon those norms for some other moral-ethical system, you will probably experience some uneasiness and indecision until you have resolved the conflict in some satisfactory way. As long as you are genuinely undecided about whether to follow the norms you have always known or the ones which you are thinking about adopting, you will be experiencing the state of normlessness to some degree.

Isolation. This refers to an individual's detachment from popular cultural standards. The person who is isolated in this sense feels estranged and apart from his society. Whereas the normless person is without norms to govern his behavior, the isolated individual does not share the norms of the dominant culture in which he resides. He may or may not be normless. According to Seeman, the isolated individual will assign "low reward value to goals or beliefs that are typically highly valued in the given society."

All individuals do not become isolated in the same way. Some choose to be isolated because they do not wish to share the norms of the dominant culture and others have isolation imposed on them. It is said that many intellectuals are isolated by choice because they often follow their own norms rather than accepting the norms of the dominant culture. Other individuals in society may have isolation forced on them because the main body of the culture does not wish to include them. It is true that these individuals who are out of the mainstream may share the cultural norms of the dominant culture, but they will remain socially isolated from the mainstream as long as they are systematically excluded. Parenthetically, though it is possible, it is very unlikely that individuals who are systematically excluded from the cultural mainstream will share the norms of the dominant culture that is excluding them.

The following are a few items from a questionnaire developed by

Nettler (1957) to measure isolation from popular cultural norms. Some of the questions she asked were: Do national spectator sports (football, baseball, hockey) interest you? Do you think religion is mostly myth or mostly truth? Do you think that most married people lead trapped (frustrated or miserable) lives? According to Nettler, those who do not share dominant American norms would not be interested in spectator sports, would consider religion mostly myth, and would believe that most married people are leading frustrated or miserable lives. Naturally, as cultural norms change, questionnaires such as Nettler's need to be changed. The questions are merely included here to give you a better idea of what is meant by the term "isolated from general cultural norms."

Self-estrangement. An individual who is estranged from himself experiences himself as an alien. He does not know himself. He lives for others; not for himself. According to Seeman, the self-estranged person is one whose behavior is dependent on future rewards. He works only for the money he can make. He behaves in the presence of others only for the reaction which he can get from them. David Riesman (1950) in his book, **The Lonely Crowd,** described this kind of "other-directed" individual who behaves in terms of external demands and who does not listen to himself to determine how to act or what to believe. The term "self-estrangement" presumes that each of us has deep down within ourselves an inner self which consists of what we really are, what we really think, what we really believe. To the extent that we are "out of touch" with that inner self, we are self-estranged. For instance, you may have chosen a major in college because you think that it will enable you to get a better job although you would really prefer a different major. The external reward of "good job" in this case may have caused you to reject the wishes of your inner self and to choose in favor of the external rewards. Others find themselves in fields of study which are not of particular interest to them because their parents have pressured them into those fields. We're not trying to say that making any one kind of decision based on external criteria will result in self-estrangement. However, we would suggest that over a period of years individuals develop patterns of behavior that are "other-directed" and that as a result these people become very much out of touch with their inner selves. Repeated behavior of this sort over time could result in self-estrangement.

It is possible for people who follow society's norms unthinkingly to become self-estranged. For instance, they might like what they are supposed to like and do what they are supposed to do because everyone in society does these things. In fact, this is a very common occurrence. Many people go through life doing what everyone else does without thinking about whether or not they believe they should do those things. That is, many people would respond to Nettler's questionnaire about societal norms in the way that most people in society would, but they would respond merely because they have been unthinkingly enculturated rather than because they have reached individually thought-out responses which happen to coincide with society's norms. To the extent that an individual embraces behaviors and norms which he himself does not believe in, he is self-estranged and alienated.

Karen Horney (1950) has presented a useful analysis of how individuals come to be self-estranged. She described the "idealized self," which is a "perfected" version of the self that we set up if we find that our real selves are not tolerable. The idealized self is not the real self. It is a dream or fantasy of the self that an individual entertains. Because people are not perfect, the idealized self is an unrealistic image that cannot be attained. By contrast Horney also discusses the "real self." The real self is made up of our "intrinsic potentialities" which is a "central inner force, common to all human beings and yet unique to each, which is the deep source of growth."[4] Her definition is admittedly vague, but the idea is that the real self consists of that which we really are, rather than that which we would like to be or which we are told to be. While there is no empirical evidence for the existence of the real self any more than there is such evidence for the existence of the soul, the concept makes sense in terms of common language usage when we speak of "being true to ourselves." Throughout the rest of this chapter when we refer to the term "real self" we mean it to refer to Horney's concept.

Dehumanization

In **Sanctions for Evil,** Sanford and Comstock refer to dehumanization as "both the cause and effect of social destructiveness."[5] We

[4]1950, p. 17.
[5]1971, p. 7.

believe that dehumanization occurs whenever the other is seen in any way as less than human. As a defense against emotional involvement, dehumanization entails "a decrease in a person's sense of his own individuality and in his perception of the humanness of other people."[6]

Dehumanization can be functional or it can be maladaptive. Functional dehumanization is dehumanization which serves a useful function. For instance, Bernard, Ottenberg, and Reidl (1971) point out that it may be very functional for a medic on the battlefront to see his maimed and suffering patients as something other than fellow human beings. If he should confront these patients in their full terror and fully acknowledge the horror of what is going on around him, he might not be able to perform his important healing function. On the other hand, maladaptive dehumanization does not serve a socially beneficial function and instead tends to foster destructive behavior. The more the other is dehumanized in a maladaptive way, the easier it is to commit atrocities against him. Early American settlers used to shoot native Indians with as little concern as they shot deer because they did not see the Indians as fellow human beings but rather as animals.

Bernard, Ottenberg, and Reidl discussed five results (and causes) of maladaptive dehumanization. They are: (1) increased emotional distance from others; (2) diminished sense of personal responsibility for the consequences of one's own actions; (3) increased involvement with procedural problems to the detriment of human needs; (4) inability to oppose the dominant group attitudes and pressures; and (5) feelings of personal helplessness and estrangement. The person who does not experience himself in his human complexity, who ignores or suppresses large portions of his own unique personhood will be that much less human. He will have effectively dehumanized himself. He will also be self-estranged to the same extent. If a person dehumanized himself by denying his own unique personhood, then he will inevitably dehumanize others. We believe that this is very much related to the idea that we cannot love others unless we love ourselves and that we cannot truly respect others unless we respect ourselves. For until we can acknowledge ourselves and our own uniqueness, we will be incapable

---

[6]Ibid., p. 102.

of acknowledging the uniqueness of others. Furthermore, it seems that the more we dehumanize others, the more likely it is that we will dehumanize ourselves.

The person who is dehumanized is very other-directed and experiences feelings of helplessness. These are factors that are experienced by persons who are alienated. In addition, the dehumanized individual experiences feelings of self-estrangement. As noted above, these feelings result from not acknowledging one's own full and complex self. This means that the person who is dehumanized is alienated and vice versa, though we do not think that these two terms should be considered synonymous since some of the other results of dehumanization need not necessarily accompany the alienation of self-estrangement.

We would conclude this section by pointing out that dehumanization can be very dangerous because it can result in great violence against our fellow man. Whenever there is danger of dehumanization occurring, we believe it would be wise to do something to prevent its occurrence.

For instance, one way of dehumanizing others is to work to convince ourselves that they are less than human. We have strong personal feelings about people calling policemen "pigs" and against people who call black people "niggers." Why? Simply because it's a lot easier to throw a rock at someone who is less than human, who has many despicable traits. Through name calling it is possible to build up a rigid category system in relation to the other (stereotype) and to use that mental operation to excuse oneself for doing violence to the other. It is a lot easier to maim and kill "hippies," "niggers," "kikes," "pigs," "gooks," and "chinks" than it is to maim or kill fellow human beings.

Alienation, dehumanization, and communicating personally

Lack of adequate personal communicating is both a cause and an effect of alienation. It is a cause because people who do not get enough personal communicating tend to become alienated. It is an effect in that those individuals who are alienated tend to become less capable of engaging in personal communicating.

Powerlessness. In the next chapter we show that an adequate amount of personal communicating is necessary for psychological health to develop and be maintained. Since psychologically healthy people tend to have great feelings of control over their lives, and personal communicating tends to foster psychological health, personal communicating bears this relationship to powerlessness. In addition, it has been noted earlier that there are detrimental effects when one is not sufficiently validated, or is not responded to as the unique human being that he is. It seems logical to conclude that if an individual is not validated by others very often then he is not having an impact on them. His presence and his actions do not have much effect on others. They respond as if he were not there or, if they do respond, they may respond tangentially as if they had not heard what he said. He is not taken seriously. In this sense, then, if a person is often and repeatedly invalidated by others he may come to view himself as interpersonally powerless. This means that those who are not validated are powerless in the sense that they do not have the power to affect other human beings with whom they interact. This is an important way in which personal communication is related to the powerless dimension of alienation.

Meaninglessness. While the relationship of feelings of meaninglessness to personal communication are not very clearcut, it can be noted that psychologically healthy persons who engage in adequate amounts of personal communication are less likely to experience the world as meaningless or, if they do experience the world in this way, they are less likely to be greatly disturbed by it. By this we mean that they may experience the world as relatively meaningless because like the existentialist philosopher, they genuinely cannot make logical sense of the things that go on, but at the same time they are capable of viewing the world in this way and not being disturbed by it because they are aware that they can do nothing about it.

Normlessness. If the "man-in-the-middle" analysis is a good one, then there is a good possibility that individuals who communicate personally with sufficient frequency may experience feelings of normlessness. We say this because personal communicating tends to result in psychological growth for people. This means that these psychologically growing individuals will be experiencing changes in the ways in which they view the world. They will also experience changes in the ways in which they want to act. They may find, therefore, that the old norms against which they previously tested their attitudes and behaviors are no longer adequate. Should this occur, they will have the feelings of the man-in-the-middle who has abandoned an old set of norms and who is seeking other norms to replace those which he has abandoned. When these kinds of psychological changes are not happening for the individual, however, the person who engages in sufficient personal communication will be less likely to have the kinds of feelings of normlessness that less psychologically healthy individuals experience. We say this because the more psychologically healthy person is more likely to look internally for his norms of behavior rather than externally. In doing this he is less likely to be influenced by changes in the prevailing norms for behavior. He will be less likely to join in passing fads. In the long run, his personal norms are more likely to be more stable than are those of his more "other directed" contemporaries.

Isolation. Given the norms of twentieth-century America, and most of the organizations found within twentieth-century America, it is probable that the most psychologically healthy individuals are estranged from society and from many popular cultural standards. As noted earlier, the norms of society tend to discourage honesty and, therefore, are discouraging of personal communication. We might even go so far as to say that those who engage in a lot of personal communicating are violating norms of our society to which most persons adhere. We hope, however, that from the following discussion of the many varied factors in our society that foster alienation and mental unhealth you will concede that it might be good if people violate some societal norms that can damage them psychologically if blindly followed. No doubt, one of the prime reasons that more personal communicating does not occur is because the prevailing norms of society are as they are. Although this chapter may sound pessimistic and you might wonder if there is any hope at all of ever creating and maintaining a society in which individuals can be more open and honest, we might remember that societal norms do change and as Toffler has pointed out, they are presently changing at an ever-increasing rate. So there is the possibility that these norms will change.

Self-estrangement. This is the dimension of alienation that is most directly related to personal communicating. As noted earlier, personal communicating requires honestly reflecting how you think you are at the given moment, but we also noted that the most personal communicating occurs when there is a good deal of coincidence between how you think you are at the given moment and how you really are. For instance, the person who is very self-estranged does not know himself and will not know how he really is. It will, therefore, be impossible for him to communicate with maximum personalness. He will be able to reveal how he thinks he is (as we all can) but this will not coincide very closely with his real self. The discrepancy is directly related to the ultimate degree of personalness with which an individual can communicate.

The relationship of personal communicating to self-estrangement is largely due to the role that personal communication plays in the development of self-knowledge. Because of this it is very easy to see how personal communicating is both a cause and effect of the alienation of self-estrangement. When we communicate with others, personally or otherwise, we get feedback from them. From this feedback we get an idea of who and how we are. Others can only respond to what we let them know of us. Therefore, the more we try to communicate personally and to let others see more of ourselves through self-disclosure the more likely it is that we will get accurate feedback about ourselves. The better the feedback about ourselves, the better we can come to know ourselves. It, therefore, follows that the more honest and open we can be, the greater are our chances for enhancing the amount and quality of self knowledge that we gain. In this way we can come to know ourselves better and decrease the chances of being self-estranged.

Dehumanization. The relationship of personal communicating to dehumanization is most apparent in the ways in which individuals do or do not acknowledge or respond to one another's uniqueness. To the extent that the other is not seen and responded to as a unique individual, he is not being seen as a fellow person and is being dehumanized. To the extent that we see, appreciate, and respond to our own uniqueness and the uniqueness of others, we diminish the chances that either we or the other will suffer dehumanization. For us to validate the other it is necessary for us to see him as the unique person that he is. So in this way when we communicate personally we diminish chances of dehumanization.

Personal communicating is directly related to the alleviation of alienation and dehumanization, yet a problem exists for one who is highly dehumanized and/or alienated. The highly alienated or dehumanized person has become that way because he has not communicated personally with sufficient frequency. At the same time because the individual is alienated or dehumanized, he will be incapable of communicating personally. He will be too self-estranged to be able to be very honest. It is as if a vicious and self-perpetuating cycle is in motion and cannot be broken. The person is alienated from lack of personal communicating and this alienation makes him relatively incapable of communicating personally so that he can alleviate his alienation. As far as we know, the primary way to break this cycle is for the alienated or dehumanized person to get with someone who is more psychologically healthy than he and who is capable of communicating personally. This psychologically healthy person might be a friend or he might be a counselor who is paid for his time. In either case being with another who is capable of personal communicating should enable the alienated individual to himself become more able to communicate personally. Carl Rogers pointed this out in his book, **On Becoming a Person**. Rogers maintained that if he were in a relationship with another person in which he was genuine and transparent about his own feelings (honest) and showed a warm acceptance of the other person and an ability to see how the other person sees the world and himself (validating), then the other person in the relationship tends to become able to experience and understand aspects of himself which he had previously repressed, to become a more unique, better-integrated, self-directing and self-confident individual who is more understanding and more accepting of others.[7]

Research about alienation and communication

Very little research has focused on the relationship of alienation to communication behaviors. That which has, has not addressed itself to the kinds of issues that are of primary concern here. Still, there may be some value in a brief examination of this research.

Seeman studied the relationship of powerlessness to information acquisition. The subjects in this study (Seeman, 1963) were

[7]1961, pp. 37–38.

eighty-five inmates in a reformatory who were given a test to measure their feelings of powerlessness. Six weeks later they were presented with twenty-four information items dealing with the immediate reformatory situation, parole matters, and long-range opportunities involving the relatively distant future (e.g., employment trends). These critical information items were presented to the inmates under the guise that they were to rate them for "interestingness." After making the interestingness ratings they were given a test which asked about the twenty-four items in multiple choice format. Overall Seeman found that those who expressed greater feelings of powerlessness learned less information. (There was no relationship between I.Q. and alienation, so this was not a confounding factor.) He concluded that those with higher expectancies that they could control their destinies (more powerful) showed greater interest and more learning when presented with potentially relevant information.

McCloskey and Schaar conducted an extensive survey of over 2,500 people throughout the country to try to determine factors in individuals which might lead them to perceive that society is in a chaotic, normless state. They developed a nine-item anomy scale (anomy or "anomie" is a term used to refer to feelings that society is generally turbulant and normless) and administered it through a Gallup poll along with over fifty other scales designed to measure various personal attitudes, orientations and characteristics. They concluded that the tendency to perceive **society** as "normless, morally chaotic and adrift" was systematically related to **the individual's** intellectual and personality characteristics. They concluded:

> Thus, persons whose cognitive capacity is for some reason deficient are more likely to view the society as disorderly and bewildering, and to deplore the incoherence of its value system. Similarly, persons strongly governed by anxiety, hostility, and other aversive motivational and affective states suffer not only from impaired cognitive functioning but also from a tendency to distort their perceptions of social "reality" to accommodate poorly to social change, complexity, and ambiguity, and—through the projection of their anxieties, fears and uncertainties—to perceive the world as hostile and anxiety-ridden. **These personality dispositions also reduce their chances for effective interaction and communication,** hampering further their opportunity to learn the norms and to achieve a more coherent sense

of how the society works. A further hinderance to effective interaction and socialization results from the holding of extreme or deviant views.[8]

While their primary concern was with psychological factors in the individual, McCloskey and Schaar found evidence supporting an important relationship between alienation and communication behavior.

Two studies have attempted to provide more specific empirical evidence for the relationship of alienation and interpersonal communication. Heston (1972) classified her subjects as alienated or normal based on their responses to two different measures of alienation. One (Srole, 1956) measured feelings of normlessness (anomie) and the other (Dean, 1961) measured feelings of powerlessness, normlessness, and social isolation. She then arranged for the subjects to appear to take part in an experiment by being interviewed and had a male confederate-interviewer invade the personal space of half of the alienated and half of the nonalienated by moving to sit within one foot of them. For the other half he sat at least four feet away. When she had subjects write about the experience, she found that the alienated subjects revealed a greater "non-person orientation" than did the normals. (Unfortunately this variable was measured by computing the ratio of statements mentioning the interviewer-confederate to the total number of statements with no mention of the reliability of the measure.) She also found that trait anxiety was positively related to the alienation measures. Lastly, she found no support for her hypothesis that the alienated attribute credibility to others differently than do normal people.

In a second study, Heston and Burgoon (1973) again used the same two measures of alienation in an attempt to examine the relationship of alienation to unwillingness to communicate, communication apprehension, and communication behavior in small groups. They found that alienation was not significantly related to the communication interaction dimensions of verbosity, interest, relevance, or tension. Their scale for measuring unwillingness to communicate was a better predictor of communication behavior than were the alienation scores.

[8]1965, p. 39, emphasis added.

Some variables related to alienation and communication

The theoretical literature suggests that alienation is related to communication behavior in general and personal communicating in
particular, yet there is almost no research which has examined
specific aspects of these relationships. This section will examine
several variables which have been discussed by theorists and
which seem particularly important for those who would understand
the relationship of alienation to communication. Though there is
little empirical support for the assertions of some of these theorists, it seems valuable to highlight the variables which they have
considered important.

Size of social structure. Tremendous recent increases in population and in the size and complexity of contemporary society have
been accompanied by factors which are said to influence both
alienation and communication. C. Wright Mills believes the kind of
society in which we live to be one which fosters alienation. He feels
that the best society is one in which there is a natural and peaceful
harmony of interests of people composing various segments of the
population, in which rational discussion takes place among individuals before action is taken, and in which, after deliberation,
the public sees that its representatives carry out its will. Mills
claims that America's forefathers anticipated such an ideal society
when they founded this nation. Today, however, we are drifting
steadily toward a "mass society." According to Mills the mass
society has four characteristics: (1) far fewer people express opinions than receive them, with individuals becoming an abstract
mass which receives impressions from mass media; (2) it is difficult or impossible for individuals to respond to official information immediately or with any effect; (3) opinions are controlled by
authorities who organize and control channels of action; and (4)
the mass has no autonomy from institutions because agents of
authorized institutions penetrate the mass at many points.

In such a society, the dominant form of communication is formal
media over which persons communicate impersonally to millions of
people whom they probably will never meet or see face-to-face.
Mills sees mass media as one of the prime factors in the creation
and maintenance of the mass society. Under the conditions of the
mass society he believes that "the public is merely a collectivity of

individuals, each rather passively exposed to the mass media and rather helplessly opened up to the suggestions and manipulations that flow from these media."[9]

Mills claims that we have developed a kind of psychological illiteracy which has been facilitated by exposure to mass media. As a result of excessive exposure to these media we get less experience firsthand. This tends to cause us to place less trust in our own experiences. A simple example of this is the typical television viewer who listens carefully to the newscaster's analysis of a President's state of the union remarks rather than making his own judgments about what the President has said and what the remarks mean.

It is true that media could provide us with the opportunity to compare among analyses presented and to reach better decisions. However, this presumes that we actually do compare and that the media really do offer a variety of content. Mills considers both these presumptions unlikely.

Technology in today's society is another factor said to influence both communication and alienation. With the introduction of mass production and its accompanying large factories and machines the individual worker has become more alienated. As mentioned earlier, Marx was one who very early saw that the conditions of working men under industrialization was causing alienation. When working in large factories individuals are estranged from the products of their work. This tends to happen because assembly-line techniques have resulted in jobs in which workers deal with only a small part of the final product. In Detroit, those working in the auto industry might spend all day putting together parts of engines with no conception of how these parts function in the completed end product. In this way, the individual is alienated from the products of his work and has a tendency to see his daily work activities as meaningless. There are other ways in which work is seen as meaningless. If people take no pride in what they produce but merely produce to produce, they will have a greater tendency to feel that their work is meaningless. Erich Fromm (1947) discussed what he calls the "production orientation" in which people produce only so that they can make money so that they can consume. When this is done, the

[9]1962, p. 208.

work that is done to earn money becomes only a means rather than an enjoyable and worthwhile end in itself. When activities are carried out as means, they tend to be experienced as meaningless.

In **The Making of a Counter Culture,** Roszak (1969) described one of the ways in which increased technology has increased feelings of powerlessness. He called it "rule by experts." The increase in technology and the increased complexity of organizations which has accompanied technology makes the average person feel that he does not know very much about how things operate. As a result he feels less confident in his decisions and less trusting of his own judgment. Instead of attempting to figure things out for himself, the average citizen defers to the judgment of experts who he believes are the only ones with enough information and knowhow to make decisions. Consequently, in many areas of daily life the typical citizen feels powerless to make decisions or to act. He believes that only the "experts" are able to gain access to and to understand the tremendous amounts of information which technology now makes it possible to generate.

With the rise of technology there has been an increase in bureaucracies and in the size of institutions. Factories today are bigger than ever before. Companies are bigger. Government is bigger. In these bigger institutions the individual tends to become less important. So many people are involved in any given enterprise that it becomes more difficult to take any single individual into account, to hear from individuals or to know and validate any single individual's perceptions and judgments about what is going on. Consequently, small groups of people assume the responsibility of running large institutions. Most others tend to feel powerless because they really are unable to alter the course of these institutions or to resist the influence of these institutions on their lives.

Another thing that happens in large organizations that helps foster feelings of powerlessness is that while the power has really become centralized in a few men, it **appears** to get diffused. When this happens the source of power is difficult, if not impossible to locate: it seems as if no one is responsible for decisions that are made. In institutions in which power seems to be widely diffused it is difficult to know whom to go to for making complaints or suggestions about how the institutions are run. The common response is: "That's not our department."

Needless to say, large universities are bureaucracies of this sort, and it has been argued that one of the major reasons for student unrest in the late 1960s and early 1970s was student feelings of powerlessness in these large bureaucracies (Cox, 1968). Since frustrated students could not identify legitimate channels for communicating their feelings, complaints, and suggestions about the university they did such things as sit in presidents' offices or boycott classes in attempts to force the "system" to hear what they had to say.

Messages that discourage development of the real self. The "psychological illiteracy" alluded to by Mills not only affects individual capacities for decision making, but also is reflected in our experiencing of ourselves. According to Mills, media tell us who we are, what we want, how we can become the way we want to become, and how to feel that we have become the way we want to become even if we haven't really become that way. Television stars stand as role models for millions of developing youngsters while the sets through which they flit are seen as ideals to which one must aspire if one is to be the "right kind of person."

Beyond the general tacit influences of media, advertising has been highlighted as a specific source of messages which discourage the development of the real self. Many people are never able to discern what they really want in life or who they are because they have been greatly influenced by advertising. Advertising works hard to encourage us to believe that the way to have successful lives and interpersonal relations is through the purchase of products that will make us more attractive and appealing to others. Advertising encourages us to think that we are in some way inadequate but that we will become adequate and attractive if we will only buy the product being advertised. The message is clear. Our selves are not adequate or likable. The way to become likable is to purchase new selves that others will find more appealing.

Marcuse (1964) in **One-Dimensional Man** speaks of false needs, and it is precisely these false needs that advertising encourages. As a result of overly stimulated false needs, we become less capable of discerning what we really need and want. Newlyweds buy thousands of dollars worth of furniture whether or not they can afford it because they have learned from media and advertising that young couples are supposed to have nice furniture if they are "making it" in our society.

Over two decades ago Vance Packard (1951) explained the

concept of "conspicuous consumption" and presented case histories which described how companies work to convince consumers that they "need" what they do not need or that when they buy a particular product they are also buying a new definition of themselves.

Two groups that have been particularly hurt by advertising and by popular conceptions of themselves portrayed in media are women and Blacks. In their book, **Black Rage,** psychiatrists Grier and Cobbs (1968) present their analysis of the effects that white-dominated media and media-fostered images have on the self-conceptions and feelings of adequacy of Blacks. For instance, they point out that media fosters the idea that the standard of beauty in the culture includes being white or light. Of course, Black Americans have more recently been transcending those old conceptions of beauty and have undergone much psychological work to convince themselves and others in society that indeed black is as beautiful as white.

Betty Frieden (1963) in **The Feminine Mystique** and more recently Germaine Greer (1971) in **The Female Eunuch** present essentially the same message as do Grier and Cobbs. Whereas Grier and Cobbs note that Black people had accepted the "popular" conceptions of success and beauty that were fostered by advertising and media, women have fallen into the same psychological trap. Women have generally accepted a stereotype of femininity that often is not in accord with the genuine feelings, attitudes, or interests of many individual female persons. Lured by media's conception of what it takes to be a good woman, they have ignored their real selves and instead have pursued the ideal portrayed in advertising and media in general. Both Frieden and Greer point out the unfortunate results of this pursuit.

It appears to us that a similar psychological dynamic is at work with the various people who have suffered from the pursuit of false needs which are stimulated by advertising and media. In all cases some sort of stereotypical idea is presented, but for most individuals, at least some aspects of the stereotype does not fit. This has led people of all sorts on an unfortunate path in pursuit of something which they are not. Many Blacks have worked hard in trying to be more white. Many women have ignored their real desires and have pursued the conception of femininity which is prevalent on the media. Many quiet, insecure male adolescents have attempted to prove to the world that they are aggressive and masculine by purchasing high horse-powered automobiles that they drive in unending circles around their local drive-ins. In all of these cases the people involved have ignored or minimized the genuine desires and needs of their real selves and have instead sought falsely stimulated needs and desires in order to make themselves into something which they are not by nature. To the extent that they pursue false needs rather than real needs they become alienated from themselves. They become out of touch with themselves. They do not really know what they want or who they are.

Try a little experiment in relation to mass media. For a minimum of one or two weeks, don't watch any television or listen to the radio. At the end of that period, when you first start to watch television or listen to the radio again, be sure that you are alone and then really pay close attention to what is presented. Think about your reactions. In addition, during the time you are engaging in your "media fast" notice how you spend your time. Do you seem to have more time? Are you bored? To make the fast a bit more radical avoid all contact with mass media of all sorts, including newspapers and magazines.

Personality. Some individuals have personalities that lead them to engage in actions that take them out of themselves and lead them toward alienation. For instance, one who has a strong proclivity toward conforming to the wishes of others may do so because of basic feelings of insecurity or feelings of being unworthy of the love and approval of others. Those experiencing these feelings of inadequacy and inferiority tend to seek the approval of others by concealing how they really think and feel and by presenting some sort of false self to others which they think the others will like. While this may appear to be an attractive approach which seems to work, on closer examination it can be shown to be self-defeating and dysfunctional in terms of the goals of gaining approval and acceptance from others. If you put forward a false front to others and they respond with acceptance or approval, you may have temporarily relieved some of the anxiety of letting others know you for a while but you will not have made any progress at all toward becoming more accepted or liked by others. The best others can do when you present a false self is to accept that false self. The big question of whether or not you yourself are accepted (or acceptable) remains unanswered. Since others do not know you but only the false self you present, the best they can do is respond to that false self. Presenting false fronts results in estrangement from others because you are maintaining a barrier of dishonesty between yourself and others and are thereby preventing them from knowing you. Since they cannot know you, they cannot approve of you or accept you. They cannot even respond to you. In the meantime, if you are consistently dishonest about your real thoughts and feelings long enough, you may come to be self-estranged as you may, after a while, have difficulty distinguishing your real self from the false self you present so regularly to others.

Besides insecurity, another feeling that leads us to be dishonest and to behave in ways that are not in accordance with our real thoughts and feelings is that of distrust. If we believe that others cannot be trusted and that they are out to get us at every turn, then it is unlikely that we will reveal our real selves to them. It is more likely that we will censor what we present and will conceal information that we think may be used against us.

References

Bernard, Viola W., Percy Ottenberg, and Fritz Reidl. 1971. "Dehumanization," in **Sanctions for Evil.** San Francisco: Jossey-Bass. N. Sanford and C. Comstock, eds., 102–24.

Cox Commission Report, 1968. **Crisis at Columbia.** New York: Random House Vintage.

Dean, Dwight G. 1961. "Alienation: Its Meaning and Measurement," **American Sociological Review,** 26:753–58.

Durkheim, Emile. 1951. **Suicide.** New York: The Free Press of Glencoe (originally published 1897).

Frieden, Betty. 1963. **The Feminine Mystique.** New York: Dell.

Fromm, Erich. 1947. **Man for Himself.** New York: Holt, Rinehart & Winston.

Greer, Germaine. 1971. **The Female Eunuch.** New York: McGraw-Hill.

Grier, William H. and Price M. Cobbs. 1968. **Black Rage.** New York: Bantam.

Heston, Judee K. 1972. "Effects of Personal Space Invasion and Anomia of Anxiety, Nonperson Orientation and Source Credibility," paper presented at the annual conference of the Speech Communication Association, Chicago.

———— and Michael Burgoon. 1973. "Unwillingness to Communicate, Anomia-Alienation and Communication Apprehension as Predictors of Small Group Communication," paper presented at the annual conference of the Speech Communication Association, New York.

Hoffer, Eric. 1951. **The True Believer.** New York: Harper & Row.

Horney, Karen. 1950. **Neurosis and Human Growth.** New York: W.W. Norton.

Josephson, Eric, and Mary Josephson (eds.). 1962. **Man Alone.** New York: Dell.

Marcuse, Herbert. 1964. **One-Dimensional Man.** Boston: Beacon.

McCloskey, Herbert, and John H. Schaar. 1965. "Psychological Dimensions of Anomy," **American Sociological Review,** 30:14–40.

Mills, C. Wright, 1962. "The Mass Society," in **Man Alone.** New York: Dell. E. and M. Josephson, eds., 201–26.

Moustakas, Clark. 1961. **Loneliness.** Englewood Cliffs, N.J.: Prentice-Hall.

Nettler, Gwynn. 1957. "A Measure of Alienation," **American Sociological Review,** 22:670–77 (December).

Packard, Vance. 1951. **The Hidden Persuaders.** New York: Pocket Books.

Riesman, David. 1950. **The Lonely Crowd.** New Haven, Conn.: Yale University Press.

Rogers, Carl. 1961. **On Becoming a Person.** Boston: Houghton Mifflin.

Roszak, Theodore. 1969. **The Making of a Counter Culture.** New York: Doubleday.

Sanford, Nevitt, and Craig Comstock (eds.). 1971. **Sanctions for Evil.** San Francisco: Jossey-Bass.

Seeman, Melvin. 1959. "On the Meaning of Alienation," **American Sociological Review,** 24:783–91.

_____. 1963. "Alienation and Social Learning in a Reformatory," **American Journal of Sociology,** 69:270–84.

Srole, Leo. 1956. "Social Integration and Certain Corollaries: An Exploratory Study," **American Sociological Review,** 21:709–16.

EIGHT

Psychological health and communicating personally

In this chapter we describe the relationship of psychological health and communicating personally. In Chapter 7 we said that a **deficiency** in personal communicating is both a result and a cause of alienation. Here we will explain that psychological health is both a result and cause of **adequate** personal communicating. In a sense, then, these two chapters deal with the same issue—the relationship between a person's psychological state and his communication behavior—but approach it from opposite vantage points.

First we present a description of the healthy personality derived from the same humanistic, social-psychological orientation toward the person that has characterized our earlier discussions. After identifying some of the general characteristics of the healthy personality, we describe the ways in which those characteristics are related to the individual's communication behavior with particular attention to the role played by personal communicating in the fostering of psychological health.

The healthy personality

Before launching into a specific description of the characteristics of the healthy personality, it is important to clarify two points. First, realize that the description of healthy personality presented here is only one of several possible ones which could be offered. Not everyone would agree with this characterization of healthy personality. And that leads to the second point: it is important that you be aware of the major assumptions underlying our orientation toward human personality. The way in which a theorist describes any personality, healthy or otherwise, depends on the orientation from which he works. Our orientation is derived primarily from those personality theorists and psychoanalysts who are humanistically/existentially/social-psychologically oriented. You are probably familiar with their names by now since we have referred to their works a number of times already. They include Abraham Maslow, Carl Rogers, Rollo May, Kurt Goldstein, Harry Stack Sullivan, Karen Horney, Erich Fromm, Carl Jung, and others.

Four major assumptions underlie our orientation toward human personality: (1) each human being has the potential to live an authentic existence; (2) a person comes to live an authentic existence through his interactions with other persons; (3) human nature is not basically bad; and (4) the normal personality is not necessarily a healthy personality.

To say that man has the potential to live an authentic existence is to say that each of us has the capability to live so that our existence is in accord with our true individual natures (Bugental, 1965). It means that each person has the potential to develop to the point where he is "self-actualized" or has the "full use and exploitation of (his) talents, capacities and potentialities." Maslow claims that self-actualizing persons seem to be "fulfilling themselves and to be doing the best that they are capable of doing."[1] Other theorists have used different terms to refer to essentially the same phenomenon as "authentic existence" or "self-actualizing." Karen Horney (1950) used the term "self-realization" and has spoken of the person being true to his real self. Carl Jung described the end product of psychological development as "individuation" (Jung, 1968). In this chapter we will use terms such as "healthy personality," "living the authentic existence," and "self-actualizing" as synonymous and interchangeable.

The social-psychological dimension of our orientation shows it-

[1]1970, p. 150.

self when we say that man comes to live the authentic existence and to actualize his human potential only through interaction with his fellowmen. As Maslow put it (and as we have reiterated throughout this book), ". . . every person is a psychotherapeutic influence or a psychopathogenic influence on everybody he has any contact with at all."[2] It is this notion that is behind some of the current thinking in the field of counseling which claims that the most important factor determining whether or not a person is helped by his counselor is the kind of relationship that develops between the two **as persons.**

In a very interesting book entitled **Wolf Children and the Problem of Human Nature,** Malson (1972) makes the point that man is not human by birth but that he becomes human by living in community with other people. The basis for this position comes from Malson's analysis of reports of the development of children who had lived for several years among animals without significant human contact. He compiled a list of 53 recorded cases of children who, like the legendary Romulus and Remus, had been abandoned or had wandered away at very early ages and were adopted by wild animals. Although most had been adopted by wolf packs, Malson's list also includes children who survived living with sheep, bears, panthers, baboons, wild boars, and gazelles.

All of these "feral children" were more like animals than humans when they were found and almost none of them ever managed to make up for the years of social and intellectual development they had lost while deprived of human contact. Malson's analysis of these cases led him to a conclusion similar to our second basic assumption: human beings only become fully human through their contact with other people. In Malson's words, "for man the lessons and examples which he requires are provided only by his human surroundings and by the magic of his relationships with others . . . [without these] . . . there is scarcely the possibility of man, let alone the promise."[3]

The third assumption of our orientation toward personality is that human nature is not innately bad. This premise differs from that of earlier psychoanalysts. For instance, Freud believed that

[2]1965, p. 77.
[3]1972, p. 80.

man's nature consists at its most fundamental level of an irresponsible, antisocial "id" which must be controlled by his "super-ego"
so that society can function and man can survive with his fellows
(Hall, 1954). Rather than taking this view, we prefer Maslow's
(1968) view that human nature is at least neutral with the potential
for both good and evil.

While the issue of good and evil in human nature is not going to
be resolved once and for all in these pages, we offer the following
as one way to account for the fact that people sometimes behave
well and sometimes badly. Maslow (1970) suggested that human
behavior is largely devoted to satisfying "needs" and that these
needs arrange themselves in a hierarchy from the simplest to the
most complex. The levels of this need hierarchy are: physiological,
safety, love and belonging, esteem, and self-actualization. According to Maslow, each of the lower needs must be satisfied before the
higher needs come to our attention and demand satisfaction. In
other words, we will not become self-actualizing until our lower
needs are generally met. When we are motivated to fulfill "lower"
needs and are not self-actualizing, we are likely to do things commonly considered evil, particularly when that which is needed to
fulfill the lower needs is in short supply. For example, Turnbull
(1972) describes the almost completely uncaring and antisocial
way in which members of a tribe treated one another during a
period of extended drought and famine. On the other hand, Maslow
describes those whose basic needs are met and who are self-
actualizing as living lives of compassion, consideration, and moral
goodness. We conclude that although people sometimes behave in
an evil manner, this does not prove that human nature is funda-
mentally evil. Rather it indicates an interaction between human
beings trying to fulfill one or more of their basic needs and environ-
mental conditions. Rather than flatly distrusting human nature, we
believe that persons whose basic needs are adequately met or who
are in an environment where they may be met without evil behavior
will allow their natural selves to actualize. Therefore, we see it as
a good thing when a person trusts his inner feelings rather than
suppressing them. We support Maslow's exhortation, "Be healthy,
and then you may trust your impulses,"[4] because if you are healthy,

---

[4] 1970, p. 179.

your impulses will more often than not lead you to do that which is both good for you and good for others.

Our fourth assumption is that the healthy personality is not necessarily the same as the normal personality. Many factors in society act to encourage us to behave in ways and to hold attitudes which foster alienation and diminish chances for healthy functioning. These factors work on all members of society and as a result there exists a discrepancy between most members of society and the optimally healthy personality.

In this discussion of our assumptions about persons, we have described the potential of becoming "actualizing" or "authentic." This indicates the possibility of movement among states of more and less actualization, and that's the point: people are always in the process of moving toward or away from authentic existence. Self-actualization is not an end state which can be reached once and for all, but a type of developing. It is, therefore, misleading and inaccurate to assume that some persons are self-actualized and others are not. Differences between persons are relative, not absolute: some persons are healthier than others; some engage in healthier behaviors than do others; some hold attitudes that foster moving toward authentic existence more than do others. We suggest that rather than conceiving of psychological health in an either/or fashion, you conceive of it as a continuum with endpoints that are never reached. No person ever completely understands himself or realizes all of his potentials and becomes completely self-actualized. At the same time probably no person is ever completely nonself-actualized—everyone is somewhere on the continuum. Further, persons do not remain at the same point on this continuum. Depending on what is happening, we may be much more actualizing at some times than at others.

General characteristics of the healthy personality

In this section we will outline general characteristics of healthy persons. As compared with most people, psychologically healthy people are: more aware; more accepting; more willing to make decisions; more willing to act on their decisions; and more willing to take responsibility for their actions.

Awareness. Self-actualizing, or authentic persons are generally more aware than others of that which goes on around them. Since they are secure, they have less reason than others to block their perceptions or to avoid aspects of the world. They can be more open to their experiences because they have less need to protect themselves and their ideas by misperceiving potential threats.

Maslow hypothesized that this capacity to perceive better than other persons might lead to better capacities to reason, to be logical, and to come to valid conclusions. In the **Psychology of Science** Maslow (1966) suggested that because of this relationship the level of self-actualization of scientists might influence the quality of their scientific work: the more psychologically healthy the scientist, the more likely he is to produce valid scientific conclusions due to his greater capacities for reasoning and perception. The same reasoning would seem to apply to all other professions in which success depends on valid intellectual work.

Another factor related to better perception is the capacity of self-actualizing persons to remain undisturbed by complex, ambiguous or apparently unstructured situations or stimuli. Psychologically healthy persons tend to be cognitively complex and therefore less bothered if they perceive that a situation or life itself seems inexplicable.

Acceptance. Psychologically healthy persons are more accepting of others, of themselves, and of the world in general. They see human nature as it is rather than as they wish it to be. This does not mean that they condone evil or that they are uninterested in improving things; it means that they recognize that in some circumstances persons behave in ways that are dysfunctional for themselves and for others. They themselves do not wish to behave in these ways, but they recognize that on occasion they might and that if they do there is nothing they can do to take back their behavior. They can only be aware of what they have done and hope they will not do it again.

Self-actualizing persons accept themselves as they are. They see themselves in their full complexity, accepting the many different facets of themselves. In contrast with the disturbed person as described by Horney (1950), the healthy person does not have an unrealistically idealized notion of himself which he attempts to maintain. Rather, he is aware of who he is and accepts himself. We could say that the healthy person's attitudes toward himself are self-validating. Though he will wish to change some of his behavior to further his development as a person, at the same time he feels adequate as a person.

There are many pitfalls in the development of persons which make it difficult to come to an attitude of acceptance of ourselves and others. In Harry Stack Sullivan's (1953) discussion of early development, he used the term **dissociation** to refer to what happens when parts of the self are not approved by significant others. Sullivan maintained that in order to avoid anxiety and feel secure we remove these disapproved parts of our selves from our personal awareness and act as if they do not exist. If we do this long enough we forget that they ever existed in the first place and they come to be dissociated. According to Sullivan the healthy development of the personality is directly related to dissociation with more actualizing persons dissociating less of themselves than others.

Since Thomas Harris was a student of Sullivan's, it is not surprising that his writings reflect an idea very similar to Sullivan's. According to Harris (1967), there are four possible positions we can take in relation to acceptance of ourselves and others. These are: I'm not OK, you're OK; I'm not OK, you're not OK; I'm OK, you're not OK; and I'm OK, you're OK. The most common position for persons is "I'm not OK, you're OK" which Harris believes is a natural outgrowth of a normal childhood. The "I'm not OK" portion of this position results from the necessary reprimands and corrective instructions which parents give to children in order to protect them when they are too little to protect themselves. Not understanding the reasons for these statements from the parents, the child concludes that he is not OK as a person. The "You're OK" aspect of this position comes from the child's response to the rewarding experiences with his parents such as being fed and held from which he concludes that others are OK.

Harris says that the other two "not OK" positions result from abnormalities in heredity or environment during childhood. The result is that each of us adopts one of the three "not OK" positions at the unconscious and nonverbal levels before we have mastered language. According to Harris these positions tend to stay with us unless we later make a conscious decision to adopt the "I'm OK, You're OK" position of the healthy personality and come to greater acceptance of ourselves and others.

Willingness to make decisions, act, and take responsibility.
Deciding, acting, and taking responsibility are very closely interrelated. Based on the greater information which they acquire
through greater awareness, healthier persons are more willing to
make decisions and to act on those decisions. Further, the person
leading the more authentic existence is more willing to take responsibility for his life. He realizes that, in large part, his life is what he
makes of it, and this attitude is an important underlying factor in
his behavior. He realizes that he is always making decisions and
taking actions but prefers to make conscious decisions and to take
courses of action based on these conscious decisions.

In **Sanity, Madness and the Family,** Laing and Esterson discussed the notions of **process** and **praxis** and point out that human
interactions are usually attributed to one of these phenomena.
Those things attributable to process seem to have no specific
source or cause. They just happen as if they emanate from no-
where. On the other hand the term "praxis" is used "when what is
going on in any human group can be traced to what agents are
doing . . ."[5] In families which produce persons who are diagnosed
as schizophrenic there is a much greater tendency to have things
happen by process rather than by praxis. In such families decisions
are made and things happen, but no one takes responsibility for
these decisions and activities. In society at large it is not hard to
find many examples of process at work. Most cities have at least
one freeway which no one seems to want and which everyone
seems powerless to stop. These freeways almost seem to propose
and construct themselves. No one takes responsibility for initiating
them or having them constructed.

Discussing what she called "neurotic claims," Horney (1950)
described how neurotic persons do not take responsibility for their
actions. Instead, they tend to make unrealistic demands (neurotic
claims) on their environment, expecting that the world will take
care of them. If things go wrong, they do not take responsibility.
Rather, they blame the world for letting them down. A simple example of this kind of behavior is the person who continually is late for
work or class and who offers the excuse that his bus does not arrive
on time without ever acknowledging that it is **he** who has decided

[5]1970, p. 22.

to take the bus which arrives consistently late and **he** could choose to take an earlier bus. Such a person is avoiding taking responsibility for his own decisions and actions. Naturally all of us do this to some extent. However, psychologically healthy persons do it less frequently than most others, and some psychologically disturbed people do it almost all the time. .

Interaction characteristics of the healthy personality

Let us consider now the attitudes of the healthy person toward others and how he interacts with them. We shall attempt to summarize the views of various theorists which examine the most important aspects of the healthy person's ways of relating to others. As we proceed, some of the relationships of communicating personally and psychological health will become apparent because much of what these theorists have had to say about interactions of healthy persons bears an obvious relationship to communicating personally.

Close yet autonomous. According to Maslow, psychologically healthy persons are generally more autonomous than others. They are highly independent and self-sufficient and thus have an easier time in trusting their perceptions and decisions. In Reisman's (1950) terms, they are more "inner-directed" which means that they tend to be less swayed by the thinking of the crowd. These attitudes sometimes make the self-actualizing person seem somewhat detached.

Although healthier persons are less dependent on others and more detached from others in some ways, they are capable of maintaining "deeper and more profound interpersonal relations than any other adults."[6] This capacity for extremely close interpersonal relations is probably related to yet another characteristic which Maslow attributes to healthier persons. This is a general attitude of **gemeinschaftsgefühl**. This term, borrowed from Adler, refers to a general attitude of brotherhood and oneness with mankind.

Caring. According to Mayeroff, the psychologically healthy person cares for himself, for others and for the important projects in

[6]1970, p. 166.

his life. Mayeroff defines caring as acting toward another person in such a way that the other is helped to grow and actualize. This caring is based on knowledge of the other and is gained through an open and trusting approach to the other. The healthy person is able to relate caringly with others because he is willing to take the time necessary to get to know the other. He is humble in realizing that he does not know all there is to know about others or himself and so is ready, willing, and courageous enough to explore unknown regions of himself and others in order to gain greater knowledge of them.[7]

Mayeroff asserts that caring brings about psychological health and tends to result from psychological health. If one is cared for, he becomes healthier, and if one is healthy, there is a tendency to care more for others. As a result of this capacity to relate to others and to himself in a caring way, the psychologically healthy person comes to know and to accept himself and others; to accept life, which he perceives as ordered; and to feel that the experience of living has intrinsic meaning.

Flexibility. In earlier chapters we discussed at length the ways in which persons go about establishing relationships with others. Flexibility allows healthier persons to relate in different ways with others. According to Leary, when we interact with others we try to establish particular kinds of relationships. He suggests that we can look at the **interpersonal motive** as the basic unit in interaction to focus on the kind of relationship a person is trying to establish with others. This attempt to establish a particular kind of relationship goes on at what we have called the relational level of communication. As Leary says: "Behind the superficial content of most social exchanges it is possible to determine the naked motive of communications: I am wiser; I am stronger . . ."[8] These interactions which work toward the establishment of relationships with others are carried out intentionally and spontaneously. They constitute our natural ways of being with others.

All persons show preferences for particular kinds of relationships and exhibit these preferences in the ways in which they interact with others. However, more self-actualizing persons generally demonstrate many different kinds of responses to others and

[7]1971, pp. 13–28.
[8]1965, p. 148.

are more capable of living comfortably in many different kinds of relationships. Thus flexibility of interaction reflected by the capacity to react flexibly, adaptively, and appropriately is another important interaction characteristic of the healthier person. The less healthy a person is, the less likely he will be to tolerate various kinds of relationships with others. The person who must **always** be defined as the baseball expert to others provides a simple example of rigidity in capacities to relate. In the extreme are many mentally ill persons who have come to the point where they rely on only one kind of interpersonal technique.

Another explanation of Leary's basic idea can be found in the literature of Transactional Analysis. In **Games People Play,** Eric Berne (1964), the founder of Transactional Analysis, suggested that the human personality is made up of three ego states: the Parent; the Adult; and the Child.[9] According to Berne, we may interact with others from any of these three ego states or orientations. When we are doing what most people simplistically refer to as "mature," we are reacting from the Adult ego states; when we tend to follow the traditions of society and of its institutions we are responding from the Parent ego state; and when we are emphasizing our intuition, creativity, spontaneity, we are responding from the Child ego state.

Like Leary, Berne maintains that the healthier personality acknowledges these different aspects of himself and is capable of flexibility in his interactions with others. The less healthy person is more locked into one of the three ego states because he is most comfortable with a particular kind of relationship with others. Berne maintains that one kind of behavior tends to elicit a certain kind of behavior from the other, so the insecure person who is comfortable with only one kind of relationship with others will work very hard to try to evoke the other to respond in such a way that the kind of relationship he (the insecure one) prefers can result. In Berne's terminology, the person who must always be right and who assumes the role of resident critic is interacting from his Parent ego state and in doing so is attempting to induce others to respond as less responsible Children who will allow him to be in charge.

This interpersonal factor is related to some of the general char-

[9]Following the procedure of those who write about Transactional Analysis, when the ego states are referred to, the words **Parent, Adult,** and **Child** are capitalized.

acteristics of the healthy person. The person who seeks to structure his relationships in only one or a few ways is defining himself in narrower terms than the person who is able to conceive of himself comfortably in many different relationships with others. In his flexibility with interpersonal relationships, the healthy person is acting on his greater awareness and acceptance of the many different aspects that make up his complex self.

Congruence. According to Carl Rogers,[10] the basis of the communication of healthy persons is congruence. By congruence he means that there is a matching of experience, awareness, and communication. The healthier person is the one who is more congruent. He has a greater awareness of his experiencing at any given moment. At the same time he is more capable than most of us of taking the risk entailed in letting others know what he is experiencing, by communicating with them openly and honestly. Messages generated by the congruent person are characterized by their clarity and straightforwardness. Having devoted all of Chapter 4 to an extended discussion of honesty, we will only remind you here that Jourard (1971) considers the ability to disclose information about one's self to at least one significant other as characteristic of the healthy person. When the person discloses about himself, by definition, those disclosures are congruent communications.

Empathy. As a receiver of messages the healthy person exhibits greater empathic understanding of the other than do most others and he is more willing to take time to listen carefully to what the other has to say (Rogers, 1961). Since he is more in touch with the many complex aspects of himself, he is better able to understand the various aspects of the other which the other attempts to make known in his communications.

Satisfying communication. In three volumes (Ruesch and Bateson, 1968; Ruesch, 1972; and Ruesch, 1973), Jurgen Ruesch outlined a theory of mental health and therapy in which the ability to communicate in a satisfying way is considered virtually synonymous with one's level of psychological health. Ruesch claims that the traditional practice of psychoanalysts of diagnosing and labeling "mental illnesses" is not particularly useful and suggests that

[10]1961, pp. 338–46.

instead an analysis be made of communication behaviors of persons who are disturbed.[11]

Ruesch divides communication into the three major activities of perception, evaluation, and transmission and claims that the first job of diagnosis is to determine which of these is most impaired in the disturbed person. This is no simple task, for the three activities work as an interrelated system. When one is malfunctioning, the others are also disturbed. In looking for disturbed communication, however, Ruesch does provide some guidelines. Generally he says, disturbed communication consists of "messages that occur at the wrong time or at the wrong place, or that are quantitatively not matched to the input characteristics of the other person."[12] He summarized this definition in a little poem:

> Too much,
> Too little,
> Too early,
> Too late,
> At the wrong place,
> Is the disturbed message's fate.[13]

If communication analysis is accurate and therapy is successful, the person will be able to communicate in ways that are satisfying both to himself and to others. Thus Ruesch's goal for therapy is just about identical with Rogers' notion of congruence. Ruesch says successful therapy will "enable the patient to experience fully, to accept what he has experienced and to share these experiences with others."[14] This view supports our contention that good communication begets good communication. Therapy consists of interacting with the therapist who is himself a good communicator and who is capable of pointing out things to the client about his communication behavior.

We have attempted to show you how the communication of healthier persons differs in systematic ways from that of most others. As a result of the information we have presented we wish

[11]1973, p. 296.
[12]1972, p. xiii.
[13]Ibid., p. 41.
[14]1973, p. 37.

to draw the conclusion that psychological health bears a positive relationship to the frequency with which persons communicate personally. After seeing that many other different theorists have claimed that more actualizing persons are more caring, more capable of establishing and maintaining deep personal relationships, and more congruent in their communication we hope that you will not feel that our analysis is superfluous and merely redundant of their ideas. Our goal in formulating a theory of personal communicating is the development of a theory which simply and explicitly outlines the role of communication in the development of significant human relationships, such as love and friendship, and the role of this specific kind of communication in the psychological development of people. So far in this chapter we have attempted to support the notion that healthier persons communicate personally more frequently than do others. In the next section we will present evidence which we believe supports the corollary notion that being with others who communicate personally tends to foster psychological health.

Becoming healthier and communicating personally

While psychological health seems to be related in important ways to all kinds of communication, it seems to bear a particularly important relationship to our capacities for communicating personally. We believe that psychologically healthier people tend to communicate personally more frequently than normal people and that they have become as healthy as they are because they have experienced relationships with significant others who have communicated personally with them.

There is almost no research or theorizing (beyond ours) which directly addresses this issue. However, many different therapists and counselors have written about the growth-promoting effects of communicating personally in the client-therapist relationship. Therefore, this section will focus on theory and research from these people who have worked specifically in the therapeutic environment. They constitute the basis of our thinking about communicating personally, and though their theoretical statements, observations, and research have their basis in environments and relationships designed primarily to be therapeutic, they have claimed that their ideas apply to everyday interaction situations between normal people who do not suffer from gross disturbances. We also see this direct relationship between communication that takes place in helping situations and communication in everyday life. It is our belief that the communication that takes place in the therapeutic environment is no different from communicating personally and that the purpose of therapy is the training of the client in the skills of communicating personally. We therefore feel comfortable in drawing from the theorizing and research of these counselors in substantiating the relationship between communicating personally and psychological growth.

An important basis for our thinking about communicating personally comes from the writings of Carl Rogers. In 1957 Rogers outlined what he believed to be the "necessary and sufficient Conditions" for bringing about psychological change (psychological growth) in persons. He said:

> For constructive personality change to occur, it is necessary that these conditions exist and continue over a period of time:
> 1. Two persons are in psychological contact.
> 2. The first, whom we shall term the client, is in a state of incongruence, being vulnerable and anxious.
> 3. The second, whom we shall term the therapist, is congruent or integrated in the relationship.
> 4. The therapist experiences unconditional positive regard for the client.
> 5. The therapist experiences an empathic understanding of the client's internal frame of reference and endeavors to communicate this experience to the client.
> 6. The communication to the client of the therapist's empathic understanding and unconditional positive regard is to a minimal degree achieved.
> No other conditions are necessary. If these six conditions exist, and continue over a period of time, this is sufficient. The process of constructive personality change will follow.[15]

This statement from Rogers embodies the basic elements of Rogerian client-centered therapy. While this is only one mode of therapy, we are particularly impressed with Rogers' emphasis on

[15]1957, p. 96.

the communication relationship between the persons involved. Additionally, it is important to our interests in everyday interpersonal communication among normal people because Rogers' client-centered approach is the fundamental position taken by leaders in basic encounter groups which are designed for normal persons who would like to become healthier. So while we are not certain that this kind of communication relationship works for all kinds of people there is quite a bit of consensual validity among therapists and encounter group leaders that this is a good way to proceed with fairly normal people.

If you're interested in further reading about this kind of therapy and its applications, we suggest **Dibs: In Search of Self** by Virginia Axline. Axline is a client-centered child therapist and this book is an account of her work with Dibs, a disturbed child. It is highly readable, almost like a novel, and provides good insight into how client-centered therapy works and how it operates over time.

More recently Carkhuff has made some significant advances beyond Rogers' initial work and as a result has suggested his own list of "core dimensions" of counselor behavior which facilitate self-exploration and psychological growth on the part of others. After reviewing literature about different kinds of therapies and their effects, Carkhuff and Berenson (1967) claimed that for any therapy to be successful in bringing about better psychological functioning the following core dimensions must be present: empathy; respect; genuineness; and concreteness. These core dimensions are similar to Rogers' necessary and sufficient conditions. One advantage of the core dimensions, however, is that Carkhuff and his colleagues and students have conducted many different research studies which have verified that the core dimensions really do foster self-exploration and psychological growth.

Since Rogers' and Carkhuff's basic concepts are very similar, we will discuss the relationship of both schemes to our concepts of honesty and validation. Empathy is related directly to the concept of validation, but it does not involve quite so much. When we are empathic, we understand how things are with the other person. As such, empathy is a precondition for validation. In validating the other we not only let him know that we understand how he is, but we also let him know that based on this understanding we accept him as a person.

Respect and positive regard are similar concepts. According to Carkhuff and Berenson, when we attempt to understand the other we communicate our respect for him as a person by letting him know we think he is worth taking the time to understand. As we see it, validation is a higher level concept which includes both empathic understanding and respect for the other's integrity as a person.

Carkhuff's conception of genuineness is essentially the same as our concept of honesty and seems to be implied in Rogers' notion of congruence. It consists of being open with the other and in freely letting the other know how we are at the given moment. Carkhuff and Berenson claim that ". . . the basis of the entire therapeutic process is the establishment of a **genuine** relationship between therapist and client."[16]

The fourth core dimension of counselor behavior is concreteness. This is related to genuineness and has to do with **how** things are related. In being concrete with another we speak directly and fluently about our feelings and experiences.

Carkhuff and Berenson claim that the core dimensions are contagious in much the same way Rogers claims that congruent communication begets congruent communication, and we have maintained that communicating personally tends to foster personal communicating on the part of others. As a final point of similarity, we, Carkhuff and Berenson, and Rogers all maintain that the kind of communicating we are talking about can only come as a genuine expression of our true feelings about the other. We'll admit you can fool some of the people some of the time, but on a long-term basis personal communicating must be an expression of your real self.

Since the core dimensions are so similar to our basic factors of honesty and validation, we believe it is reasonable to consider the research done by Carkhuff and his colleagues as support of our own position for it seems to us that all four of their dimensions are either explicit or implied in our two.

Now we would like to outline an important recent study which supports our claim that communication climates in which persons experience honesty and validation foster psychological growth. This study was conducted by Lieberman, Yalom, and Miles (1973) and is comprehensively summarized in their book, **Encounter**

[16]1967, p. 29, emphasis added.

Groups: First Facts. In the study they compared the effects of various kinds of encounter-type groups on college students at Stanford University. Using a stratified random sampling method based on sex, class year, and previous encounter group experience, 210 volunteer students were assigned to one of eighteen different groups. Sixty-nine students, similar to the experimental subjects, served as a control group. All of the group leaders had had years of experience and "were uniformly esteemed by their colleagues as representing the best of their approach."[17] All of the groups met for a total of approximately thirty hours, a common length for encounter groups. Since it was assumed that the kind of theoretical orientation of the leader's approach would be a major influence on participants, the groups represented ten different approaches.[18]

To determine if the groups had had any impact on the participants, Lieberman and his colleagues collected great masses of information. The subjects filled out questionnaires before the groups began, after each group session, immediately after the series of group meetings had been completed, and six to eight months after the groups had been completed. Among other things, the questionnaires before the groups asked how the subjects viewed themselves, their attitudes toward encounter groups, how they perceived the norms in their groups, specific others in their groups, and their leader. After each group session, the questionnaires asked if anything that had occurred during the session had been particularly meaningful, what it had been, and why it was deemed significant. When the groups were completed, the pretest questionnaires were administered again and the subjects were asked if they believed the group experience had been helpful or harmful to themselves and others.

The group leaders also filled out questionnaires about themselves, the groups in general, and individual members of their groups. In addition the researchers solicited responses to questions about the participants from persons who the participants said knew them well and were in a position to report if there were any changes in them as a result of the group.

To determine what went on in the groups all of the sessions of

---

[17]Lieberman **et al.,** 1973, p. 11.
[18]If you're interested in the kinds of groups represented and a brief description of the orientation of each, see Lieberman **et al.** (1973), pp. 11–13.

all of the groups were recorded and two observers attended each group session and rated the groups on several dimensions. After collecting all of the data from these different sources the researchers looked over information about each participant (they did not know any of the participants or which groups they had participated in) and made a composite judgment about whether or not he had changed. As a result of this judgment each participant was placed into one of five large categories which ranged from high positive change through no change to the "casualties" who seemed to have undergone marked psychological deterioration since beginning their groups.

One important general conclusion was that there did not seem to be any systematic relationship between the outcome subjects experienced and the kind of group orientation the group was supposed to have had. Instead the tapes revealed that in reality there was not a great deal of difference in the ways in which the different leaders behaved in their groups in terms of formal approach. In some cases two leaders claiming different orientations were more similar in conducting groups than the two who claimed to share the same orientation. What **was** more important was the style of the individual leaders as persons rather than the theoretical positions they claimed.

Overall the composite ratings indicated that about a third of the participants showed positive psychological change, a little more than a third had experienced no change, and approximately fifteen percent had deteriorated psychologically. The remaining persons had dropped out of their groups and were not included in this portion of the study. When the change scores for the various groups were analyzed, however, it became apparent that the groups differed widely. In essence, there had been seventeen different learning environments (two of the groups had been combined) and each seemed to have produced different kinds of impacts on participants. Accordingly, Lieberman **et al.** looked more closely at individual participants, groups, and their leaders in an attempt to see if any generalizations could be drawn which would help explain what had produced the various outcomes for participants.

Given the large amount of data collected, there were many different conclusions drawn based on this more specific analysis. We will focus only on those which are particularly related to our contention that experiencing a communication relationship characterized by honesty and validation results in psychological growth.

One particularly relevant conclusion had to do with the styles of the group leaders. Lieberman **et al.** took responses from the subjects about how they perceived their leaders and their leaders' behaviors and applied factor analysis to them. (Factor analysis is a statistical technique which groups similar items together based on people's responses to them. Each group of items constitutes a "factor" and the researcher looks at the items which are together and gives the factor a name based on what seems to be similar in the content of the items.) They found when they factor-analyzed twenty-seven different items about leaders the items fell into four groups which were taken to represent important leadership functions. These four functions were: Emotional Stimulation, which had to do with the leader's revealing of his own feelings and personal values and the degree to which he challenged and confronted others; Caring, which emphasized protecting others and the offering of love, support and friendship; Meaning-Attribution referred to the providing of concepts helpful to participants in understanding and clarifying their experiences; and Executive Function, which reflected the degree to which the leader set rules and gave directions to the group.

Generally they found that leaders who were high on caring and meaning-attribution while moderate in the other two functions were the best leaders. In their groups many people experienced positive change with almost no casualties. The most detrimental groups in which several people deteriorated psychologically with almost no one making positive growth had leaders who were cold and impersonal and excessively high in carrying out executive functions and in aggressively challenging participants. Though they found that the four leader dimensions did interact with one another so that the ways in which they were combined in any leader made a difference, they also concluded that **"the two central functions without which leaders rarely were successful, are sufficient Caring and Meaning-Attribution. A combination of high levels of affectional behavior and high levels of cognitive input are critical."**[19]

[19]1973, p. 241, boldface added.

For high learners the most prevalent changes came in the areas of interpersonal openness and increased self-esteem. Generally they were persons who had had realistic expectations about what the group might accomplish for them. In the groups they had ample opportunity to give and receive feedback about themselves and others. Their general increase in levels of interpersonal openness and increased self-esteem reflected directly on their behavior in the group. In the group they generally revealed more of themselves than they had in the past and when they did, they felt support and understanding from the leader and their fellow participants.

Looking at the casualties leads to the same general conclusion but from a different angle. Of the casualties, the majority reported being most negatively influenced by being attacked for their values or behaviors. They did not feel much in common with others in their group. They felt rejected, that others did not make an effort to understand them, and that they were not understood or cared for as persons. This kind of feeling was particularly devastating when they opened up and tried to be especially honest about themselves and others and were responded to with contempt or indifference. One participant's comments characterize this feeling rather straightforwardly:

> It disturbed me to see people reject me when I started opening up. Even more the leader's lack of genuine warmth unsettled me. The group became much more hostile to me the more I participated, and it was hard for me to feel a part of the group. I was mostly irritated with the way the leader sponsored a clique within the group. I felt like I was at a fraternity rush party, and had to b.s. in order to make it. I would not have felt sincere if I had tried to be accepted thusly.[20]

This comment reflects another of the major factors contributing to casualties, coercive expectations. Both of these factors are invalidating of the person. They say to him, "We do not care about you. You are not all right as a person. If you tell us how you really are, we will reject you as a person. We expect you to be a certain way and you are not."

We take this additional data as further support of our contention that honesty accompanied by validation results in psychological

[20]Ibid., p. 188.

growth for persons and that the lack of honesty and validation is likely to retard psychological growth and possibly bring about psychological deterioration. In honest and validating relationships we feel a generally caring, support, and understanding from others which gives us the courage to disclose more about ourselves, to explore our inner selves more deeply than usual, and to seek and give feedback about ourselves and others.

Summary

In this chapter intrapersonal and interpersonal characteristics of psychologically healthy persons have been examined. Generally we have attempted to show the cause/effect relationship between communicating personally and psychological health. Through a summary of various theoretical statements and research efforts we have tried to show how psychologically healthy persons might be expected to communicate personally more often than others and that exposure to personal communication is likely to foster psychological health.

References

Axline, Virginia. 1967. **Dibs: In Search of Self.** New York: Ballentine.

Berne, Eric. 1964. **Games People Play.** New York: Grove Press.

Bugental, J.F.T. 1965. **The Search for Authenticity.** New York: Holt, Rinehart and Winston.

Carkhuff, Robert R., and Bernard G. Berenson. 1967. **Beyond Counseling and Therapy.** New York: Holt, Rinehart and Winston.

Hall, Calvin S. 1954. **A Primer of Freudian Psychology.** New York: World Publishing Co.

Harris, Thomas. 1967. **I'm OK, You're OK.** New York: Harper and Row.

Horney, Karen. 1950. **Neurosis and Human Growth.** New York: W.W. Norton.

Jourard, Sidney. 1967. **Personal Adjustment.** 2nd ed. New York: Macmillan.

––––––. 1971. **The Transparent Self.** Rev. 2nd ed. New York: Van Nostrand.

Jung, Carl G. 1968. **Analytical Psychology: Its Theory and Practice.** New York: Random House.

Laing, Ronald D., and A. Esterson. 1970. **Sanity, Madness and the Family.** 2nd ed. Baltimore: Penguin.

Leary, Timothy. 1965. "The Theory and Measurement Methodology of Interpersonal Communication," **Psychiatry,** 18:147–61.

Lieberman, Morton A., Irvin D. Yalom, and Matthew B. Miles. 1973. **Encounter Groups: First Facts.** New York: Basic Books.

Malson, Lucien. 1972. **Wolf Children and the Problem of Human Nature.** New York: Monthly Review Press (originally published as **Les Enfants Sauvages** by Union Generale d'Editions, Paris, France, 1964).

Maslow, Abraham. 1965. **Eupsychian Management.** Homewood, Ill.: Dorsey Press.

––––––. 1966. **The Psychology of Science.** Chicago: Henry Regery Co.

––––––. 1968. **Toward a Psychology of Being.** 2nd ed. New York: Van Nostrand.

––––––. 1970. **Motivation and Personality.** Rev. 2nd ed. New York: Harper and Row.

Mayeroff, Milton, 1971. **On Caring.** New York: Harper and Row Perennial Library.

Reisman, David. 1950. **The Lonely Crowd.** New Haven, Conn.: Yale University Press.

Rogers, Carl R. 1957. "The Necessary and Sufficient Conditions of Therapeutic Personality Change," **Journal of Consulting Psychology** 21: 95–103.

————. 1961. **On Becoming a Person.** Boston: Houghton Mifflin.

Ruesch, Jurgen, and Gregory Bateson. 1968. **Communication: The Social Matrix of Psychiatry.** New York: W.W. Norton (originally published 1951).

————. 1972. **Disturbed Communication.** New York: W.W. Norton (originally published 1957).

————. 1973. **Therapeutic Communication.** New York: W.W. Norton (originally published 1961).

Sullivan, Harry S. 1953. **Conceptions of Modern Psychiatry.** 2nd ed. New York: W.W. Norton.

Turnbull, Colin M. 1972. **The Mountain People.** New York: Simon and Schuster.

Watzlawick, Paul, J.H. Beavin, and D.D. Jackson. 1967. **Pragmatics of Human Communication.** New York: W.W. Norton.

NINE

Personal communicating in everyday life: some pioneering research

Though most of the existent research about communicating personally has been the work of therapists and counselors and has been carried out in environments designed to be therapeutic, some research pertinent to looking at personal communicating in everyday interaction situations is beginning to appear. So while some of our theoretical formulations are ahead of the data and yet to be tested, the research tools needed for this testing are beginning to be developed and research studies are now being done which bear directly on our primary interest—the role of everyday communicative interaction in the psychological development of persons.

Research tools

Two studies have recently been completed which should help pave the way for further research about relational communication and communicating personally by providing coding systems which include categories for relational, rather than content, aspects of messages.

Mark (1971) made the initial effort and based his work on that of Sluczki and Beavin (1965), who claimed that relational control

197

of communication situations is based on both the grammatical form and response style of messages. Accordingly Mark's coding system is capable of handling three different aspects of messages, each of which is assigned a digit by the coder. The first digit identifies the speaker, the second reflects which of nine grammatical structures most characterizes the message, and the third indicates the message's relationship to the statement immediately preceding it. This system is capable of identifying ten different relationships between messages. These are: agreement; disagreement; extension; answer; disconfirmation; topic change; agreement and extension, disagreement and extension; other; and laughter. Based on the three digit code, pairs of messages are then examined so that their relationship can be determined. Mark calls the relationship between two contiguous messages a **transaction** and believes it to be the most basic meaningful unit for analyzing communication. He maintains that by viewing messages within the context of the ongoing interaction in which they are made we get a better idea of how communication really works. By emphasizing the role messages play in the definition, redefinition, and reinforcement of the nature of relationships between persons and attempting to deal with the transactional nature of communication, this coding system represents an important advance in the study of communication.

It is also promising for another very practical reason. Mark has reported that with only two hours of training raters who independently rated tape recordings of dialogues had an overall average inter-rater reliability of over .90, which indicates that the raters had a very strong tendency to code the messages on the tape similarly. After analyzing the data from these dialogues, Mark concluded that his system was capable of reflecting relational differences among couples and that it was "effective in analyzing at least dyadic communication at the relationship level in order to uncover what appear to be some unique differences in the way people relate."[1]

More recently Rogers and Farace (1973) have expanded on Mark's work. They felt that his system included some confusing combinations of messages and transactional values and needed

[1]1971, p. 231.

further refinement. To correct these limitations they modified his system by changing some of the categories into which messages could be coded and altering the ways pairs of messages could be combined. These changes were made to simplify the system and to extend its capacities for reflecting the relational patterns of messages.

Both of these systems are significant for our interests in the study of relational communication and personal communicating. In addition, they reflect an important advance in thinking and studying about communication in general. By focusing on the ongoing aspects of interpersonal interaction and the "how" rather than the "what" of messages, they stress the reciprocally influential aspects of our transactions with others. As such, their transactional approach helps bring the study of communication to a closer approximation of the phenomenon of communication as we experience it.

Satisfying, good, and healthy communication

In this section we will report on three studies. They deal with satisfying, good, and healthy communicating.

Sieberg and Larson (1971) attempted to determine if there are any underlying dimensions to the communicative responses of persons with whom it is satisfying to interact. To do this they reviewed articles and books about interpersonal communication and examined the live interaction of various dyads and small groups to arrive at twenty-four categories which they believed included all possible kinds of responses which could be made to another in an interpersonal communication situation. After making up the categories, they got ninety-five members of the Interpersonal Communication Division of the International Communication Association, most of whom were professors of communication, to respond to each category with a rating of from one to six to reflect how typical or atypical the response was of persons with whom they most enjoyed conversing. They also responded to reflect how typical or atypical each response was of persons with whom they least enjoyed communicating.

To analyze the data they applied two factor-analyses, one to the responses which described those who were most enjoyable to interact with and one to the responses which described those who were least enjoyable in interpersonal communication situations. After looking at the two separate factor-analyses and applying other statistical procedures to the combined data, they determined that the same underlying dimensions were important when describing both most enjoyable and least enjoyable communicators. These analyses revealed two major underlying dimensions of interpersonal responses which distinguished most and least enjoyable interpersonal communicators. The first factor consisted of characteristics such as direct acknowledgment, clarifying, and supporting, which Sieberg and Larson termed **confirming.** The second major factor which emerged from the analyses consisted of responses such as interrupting, impersonal, incoherent, and incongruous, which they termed **disconfirming.** They concluded that their study had confirmed the theoretical position taken by many in the literature by providing empirical evidence that most satisfying interpersonal communication was with those who were confirming and least satisfying interpersonal communication occurred with those who were disconfirming.

As part of the work in developing a scale to measure effectiveness at interpersonal communication, Rossiter has recently completed a study that is similar in nature to that by Sieberg and Larson. To accumulate adjectives and phrases (descriptors) which distinguish between good and poor communicators, Rossiter and his colleagues (1973) reviewed hundreds of articles and books to find characteristics which had been attributed to good and poor communicators. They also asked over a hundred persons to write short lists of descriptive adjectives and phrases describing the best and worst communicators they knew or had known. From this they arrived at a list of 142 descriptors which had been used either in the literature or by respondents to describe good and/or poor communicators. The 142 descriptors were divided into two 71-item lists and each list was administered to 200 subjects. One hundred were asked to select the best communicator they knew or had known and to rate each item from one to three to indicate whether it applied to the person being rated "seldom," "sometimes," or "often." The other hundred responded in the same way in terms of the worst communicator they knew or had known.

Based on these responses, discrimination indices were calculated for each descriptor. These indices reflect the degree to which a descriptor is marked differently when ratings for good and poor communicators are compared. Items with high discrimination indices are marked very differently when good and poor communicators are described and thus reflect attributes which are important in distinguishing between good and poor communicators. Items with low discrimination indices are marked very similarly when good and poor communicators are described and reflect attributes which are not important for distinguishing between good and poor communicators.

The thirty descriptors which had the highest discrimination indices were then content-analyzed to determine if they could be grouped into categories which seemed to reflect major basic underlying factors which discriminate between good and poor communicators. These items seemed to fall into six major categories. The categories in descending order based on the number of adjectives in each were: **attractiveness-interestingness; caring; clarity; responsiveness; attitudes toward others;** and **intelligence.**

Based on this analysis, Rossiter and his colleagues concluded that personal aspects of the other seemed more important than impersonal factors when distinguishing between good and poor communicators in informal interpersonal communication situations. Of the six categories only two, clarity and intelligence, were not primarily concerned with attitudes and response styles of the persons being rated. These two categories included only seven of the thirty most discriminating descriptors indicating that when distinguishing between good and poor interpersonal communicators, how the other is seen as a person was much more important than how he structured his messages.

Finally, Macklin (1973) undertook an investigation which bears directly on our theory of personal communicating. He examined the relationship of psychological health and several aspects of everyday interpersonal communication behavior and attitudes. To examine this relationship he first developed scales to measure interpersonal communication behaviors and attitudes. He took a long list of statements about communication behaviors and attitudes and had over a hundred upperclassmen and graduate students in counseling and communication respond to them by reporting how frequently they engaged in the behaviors or held the attitudes mentioned. He applied factor-analysis to these responses and found he had three factors. These were: Self-disclosure, which we defined and discussed at length in Chapter 4; Expressiveness, which was made up of items which had to do with spontaneity and free and open expression of feelings; and Understanding, which included items that referred to capabilities to accurately perceive verbal and nonverbal messages from others. He then computed correlations between scores on each of these communication factors and the **Personal Orientation Inventory,** a standardized and widely used test for measuring level of self-actualization.

He found that all of the correlations were positive and statistically significant.[2] He concluded that psychological health and interpersonal communication behaviors and attitudes were related in important ways. His data suggested that more actualizing persons tend to disclose more about their personal selves to others, to be more spontaneous and free in their interpersonal interactions, and to be more accurate at interpreting messages from others than less actualizing persons. Naturally, none of this comes as a surprise to people who have read what the various theorists have had to say about the interpersonal behavior of healthy persons. The importance of Macklin's study is that he has provided us with data from the real world which supports many of the contentions which theorists have made about the relationship of communication to level of self-actualization. Specifically his findings lend support to our contention that healthier persons communicate personally more often than others by showing that they are more open, spontaneous, and understanding in their communication.

Summary

This chapter completes the presentation of our views about communicating personally. Rather than ending it with a summary we suggest you now reread Chapter 1 in which we present a general overview of our entire message. Those interested in exploration of our subject in greater depth are encouraged to proceed to the appendices, suggested additional readings, and those sources we have referenced throughout the text.

[2]The correlations between the **POI** and the communication scales were: Self-Disclosure, +.34; Expressiveness, +.45; and Understanding, +.35. None of these correlations deviated significantly from linearity.

References

Macklin, Thomas. 1973. **Interpersonal Communication and Self-Actualization**, unpublished Master's thesis, University of Wisconsin, Milwaukee.

Mark, Robert A. 1971. "Coding Communication at the Relationship Level," **Journal of Communication**, 21:221–32.

Rogers, L. Edna, and Richard V. Farace. 1973. "Relational Communication Analysis: New Measurement Procedures," paper presented at the annual conference of the International Communication Association, Montreal, Canada.

Rossiter, Charles M., Jr., Mary Ellen Munley, and Sandra L. Mazurek. 1973. "A Content Analysis of Descriptors of Good and Poor Communicators," unpublished paper, University of Wisconsin, Milwaukee.

Sieberg, Evelyn, and Carl Larson. 1971. "Dimensions of Interpersonal Response," paper presented at the annual conference of the International Communication Association, Phoenix, Arizona.

Sluczki, G. E., and J. H. Beavin. 1965. "Simetria y Complementaridad: Una Definicion Operacional u una Tipologia de Parejas." (Symmetry and Complementarity: An Operational Definition and Typology of Dyads.) **Acta Psiquidtrica y Psicologica de America Latina,** 11: 321–30.

Appendices

As appendices we present four scholarly papers pertinent to the study of personal communicating. Each extends and amplifies ideas found in the text. They are intended primarily for those students and colleagues who are interested in advanced study and/or research about variables related to our theory. Though we have not made stylistic considerations for the beginning student, they should not be beyond the capabilities of the highly motivated. Appendices A and B are reviews of literature about self-disclosure and trust, respectively. Appendix C provides an analysis of meta-communication in human relationships, and Appendix D presents some methodological considerations for the study of interpersonal communication from the transactional approach that we have advocated.

Self-disclosing communication[1]

According to Jourard (1964, p. 3), communicators continually confront the choice whether to "permit our fellow men to know us as we now are or . . . [to] seek instead to remain an enigma, an uncertain quantity, wishing to be seen as something we are not." To some extent, Jourard has posed a false dilemma because speakers reveal something of themselves whenever they speak. All messages contain information about the speaker's perception of the relationship between himself and his auditors (Watzlawick, Beavin, and Jackson, 1967), and the multiple message systems in oral speech function independently of the intended meaning. For example, nuances of word choice (Wiener and Mehrabian, 1968) and nonverbal properties of the voice (Pearce and Conklin, 1971; Pearce and Brommel, 1972) enable listeners to draw systematic inferences about the speaker.

Although speakers are frequently oblivious of and sometimes try to suppress these cues, under some conditions individuals consciously make themselves the subject of their messages. Communication behavior in which the speaker deliberately makes him-

[1]This essay was co-authored by Stewart Michael Sharp while he was a graduate student at the University of North Dakota, and published in the **Journal of Communication,** 23 (1973), 409–25. Mr. Sharp is now a clinical research supervisor for the Sandoz Pharmaceutical Company.

self known to the other is most frequently called "self-disclosure."

A considerable scholarly literature—nearly 100 articles and books since 1956—reflects a continuing concern with self-disclosing communication. Some recent communication textbooks (Brooks, 1971; Wenburg and Wilmot, 1973; Stewart, 1973) include discussions of self-disclosure, and there is widespread testimony attesting to the importance of self-disclosing communication in a variety of contexts. For example, participation in "dialogue" (Matson and Montagu, 1967; Johannesen, 1971) or "supportive" communication (Gibb, 1964) requires an ability and willingness to engage in self-disclosure. Argyris's (1962) concept of interpersonal competence identified an ability to be open and nondefensive by management personnel as an important factor in organizational effectiveness. Strong relationships between self-disclosure and friendship (Pearce **et al.,** 1973) suggest that the process of developing friendships requires mutual disclosure. Several theories of psychotherapy stress the therapeutic value of disclosure by the client and the facilitative effect of disclosure by the therapist (Jourard, 1964; Rogers, 1965). Based on the principle that meanings for messages must be created by the receiver (Barnlund, 1962) and that the receiver will be most likely to create the meaning intended by the speaker if he knows a considerable amount about him, self-disclosure facilitates understanding. In addition to these materials, self-disclosure is a prominent theme in popular celebrations of intimate personal relationships (see, for example, Luft, 1969; Culbert, 1968; Powell, 1969).

This paper summarizes the contributions of the self-disclosure literature for an understanding of self-disclosing communication. Three features of this literature reduce its value for a review from a communication perspective. First, a sizeable portion of the literature was written by psychologists who tried to measure self-disclosure as a personality trait (see Cozby, 1973). To include these studies in this review would commit the fallacy of treating communication as a thing **sui generis** (Thayer, 1963). The temptation to draw upon these materials is reduced, however, by the fact that the findings of studies based on this orientation are contradictory (Cozby, 1973). Second, those studies which examined exchanges of messages usually assumed a linear model of communication of the form: person A says something to person B with effect C. This one-way influence concept of communication has been widely discredited (Thayer, 1963; Redding, 1968) and even if these studies were conceptually acceptable, they would not be useful. As Stamm and Pearce (1971) argued in another context, the analysis of communication **effects** is not particularly enlightening about communication **behavior.** Third, quite different conceptualizations of self-disclosure and some questionable methodologies are included in this literature. Before relevant findings can be summarized, self-disclosure must be described in terms of more adequate understanding of communication and a more adequate conceptualization of self-disclosure must be developed.

Communication as transaction[2]

Recent attempts to conceptualize communication in ways which avoid the fallacies and limitations of previous models involve the notion of transaction or the closely related idea of process. An early statement of a process orientation toward communication was Berlo's (1960, p. 24) eschewal of attempts to locate "a beginning, an end, a fixed sequence of events" in communication in favor of a concept which stipulated that "the ingredients within a process interact; each affects all of the others." Such an orientation is difficult to translate into research and theory, however. After noting that Berlo himself abandoned this principle of process when he began developing his model, Smith (1972, p. 177) concluded that formal definitions of communication pay homage to "quantum relativistic" concepts of process while research designs implement Newtonian concepts of linear deterministic relationships.

Some of the implications of a transactional perspective for communication behavior were recently discussed by Stewart (1973) and Barnlund (1970). At least two transactional principles are relevant to the present attempt to summarize the contributions of the self-disclosure literature for an understanding of self-disclosing

[2]We are aware that this section is somewhat repetitious of information presented in Chapter 2. However, in making specific applications of these notions to the study of self-disclosing communication we thought it would be useful to include this brief reiteration. We are also aware that this section is somewhat repetitious of information presented in Appendix D. We have intentionally included the information in both appendices as we anticipate that some readers will not read all appendices but only those in which they have special interest.

communication. First, this perspective stipulates that people are not the same in different communication contexts. In what Barnlund (1970) called the Cartesian view of the universe, wholes are expected to be the sum of their parts, and if one knew enough about each of the participants in dyadic communication, he should be able to predict how they will behave when they confront each other in dialogue. This assumes, however, that people may be considered as clusters of traits which remain the same regardless of the immediate social relationship and which behave in consistent ways. Arguing to the contrary, Stewart (1973, p. 12) wrote that "we are who we are only in relationship to the other person(s) we're communicating with." Describing the reciprocal effect of perceived and perceiver, Ittelson and Cantril (1954, p. 3) stated that both "owe their very existence as encountered in the situation to this fact of active participation and do not appear as already existing entities merely interacting with each other without affecting their own identity." It is only a short step from Sullivan's (1953, pp. 110–11) definition of personality ("the relatively enduring pattern of recurrent interpersonal situations which characterize a human life") to an understanding that a person is what he is in any given situation in part as a function of his relationships with the other(s) in that situation. Toch and MacLean (1967, p. 56) concluded that "every human being is a product—a constantly changing product —of the situation through which he moves."

Second, this perspective stipulates that it is impossible to identify cause and effect, actor and acted-upon, beginning and end in the process of communication. Ittelson and Cantril (1954, p. 5) stressed the confusion between "stimulus" and "response" in perception by declaring that "The world **as we experience it** is the product of perception, not the cause of it" (author's emphasis). Barnlund (1970, p. 91) would dispense with models incorporating "linear causality" in communication because the concept "with its sharp demarcation of independent and dependent variables, no longer gives sensible structure to observation." "Signals," he concluded, "must be treated simultaneously as both cause and effect. . . ." A description of sequential behavior in communication which explains how message sources and receivers cannot be differentiated was offered by Hulett (1966a, 1966b). The most relevant part of the model describes "covert rehearsal" which the message "source" performs before and the message "receiver" after a message is transmitted. Covert rehearsal involves two behaviors: role-playing, in which each covertly creates some or all of the messages which might be made; and role-taking, in which each predicts the response the other would make to or meaning the other would associate with each of these potential messages. Hulett's is a model of dyadic interpersonal communication because both participants perform the same behaviors in an out-of-phase sequence, and a transactional model in that it demonstrates that the "receiver" is very much a part of selecting and encoding messages and the "source" in decoding and interpreting them.

Viewing communication as transaction depreciates the significance of the many studies of self-disclosure which focused on the discloser in isolation from the communication process (such as those attempting to identify "high" and "low" disclosers or associate particular levels of disclosure with demographic or personality variables) and those which attempted to identify "causes" or "effects" of disclosure. As a transactionalist would expect, research on disclosure as a personality trait has been inconclusive (Cozby, 1973) and findings of relationships between disclosure and age, sex and social background have not fared well in replication. **Post hoc** interpretations of "distrustful and suspicious" policemen (Jourard, 1971) and strong, silent, rational males who play a "lethal ... role" (Jourard, 1964) appear in retrospect more fanciful than factual. Rather than these approaches, a transactional communication analysis directs attention to the process occurring between the participants. It is what happens when communicators transact with each other rather than characteristics of either or both in other contexts which provides an understanding of self-disclosing communication.

A conceptualization of self-disclosure

Three recent reviews of this literature (Egan, 1970; Jourard, 1971; Cozby, 1973) drew quite different conclusions, partly as a function of the authors' preferences for various definitions of self-disclosure. Cozby (1973, p. 73) defined self-disclosure as "any information about himself which Person A communicates verbally to a Person B," while Egan (1970) differentiated between authentic self-disclosure ("story") and pseudoself-disclosure ("history"), both of which Cozby would consider the same. Jourard's (1964, 1971) verbal definitions resemble Cozby's, but his operational definitions are closer to Egan's. Confronted with Himelstein and Kimbrough's (1963) inability to predict from SDQ scores the extent to which secondary school counselors included in self-introductory speeches details about their age, military service, occupation and the like, Jourard (1971) argued that public recital of such innocuous and uninvolving facts was a "broadcasting type of self-disclosure" unrelated to the private disclosure of personal information to carefully selected others.

A number of roughly synonymous terms are used in this literature, most of which have been championed by one or more of the major contributors. The relations among "genuineness," "honesty," "story," "verbal accessibility," "self-revealingness," "transparency," "openness," "congruency" and "self-disclosure" have not been previously specified and no attempt is made here to adhere to the meanings originally associated with them.

Self-disclosure is best conceptualized as a subset of encoding behavior distinguished from three other subsets: non-disclosure, revealing, and confession. **Self-disclosure** occurs when one person voluntarily tells another person things about himself which the other is unlikely to know or to discover from other sources. Since self-disclosure is voluntary, it excludes **confessions,** or communication behavior in which personal information is elicited from a person by force, threats or use of drugs, and **revealing** behavior, consisting of unintentional cues (e.g., "Freudian slips" or nonverbal mannerisms) which express something about the person. **Nondisclosure** comprises those common communication strategies by which persons avoid being known by others. A partial inventory of these include lying (presenting false information about one's self), concealment (deliberately not presenting any information about one's self), and the cluster of behaviors Gibb (1964) identified as "defensive" (which maintain interpersonal distance between the communicators by insisting on structure, evaluation, and personal disinterestedness).

Self-disclosure includes two quite different forms of communication behavior. Some but not all divulging of personal information is an attempt to make the speaker known to his listeners. History (see Egan, 1970) describes communication strategies in which information about oneself is presented to distract, shock, or simply disinterest the listeners. Past events rather than present experiences, actuarial detail rather than subjective responses, and intellectual interpretation rather than personal involvement characterize history, and it is presented with a detached manner forbidding others to become excited about or involved in the events recounted. Honesty, on the other hand, consists of descriptions of the speaker's experience which invite the listener to share and respond empathically. Honest messages are not necessarily true—individuals are neither completely nor totally accurately aware of their experience—but they carry with them the implicit or explicit statement that they are a sincere attempt to make the speaker known to the listener (see Moustakas, 1962).

Claims for the importance of self-disclosing communication generally refer to what is here identified as honesty, but techniques for measuring self-disclosure are too crude to distinguish honesty from several other forms of encoding behavior. The most frequently used procedure, self-disclosure questionnaires (see Jourard and Lasakow, 1958), do not discriminate between information told as a stratagem to avoid being known (history) and invitations to share experiences (honesty). One important step in this direction, although far from satisfactory, is that of identifying the level of intimacy involved in disclosure about various topics (see Jourard and Resnick, 1970; Vondracek and Marshall, 1971). Content analysis of word choice (MacDaniels, **et al.,** 1971; Janofsky, 1971) or categories of content (Chittick and Himelstein, 1967; Himelstein and Kimbrough, 1963) have no way to distinguish between self-disclosure and revealingness. Direct observation of disclosure in laboratory contrived situations (Axtell and Cole, 1971; Drag, 1971; Jourard and Resnick, 1970) are perhaps best understood as the sums of confessions (to the extent that subjects acceded to the demand characteristics of the experiment), revealing behavior, history and—perhaps—honesty.

These weaknesses in conceptualization and measurement pose a problem for this review. The worst type of distortion occurs when studies which measured predominantly history, revealing behavior, and confession are summed and added to those observing honesty. To guard against this distortion, studies predominantly involving some form of encoding behavior other than honesty (e.g., Himelstein and Kimbrough, 1963; Janofsky, 1971) were excluded from this review.

Characteristics of self-disclosing communication

This review summarizes the contributions of the self-disclosure literature for an understanding of a particular type of communication behavior which is claimed to be highly significant in a variety of contexts. The weakness of this literature both in conceptualization and methodology and the demands of a transactional perspective of communication make much of the literature inappropriate for present purposes. Only materials which characterized communication behavior as it occurred in interpersonal transactions and which used a methodology which, in our opinion, was likely to measure honesty were included. Excluded materials included analyses of individual characteristics associated with disclosure, attempts to assess simple cause and effect relationships with self-disclosure as either independent or dependent variables, and studies in which the communication behavior likely included predominantly history, revealing behavior and/or confessions.

Relatively few communication transactions involve high levels of disclosure. Although no studies have tested explicit hypotheses about the generality of high levels of disclosure, inspection of the data from a number of studies indicates that very little disclosure occurs in most communication transactions and quite a bit occurs in a very few. Further, high levels of disclosure occur in specific transactions: participants in highly disclosing transactions are not necessarily highly disclosing when communicating with other persons or with the same persons at another time.

Several writers expressed concern over the infrequency of high levels of disclosure. Jourard (1967) believed that non-disclosure is the rule, only broken "when we experience it as **safe** thus to be known and when we believe that vital values will be gained if we are known in our authentic being, or lost if we are not" (p. 28, author's emphasis). If, as several psychologists believe, individuals "err" more frequently by disclosing too little rather than too much, this might indicate that members of our society overlearn communicative skills appropriate for non-disclosing relationships (lying, con-

cealment, defensiveness, etc.) and are not taught how to participate in open, disclosing transactions. In his statement of this reasoning, Laing (1967) described how persons give or withhold approval in order to "train" others to present an "edited" version of
themselves. Similarly, Jourard (1964, p. 10) wrote:

> dissemblance is learned early in life by all of us. As children, we **are,**
> and we **act,** our real selves. We say what we think, we scream for what
> we want, we tell what we did . . . some disclosures are ignored, some
> rewarded, and some punished . . . very soon, then, the growing child
> learns to display a highly expurgated version of his self to others
> . . . the public self . . . the concept of oneself which one wants others
> to believe.

An important task for researchers and teachers is to identify the
communicative processes associated with high levels of disclosure.
Some of these are described in the following generalizations from
the self-disclosure literature.

Self-disclosure usually occurs in dyads. Although levels of disclosure in interpersonal, public, and mass communication situations have not been compared in any one study, there is good
evidence that individuals are highly selective in choosing persons
to whom to disclose and that the number of communicators in the
transaction affects the probability of the development of high levels of disclosure. Jourard (1971) felt that measures of private
disclosure to family and friends were unrelated to performance in
a public speaking situation. It seems likely that the presence of
"third parties," particularly if they are uninvolved or disinterested,
inhibits disclosure. This interpretation is compatible with Caplow's
(1968) analysis of triadic social structure and is supported by
comparing disclosure in a client-therapist dyad with that between
client and therapist in a group. Hountras and Anderson (1969)
found that clients disclosed most to therapists who were empathic,
respectful, and genuine, but no increase in client disclosure occurred when the group leader in Berger and Anchor's (1970) study
was disclosing.

The specific identity of the participants affects the nature of the
transaction in ways important for self-disclosure. A curvilinear relation sometimes occurs between the closeness of the relationship
between communicators and the extent to which they disclose. Two

studies, Quinn (1965) and Murdock, Chenowith and Rissman (1969), found the highest levels of disclosure in transactions between strangers with whom no subsequent contact was anticipated and between friends who were trusted not to betray confidences. Least disclosure occurred in transactions between acquaintances who did not know each other well but with whom future association was expected. Ehrlich and Graeven (1971, p. 399) were unable to identify a characteristic level of disclosure which was consistent across situations and concluded that "it may be that prediction from past behavior with a high disclosure target to behavior with a stranger encountered in a laboratory is an inappropriate measurement strategy." From a transactional perspective, it would be strange if it were not so.

In a dyad, self-disclosure is usually symmetrical. It is unusual to find a continuing relationship in which one person has disclosed considerably more than the other, and erroneous perceptions of the extent to which both have disclosed consistently exaggerate symmetry. The best-documented characteristic of self-disclosing communication is that as disclosure by one person increases, so does that by the other (Jourard and Landsman, 1960; Jourard and Resnick, 1970; Jourard and Jaffee, 1970; Ehrlich and Graeven, 1971; Levinger and Senn, 1967; Cozby, 1972; Levin and Gergen, 1969). Unfortunately, these studies often confounded **actual** and **perceived** similarity in disclosure. In a study which differentiated between these, Pearce **et al.** (in press) found that perceived similarity in disclosure between same-sex friends and acquaintances approached unity, but actual similarity correlated at about .50 for males, .82 for females.

Two interpretations of symmetrical patterns of disclosure have been offered, both of which involve hedonic values. Jourard (1964) reasoned that persons disclose only when they feel safe; that being able to disclose is positively valued; and that disclosure by one person makes the other feel safe and able to disclose. Worthy, Gary, and Kahn (1969) interpreted symmetry in terms of Thibaut and Kelley (1959) and Homans's (1961) social exchange theory, a basic principle of which is that the outcomes exchanged by members of a dyad are of comparable value. Reasoning that persons are expected to reveal themselves only to liked or trusted others; being selected as a target for disclosure indicates that the

person is liked or trusted; and that being liked or trusted is rewarding; Worthy, Gary and Kahn concluded that being disclosed to is
rewarding and obligates the person to reciprocate. These interpretations both identify a norm of reciprocity in exchanging positively
valued behavior, but differ in two ways: Jourard describes **being
allowed to disclose** and Worthy **et al. being disclosed to** as the
positively valued behavior; and Worthy, Gary, and Kahn are much
more explicit in their interpretation of symmetry in disclosure as
a social exchange process.

**Self-disclosure occurs in the context of positive social relation-
ships.** While no one has suggested that high levels of disclosure are
common between communicators who are hostile and/or dislike
each other, considerable attention has been given toward identifying those characteristics of positive relationships most closely associated with disclosure.

One of the most commonly cited relationships is that between
affection and disclosure between communicators (see Jourard and
Lasakow, 1958; Jourard, 1959; Worthy, Gary, and Kahn, 1969;
Cozby, 1972). But both the ubiquity and significance of this relationship have been questioned. In Jourard's (1959) study of the
nine faculty members in the University of Florida School of Nursing,
the highest and the lowest disclosers were the least liked. Query
(1964) found an asymmetrical relation between affection and disclosure among a group who associated with each other for several
weeks. Although high levels of disclosure occurred in mutually
affectionate dyads, some high disclosers were not well liked. Much
the same result was reported by Taylor (1965), who observed that
roommates—particularly those who were highly disclosing—decreased in liking as disclosure increased over a thirteen-week period. Marital satisfaction was found to be affected more by communicators' favorable attitudes toward the information disclosed
than by the amount of disclosure (Levinger and Senn, 1967), and
Voss (1969) identified "shared activities" and "children and ca-
reers" as the only two of seventeen topic areas about which disclosure was related to marital satisfaction.

Pearce **et al.** (in press) were concerned to identify the role of
disclosure in same-sex friendships. Using Wright's (1972) model
of friendship, three criterion variables for friendship were measured in relation to self-disclosure: general favorability (liking);

voluntary interdependence (a behavioral criterion of friendship); and person-qua-person (a phenomenological criterion). Of these three, general favorability was **least** (r = .20 for males, .15 for females) correlated with disclosure. These results indicate that interpersonal relationships are more complex than mere liking/disliking, and that disclosure is a basic part of such relationships.

Several writers referred to interpersonal trust as a factor in disclosure, but supporting research is limited to Mellinger's (1956) study which found that members of a research organization who did not trust others communicated in such a way as to conceal their feelings toward relevant topics. Although Vondracek and Marshall (1971) found no relationship between trust and disclosure, their study had a number of methodological weaknesses, including a six-month delay between measures of trust and disclosure, a mail-out distribution of questionnaires which probably introduced a response set due to self-selection of respondents and the use of Rotter's Interpersonal Trust Scale which measures stereotypes rather than trust of particular others (see Appendix B). Conceptually, the relationship between trust and self-disclosing communication seems strong, and still awaits an adequate empirical test.

Self-disclosure usually occurs incrementally. With the exception of strangers with whom no subsequent interaction is expected (Quinn, 1964; Murdock, Chenowith and Rissman, 1969), self-disclosure usually occurs slowly, increasing as the relationship becomes more stable and permanent. Taylor's (1965) study of male freshmen roommates who had known each other for periods ranging from one to thirteen weeks generated this picture of self-disclosing communication: a relatively high level of nonintimate disclosure was followed by a gradual increase in disclosure of more intimate information. The behavioral criterion of friendship, voluntary interdependence, used by Pearce **et al.** (1973), demonstrated that disclosure co-varied with the amount of time same-sex peers spent together.

Discussion

The self-disclosure literature was reviewed from a transactional perspective of communication and a conceptualization of self-disclosure as a deliberate invitation to the other to know and share the speaker's experience. This orientation made much of the literature irrelevant and precluded drawing some conclusions which would appear to have immediate practical usefulness. For example, generalizations taking these forms were inconsistent with the assumptions of this paper: (1) persons with trait X disclose more than those with trait Y; (2) if person A does X, person B will disclose more (or less); and (3) if person A discloses, person B will do X. However, we believe that these decisions enabled us to avoid some of the confusion which would have resulted with less rigorous conceptualizations of communication and self-disclosure.

Five generalizations about self-disclosing communication were drawn. Obviously, these do not comprise all which needs to be known, but do provide a better understanding of this relatively infrequent but highly significant form of communication behavior.

A number of research and pedagogical challenges present themselves based on this review. Of particular importance is the development of techniques for educators, consultants, or counselors to increase individuals' awareness of the present and potential levels of disclosure which characterize their transactions with particular others. To the extent that high levels of disclosure facilitate organizational effectiveness, mutual understanding, helping relationships, and personal satisfaction, those whose concern is to improve communication behavior in particular situations must include a knowledge of self-disclosure in their repertoire of professional competence. This review provides some basis for diagnosing problems in self-disclosing communication. For example, transactions in which disclosure is asymmetrical or hostile, aggressive, competitive relationships are not likely to be efficient, comfortable, or characterized by high levels of understanding. After problem areas have been identified, however, the contribution which the self-disclosure literature can make to someone desiring to improve communication is limited to suggesting the direction in which change should occur (e.g., toward symmetry). An important priority for future research in self-disclosing communication is that of exploring ways in which transactions may be beneficially affected by a consultant or change agent.

References

Argyris, C. 1962. **Interpersonal Competence and Organizational Effectiveness.** Homewood, Ill.: Dorsey.

Axtell, B., and C.W. Cole. 1971. "Repression-sensitization Response Mode and Verbal Avoidance," **Journal of Personality and Social Psychology.** 18: 133–37.

Barnlund, D. 1962. "Toward a Meaning-centered Philosophy of Communication," **Journal of Communication.** 12: 197–211.

_____. 1970. "A Transactional Model of Communication," in **Foundations of Communication Theory.** New York: Harper and Row. Ken Sereno and C. David Mortensen, eds. pp. 83–102.

Berger, S., and L. Anchor. 1970. "Disclosure Process in Group Interaction," 529–30 in **Proceedings of the 78th Annual Convention,** American Psychological Association. pp. 529–30.

Berlo, D. 1960. **The Process of Communication.** New York: Holt, Rinehart and Winston.

Brooks, William D. 1971. **Speech Communication.** Dubuque, Iowa: William C. Brown.

Caplow, Theodore. 1968. **Two Against One: Coalitions in Triads.** Englewood Cliffs, N.J.: Prentice-Hall.

Chittick, E.V., and Himelstein, D. 1967. "The Manipulation of Self-disclosure," **Journal of Psychology.** 65: 117–21.

Cozby, Paul. 1972. "Self-disclosure, Reciprocity and Liking," **Sociometry,** 35: 151–60.

_____. 1973. "Self-disclosure: A Literature Review," **Psychological Bulletin,** 79: 73–91.

Culbert, S. 1968. **The Interpersonal Process of Self-disclosure: It Takes Two to See One.** New York: Renaissance.

Drag, L.R. 1971. "The Bus-rider Phenomenon and its Generalizability: A Study of Self-disclosure in Student-Stranger Versus College Roommate Dyads." Ph.D. dissertation. Gainesville: University of Florida.

Egan, G. 1970. **Encounter: Group Processes for Interpersonal Growth.** Belmont, California: Wadsworth.

Erlich, H., and Graeven, D. 1971. "Reciprocal Self-disclosure in a Dyad," **Journal of Experimental Social Psychology.** 7: 389–400.

Gibb, J.R. 1964. "Climate for Trust Formation," in **T-Group Theory and Laboratory Method.** New York: Wiley. L. Bradford, J.R. Gibb and K. Benne, eds. pp. 279–309.

Himelstein, P., and Kimbrough, W.W. 1963. "Relationship of the MMPI K Scale and a Measure of Self-disclosure in a Normal Population," **Psychological Reports.** 19: 166.

Homans, G.E. 1961. **Social Behavior: Its Elementary Forms.** New York: Harcourt, Brace and World.

Hountras, P.T., and D.L. Anderson. 1969. "Counselor Conditions for Self-exploration of College Students," **Personnel and Guidance Journal,** 48: 45–48.

Hulett, E.J. 1966a. "A Symbolic Interactionist Model of Human Communication: Part One," **Audio-Visual Communication Review,** 14: 5–34.

————. 1966b. "A Symbolic Interactionist Model of Human Communication: Part Two," **Audio-Visual Communication Review,** 14: 203–20.

Ittelson, W. and H. Cantril. 1954. **Perception: A Transactional Approach.** New York: Norton.

Janofsky, A.E. 1971. "Affective Self-disclosure in Telephone vs. Face-to-face Interviews," **Journal of Humanistic Psychology,** 11: 93–103.

Johannesen, Richard. 1971. "The Emerging Concept of Communication as Dialogue," **The Quarterly Journal of Speech,** 57: 373–82.

Jourard, S. 1959. "Self-disclosure and Other-cathexis," **Journal of Abnormal and Social Psychology,** 59: 428–31.

————. 1964. **The Transparent Self.** New York: Van Nostrand.

————. ed. 1967. "To Be or Not To Be—Existential Psychological Perspectives on the Self," **University of Florida Monographs, Social Sciences.** No. 34. Gainesville: University of Florida Press.

————. 1971. **Self-disclosure: The Experimental Investigation of the Transparent Self.** New York: Wiley.

———— and P. Lasakow. 1958. "Some Factors in Self-disclosure," **Journal of Abnormal and Social Psychology,** 56: 91–98.

———— and M.J. Landsman. 1960. "Cognition, Cathexis, and the 'Dyadic Effect' in Men's Self-disclosing Behavior," **Merrill-Palmer Quarterly of Behavior and Development,** 9: 141–48.

———— and P. Jaffe. 1970. "Influence of an Interviewer's Disclosure on the Self-disclosing Behavior of Interviewees," **Journal of Counseling Psychology,** 17: 252–97.

———— and J.L. Resnick. 1970. "Some Effects of Self-disclosure Among College Women," **Journal of Humanistic Psychology,** 10: 84–93.

Laing, R.D. 1967. **The Politics of Experience.** New York: Pantheon.

Levin, F.M., and K. Gergen. 1969. "Revealingness, Ingratiation, and The

Disclosure of Self," in **Proceedings of the 77th Annual Convention,** American Psychological Association, pp. 447–48.

Levinger, G., and D. Senn. 1967. "Disclosure of Feelings in Marriage," **Merrill-Palmer Quarterly of Behavior and Development,** 13: 237–49.

Luft, J. 1969. **Of Human Interaction.** Palo Alto, California: National Press.

MacDaniels, J.E., Yarbrough, C. Kaszmaul, and K. Giffin. 1971. "Openness: Personalized Expression in Interpersonal Communication," paper presented to the International Communication Association, Phoenix, Arizona.

Matson, Floyd, and A. Montagu. 1967. "The Unfinished Revolution," in **The Human Dialogue.** New York: Free Press. F. Matson and A. Montagu, eds. pp. 1–14.

Mellinger, G.D. 1956. "Interpersonal Trust as a Factor in Communication," **Journal of Abnormal and Social Psychology,** 52: 304–9.

Moustakas, C. 1962. "Honesty, Idiocy and Manipulation," **Journal of Humanistic Psychology.** 2: 1–15.

Murdock, Peter, R. Chenowith, and K. Rissman. 1969. "Eligibility and Intimacy Effects on Self-disclosure." Paper presented to the Society of Experimental Social Psychology, Madison, Wisconsin.

Pearce, W. Barnett. 1973. "Trust in Interpersonal Communication," paper presented to the International Communication Association, Montreal, Canada.

_____ and F. Conklin. 1971. "Nonverbal Vocalic Communication and Perceptions of the Speaker," **Speech Monographs.** 38: 235–41.

_____ and B. Brommel. 1972. "Vocalic Communication and Persuasion," **The Quarterly Journal of Speech.** 58: 298–306.

_____, P. Wright, S. Sharp, and K. Slama. In press. "Affection and Reciprocity in Self-disclosing Communication." **Human Communication Research.**

Powell, J. 1969. **Why Am I Afraid to Tell You Who I Am?** Chicago: Peacock.

Query, W.T. 1964. "Self-disclosure as a Variable in Group Psychotherapy," **International Journal of Group Psychotherapy,** 14: 107–15.

Quinn, P.T. 1965. "Self-disclosure as a Function of Degree of Acquaintance and Potential Power." Master's Thesis. Columbus: Ohio State University.

Redding, W. C. 1968. "Human Communication Behavior in Complex Organizations: Some Fallacies Revisited," in **Perspectives on Com-**

munication. Milwaukee: University of Wisconsin, Milwaukee Press. C. Larson and F. Dance, eds. pp. 99–112.

Rogers, C. 1965. "The Therapeutic Relationship: Recent Theory and Research," **Australian Journal of Psychology,** 17: 95–108.

Smith, D. 1972. "Communication Research and the Idea of Process," **Speech Monographs,** 39: 174–82.

Stamm, Keith, and W.B. Pearce. 1971. "Communication Behavior and Coorientational Relations," **Journal of Communication,** 21: 208–20.

Stewart, J. 1973. **Bridges Not Walls: A Book About Interpersonal Communication.** Reading, Massachusetts: Addison-Wesley.

Sullivan, H.S. 1953. **The Interpersonal Theory of Psychiatry.** New York: Norton.

Taylor, D.A. 1965. "Some Aspects of the Development of Interpersonal Relationships: Social Penetration Process," Technical Report No. 1, Center for Research on Social Behavior, University of Delaware.

Thayer, Lee. 1963. "On Theory-building in Communication: I. Some Conceptual Problems," **Journal of Communication,** 13: 1–27.

Thibaut, J.W., and H.H. Kelley. 1959. **The Social Psychology of Groups.** New York: Wiley.

Toch, H., and M. MacLean, Jr. 1967. "Perception and Communication: A Transactional View," **Audio-Visual Communication Review,** 10: 55–77.

Vondracek, F.W., and M.J. Marshall. 1971. "Self-disclosure and Inter-personal Trust: An Exploratory Study," **Psychological Reports,** 28: 235–40.

Voss, F. 1969. "The Relationships of Disclosure to Marital Satisfaction: An Exploratory Study." Master's thesis. Milwaukee: University of Wisconsin, Milwaukee.

Watzlawick, P., Beavin, J., and D. Jackson. 1967. **Pragmatics of Human Communication.** New York: Norton.

Weiner, M., and A. Mehrabian. 1968. **Language Within Language.** New York: Appleton-Century-Crofts.

Wenburg, J., and W. Wilmot. 1973. **The Personal Communication Process.** New York: Wiley.

Worthy, W., A. Gary, and G.M. Kahn. 1969. "Self-disclosure as an Exchange Process," **Journal of Personality and Social Psychology,** 13: 59–63.

Wright, P. 1972. "A Conceptual Model for Studies of Friendship." Unpublished paper, University of North Dakota.

The study of trust: a review of four literatures[1]

Trust—or the lack of it—is an important factor in human relationships. Several literatures attest to the difference trust makes in organizational morale, the ability of individuals to work cooperatively, and the confidence with which individuals participate in social tasks. For example, Mellinger (1956) found that communication between members of a research institute increased the extent to which they accurately perceived each other's position about relevant policy issues **only if they trusted each other.** Without trust, Mellinger concluded, each communicated in such a way as to conceal information about his own attitudes. In Deutsch's (1958) study, subjects who had no reason to distrust each other played a Prisoner's Dilemma matrix game more cooperatively when they had an opportunity to communicate, but when subjects distrusted each other communication did not increase cooperation. Wallace and Rothaus (1969, p. 379) concluded that in the absence of trust, "communication seemed more to serve the end of conflict and warfare than to function in the service of conflict resolution."

However, like many other concepts in the behavioral sciences, "trust" is poorly defined. More effort has been expended to determine the causes or effects of trust than to specify exactly what is

[1]This article appears in slightly revised form in **Speech Magazine**, 1974.

meant when the term is used. This conceptual slipperiness is in part a function of the difficulty in dealing scientifically with a concept which is important in everyday life and which has high evaluative meaning: trust has often (been viewed as a somewhat mystical and intangible factor defying careful definition" (Giffin and Patton, 1971, p. 376)

Studies of trust appear in at least four literatures, but each conceptualizes trust differently. This Appendix provides a basis for evaluating the conceptualization of trust presented in Chapter 6 and for further research by reviewing each of these literatures.

Game theory

About fifteen years ago, Deutsch (1958) noted that the word "trust" did not appear in the indices of the half-dozen "leading textbooks in social psychology." Deploring neglect of what he considered an important topic, he devised a method for studying trust and suspicion by observing the way subjects played matrix games. The literature based on Deutsch's application of game theory to social psychology is now the largest of those which are directly relevant to trust.

Deutsch defined trust as an expectation that another will behave trustworthily which "leads to behavior which he perceives to have greater negative motivational consequences if the expectation is not confirmed than positive motivational consequences if it is confirmed." The opposite of trust was identified as suspicion, or behavior which expects untrustworthy behavior and involves a choice in which less is lost if the other behaves as expected than if he does not. The requirements of these definitions are met, not accidentally, by the Prisoners' Dilemma game (PD). In the PD, two people are confronted with dichotomous choices, with the outcome for each depending on the decision made by both. Each person has an option which will confer upon him (depending on the other's choice) either a highly negative (e.g., -10) or a slightly positive (e.g., $+5$) outcome, and an option which will confer either a slightly negative (e.g., -5) or a highly positive (e.g., $+10$) outcome. The "safest" choice, in terms of risking least and standing to gain the most, is to choose the option with the -5 and $+10$ possibilities, but the PD is arranged so that if both participants choose this option, both receive an outcome of −5. Only if both choose the "high risk" option will both receive a positive outcome. (Figure 8 on page 135 is a typical PD matrix. Following Deutsch's definition, person A trusts B if he chooses 2; is suspicious of B if he chooses 1. Person B is suspicious of A if he chooses X, trusts A if he chooses Y.)

The appeal of this approach is that it is empirical and the observed behaviors appear to be unequivocal. The problem is that Deutsch has not explicated a conceptualization of trust and given an operational definition; rather, he has interpreted a particular empirical measure based on the unique characteristics of the PD game. Three criticisms of Deutsch's paradigm for studying trust are appropriate. First, Deutsch's definitions necessitate an interpersonal relationship in which the participants' outcomes are contingent on each other in the precise manner described by the PD matrix. But many social situations do not resemble the PD: options are frequently more varied than the dichotomy in the PD (see Kee and Knox, 1970) and the distribution of outcomes may differ from the PD pattern (as in the game of "Chicken": see Vinacke, 1969, p. 295). Second, trust and suspicion are not necessarily bipolar opposites. Kee and Knox (1970) questioned whether they are even appropriately considered as points along a single dimension. Consider the meaning of "distrust": is it synonomous with "suspicion"; is it a midpoint along a "trust-suspicion" continuum; or is it a completely different concept? Deutsch's formulations provide no adequate answer. Third and most significantly, the cognitive state antecedent to particular forms of behavior in the PD is not unambiguously indicated by subjects' choices (see Vinacke, 1969, pp. 296–97). Solomon (1960) identified, in addition to trust and suspicion, "exploitative play" in which one person seeks to maximize his gains at the expense of the other (in terms of Figure 8, person A is exploitative if he chooses 1 while expecting B to choose Y), and "risk-taking play" in which one person chooses the high risk option (2 or Y) even though he expects the other to take the competitive option (1 or X). Deutsch (1958) later realized that what he had identified as trusting behavior might indicate some other cognitive state, such as despair, conformity, impulsiveness or a social norm.

To reduce the ambiguity of choices in PD games, several techniques have been developed. Loomis (1959) and Solomon (1960) developed the concept of **mutual** trust, in which both the subjects' **intentions** to play cooperatively and their **expectations** that the other will make the cooperative choice are measured. Tedeschi, Heister and Gahagan (1969) analyzed sequences of behavior in the PD game to identify four "dispositions" in one of the game-players. Identifying the low-risk option (in Figure 8, the low-risk option is 1 for A, X for B) as "C" and the high-risk option (2 for A, Y for B) as "D", these sequences may occur:Such sequential

Person:	Trial 1		Trial 2		A's cognitive state ("disposition")
	A	B	A	B	
	C	C	C	–	Trustworthy
	D	C	C	–	Repentence
	C	D	C	–	Forgiveness
	D	D	C	–	Trust

analysis represents a significant advance over single trial observations, but does not rule out stratagems which encompass more than two trials.

Kee and Knox's (1970) concept of trust is not tied to any particular matrix although it is in the context of game-playing behavior. This concept differentiates **trusting behavior** (such as a choice in a matrix game) from the **subjective probability** that the other will behave trustworthily. This approach allowed Kee and Knox to distinguish between trusting behavior in which the person has little hope that the other will respond trustworthily (which these authors likened to the lifestyle of the "Peanuts" character Charlie Brown) and trusting behavior in which the person has virtually complete confidence in the other's trustworthiness. The behaviors in these two cases may be identical, but their significance for the individual are quite different. Unfortunately, Kee and Knox repeated the mistake for which they chastised Deutsch by implying that behavior had to be either trusting or suspicious. Further, they left the term trustworthiness undefined and their analysis of behavior in situations in which the trustworthiness of the other is questionable did not include strategies designed to determine or alter the probability of the other's trustworthiness. In his analysis of the development of trust, Swinth (1967) demonstrated that such attempts to clarify or change the trustworthiness of the other are essential. Characterizing high risk or cooperative behavior as ambiguous, Swinth believed that one person suggests to the other a renegotiation of their relationship by behaving ambiguously. If the other reciprocates, mutual trust may be established.

The game theory approach to trust is attractive to researchers. By instructing subjects as to what constitutes winning (individual vs. team scores, for example) and by manipulating the values in the matrix, an experimenter can easily control various aspects of the relationship between subjects. Further, empirical measures of trusting behavior are easily obtained by recording subjects' choices in successive trials and by summing subjects' scores. The easy empiricism of game playing masks conceptual equivocation, however. It is far more difficult to interpret than to observe trusting behavior in matrix games. Further research in this tradition should examine the patterns of sequential behaviors (as suggested by Tedeschi, Heister, and Gahagan, 1969) or combine measures of interpersonal perception with observations of behavior (as suggested by Kee and Knox, 1970).

Credibility

In the **Rhetoric,** Aristotle described the "ethos" or character of a public speaker as one of the three most important factors in persuasive effectiveness. Contemporary theories of persuasion similarly place great emphasis on credibility, or "the image held of a communicator at a given time by a receiver" (Anderson and Clevenger, 1963). Persuasive effectiveness is usually defined in terms of attitude or opinion change. When such changes are due to the effect of the credibility of the speaker, the audience may be said to trust the speaker (see Giffin, 1967).

The credibility literature conceptualizes trust in terms of several component parts, or "factors." Aristotle considered "ethos" as a combination of the speaker's intelligence (having correct opinions), character (honesty), and good will toward the audience (intentions or motivations). Hovland, Janis, and Kelley (1953) wrote of two components of credibility: expertness (intelligence and the extent to which the speaker is well informed about his topic) and trustworthiness ("the degree of confidence in the communicator's intent to communicate the assertions he considers most valid").

Giffin (1967) noted that Hovland, Janis, and Kelley's description of trustworthiness combined two elements which Aristotle differentiated: general good character and specific good intentions. Arguing that character may only be described in degrees of positiveness but intentions may be either negative or positive, Giffin followed Aristotle.

In a series of studies conducted during the early 1960s, Berlo, Lemert, and Mertz (1970) factor-analyzed judgments of credibility. The factors which accounted for the bulk of the variance comprised groups of questionnaire items subsequently labeled "qualification" (similar to competence or expertness) and "safety" (similar to trustworthiness). The next most important factor was dynamism, which Berlo, Lemert, and Mertz perceived as an "intensifier" of qualification and safety rather than as a separate dimension. Other writers have similarly found a dynamism factor in credibility, although they have interpreted it differently; Schweitzer (1970) suggested an "additive" function and Pearce and Conklin (1971) a curvilinear relation to other credibility dimensions.

The extent to which the audience likes the speaker also affects their readiness to change their attitudes in response to his urging. The "congruity principle" devised by Osgood and Tannenbaum predicted a movement toward "balance" when a liked speaker endorsed a disliked position (1955). At least three studies, Stone and Eswara (1969), Pearce and Conklin (1971), and Brommel (1972), found that liking varied independently of credibility measures. Unfortunately, the relation between liking and the dimensions of trustworthiness, competence, and dynamism is not clear. While all four may be subsets of the concept credibility, it seems more likely if less parsimonious that liking and credibility are comparable subsets of person perception.

The most significant contribution of the credibility literature is its demonstration that trust is multifactorial. However, this literature has not satisfactorily determined the relationships among various credibility factors and between credibility factors and trusting behaviors.

Sensitivity training/encounter groups

In his discussion of encounter groups, Rogers (1970) identified a slowly building sense of trust as "one of the most common developments." Similarly, Egan (1970) specified "the formation of a climate of trust" as one of the foremost objectives in the early stages of group interaction. According to Gibb (1964) the function of T-Groups is to "augment . . . personal learning" which involves four "modal concerns." The first of these, acceptance, must be achieved before the others (data, goal, and control) and trust is an important part of the ability to accept others. The therapeutic and enabling processes thought to occur in groups require the existence of a high level of reciprocated trust.

Although this literature is not marked by rigorous attempts to specify the meaning of trust, it is possible to extract the sense in which the term is used. A person is said to trust another if he feels that the other will, without attempts to control or direct him, act in ways beneficial both to the person doing the trusting and to himself. Discussing the risk involved in trusting others, Gibb (1965) used as synonymous with "deep trust and confidence" the phrase "feels that people left to themselves will be creative and effective." Elsewhere, Gibb (1964) described "accepting" the way oneself and others are as an indication of trust, and attempts to persuade, give advice, or disassociate as manifestations of distrust. In a statement of his operating assumptions, Rogers (1970) described his trust for groups and individuals in therapy as a belief that good things would happen if he were not "directive" or controlling and had no specific goals toward which he channeled the other(s). Egan (1970) described "contracts" (written agreements about behavior within the group) as useful partly because they provide a needed element of predictability in the behavior of other group members which allows trust to develop quickly.

The most explicit treatment of trust in this literature is that by Giffin and Patton (1971), who differentiated between the attitude of trust, defined as "the introspective orientation which is a potential for action," and trusting behavior. Trusting behavior occurs when a person is (1) relying on another, (2) risking something he values, and (3) attempting to achieve a desired goal. As a paradigm for the study of trust, this identifies four relevant topics: (1) the characteristics of the person who trusts; (2) the perception of the other held by the person who trusts; (3) the way the trusting person perceives the degree of risk he is taking; and (4) the way the trusting person perceives the value of the goal which he is trying to achieve.

This literature provides remarkably sensitive anecdotes and descriptions of specific situations in which trust occurs, but is not based on reliable operational techniques for observing trust.

Generalized expectations of trustworthiness

Based on his theory of social learning, Rotter (1967) developed an instrument to measure interpersonal trust, defined in this case as "an expectancy held by an individual or a group that the word, promise, verbal or written statement of another individual or group can be relied upon." It is important to note that this instrument does not measure the trust between specific individuals but generalized expectations that certain classes of others (parents, teachers, politicians, psychologists, etc.) will be trustworthy (that is, match their words with their behavior).

Rotter believed that trusting behavior in any given instance is a product of the individual's generalized expectation of the trustworthiness of the other and his previous experience with the specific situation. In a novel situation, such as evaluating the Warren Commission Report on the assassination of President Kennedy, behavior is well predicted by such measures of "predispositions to believe or disbelieve which have no direct relationship to this particular social issue but which clearly contribute to determining reactions to it" (Hamsher, Geller, and Rotter, 1968).

Rotter's measuring instrument meets normal tests of reliability and validity (Rotter, 1971) and has been used to categorize various groups in terms of their trustingness (Hochreick and Rotter, 1970), determining important factors in developing trustingness (Katz and Rotter, 1969), and estimating the extent to which public announcements will be accepted (Hamsher, Geller, and Rotter, 1968). But the limitations of this technique are not difficult to identify. As a measure of generalized expectations, Rotter's interpersonal trust scale is situation-free, designed to predict behavior in a wide range of situations, but not necessarily in particular instances. Further, when the subjects have had "consistent experience" with a particular person or group, the test may "be expected not to predict at all" (Rotter, 1971). Two problems occur which make the interpersonal trust scale less useful than it might appear: it requires subjects to reify the "trusted" persons when it pertains to groups and it is inversely sensitive (becomes less reliable) to experience with the trusted individual or groups. Summated measures of trust may be useful as long as the group is undifferentiated, but if various aspects of the group are made salient (not all politicians, teachers, or journalists are alike); if the subjects are less able to reify groups because they are aware of within-group differences (for example, that some promises made by a particular politician are more believable than others); or if they have had considerable experience with specific individuals, this scale is inappropriate. Unfortunately, these include the most interesting and important situations for an understanding of communication.

Conclusion

None of these approaches to a study of trust is fully adequate for a theory of interpersonal communication. Of the four, Rotter's concept of trust as generalized expectations is least useful and the phrase "interpersonal trust" as used by Rotter seems a misnomer. The other three literatures contributed importantly to the conceptualization presented in Chapter 6. Specifically, the differentiation between the cognitive state of trust and trusting behavior follows the game theory literature. The credibility literature informs the discussion of the cognitive state of trust and all three literatures contribute to the discussion of trusting behavior.

References

Anderson, Kenneth, and Theodore Clevenger, Jr. 1963. "A Summary of Experimental Research in Ethos," **Speech Monographs,** 30:59–78.

Berlo, David, J.B. Lemert, and R.J. Mertz. 1970. "Evaluating the Acceptability of Message Sources," **Public Opinion Quarterly,** 33:563–67.

Deutsch, Morton. 1958. "Trust and Suspicion," **Journal of Conflict Resolution,** 2:265–79.

Egan, Gerard. 1970. **Encounter: Group Process of Interpersonal Growth.** Belmont, California: Brooks/Cole.

Gibb, Jack R. 1964. "Climate for Trust Formation," in **T-Group Theory and Laboratory Method.** New York: Wiley. L. Bradford, J.R. Gibb and K. Benne, eds., pp. 279–309.

_____. 1965. "Fear and Facade: Defensive Management," in **Science and Human Affairs.** Palo Alto, California: Science and Behavior. F. Farson, ed., pp. 197–214.

Giffin, Kim. 1967. "The Contribution of Studies to Source Credibility to a Theory of Interpersonal Trust in the Communication Process," **Psychological Bulletin,** 68:104–20.

_____ and Bobby Patton. 1971. "Personal Trust in Human Interaction," in **Basic Readings in Interpersonal Communication.** New York: Harper and Row. K. Giffin and B. Patton, eds., pp. 375–91.

Hamsher, J., J. Geller, and J. Rotter. 1968. "Interpersonal Trust, Internal-External Control, and the Warren Commission Report," **Journal of Personality and Social Psychology,** 9:210–15.

Hochreick, D., and J. Rotter. 1970. "Have College Students Become Less Trusting," **Journal of Personality and Social Psychology,** 15:211–14.

Hovland, Carl, Irving Janis, and Harold Kelley. 1953. **Communication and Persuasion.** New Haven, Conn.: Yale University Press.

Katz, H., and J. Rotter. 1969. "Interpersonal Trust Scores of College Students and Their Parents," **Child Development,** 40:657–61.

Kee, H., and R. Knox. 1970. "Conceptual and Methodological Considerations in the Study of Trust and Suspicion," **Journal of Conflict Resolution,** 14:357–66.

Loomis, J. 1959. "Communication, the Development of Trust, and Cooperative Behavior," **Human Relations,** 12:305–16.

Mellinger, Glen. 1956. "Interpersonal Trust as a Factor in Communication," **Journal of Abnormal and Social Psychology,** 52:304–9.

Osgood, Charles, and Percy Tannenbaum. 1955. "The Principle of Congruity in the Prediction of Attitude Change," **Psychological Review,** 62:42–55.

Pearce, W. Barnett, and B.J. Brommel. 1972. "Vocalic Communication in Persuasion," **The Quarterly Journal of Speech,** 58:298–306.

————, and R. Forrest Conklin. 1971. "Nonverbal Vocalic Communication and Perceptions of a Speaker," **Speech Monographs,** 38:235–41.

Rogers, Carl. 1970. **Carl Rogers on Encounter Groups.** New York: Harper and Row.

Rotter, Julian. 1971. "Generalized Expectations for Interpersonal Trust," **American Psychologist,** 26:443–52.

————. 1967. "A New Scale of the Measurement of Interpersonal Trust," **Journal of Personality,** 35:651–65.

Schweitzer, Don. 1970. "The Effect of Presentation on Source Evaluation," **The Quarterly Journal of Speech,** 56:33–39.

Solomon, L. 1960. "The Influence of Some Types of Power Relationships and Game Strategies upon the Development of Interpersonal Trust," **Journal of Abnormal and Social Psychology,** 61:223–30.

Stone, V., and H. Eswara. 1969. "The Likeability and Self-Interest of the Source in Attitude Change," **Journalism Quarterly,** 46:61–68.

Swinth, R. 1967. "The Establishment of the Trust Relationship," **Journal of Conflict Resolution,** 11:335–44.

Tedeschi, J., D. Heister, and J. Gahagan. 1969. "Trust and Prisoner's Dilemma Game," **Journal of Social Psychology,** 79:43–50.

Vinacke, W.E. 1969. "Variables in Experimental Games: Toward a Field Theory," **Psychological Bulletin,** 71:293–318.

Wallace, D., and P. Rothaus. 1969. "Communication, Group Loyalty, and Trust in the PD Game," **Journal of Conflict Resolution,** 13:-370–80.

Metacommunication[1]

Much of the communication that builds, maintains, or destroys human relationships is at the metacommunicative level. Metacommunication is an important phenomenon to consider for those interested in the role of communication in human relationships.

To metacommunicate is to communicate about communication. Two major types of metacommunication may be distinguished: that which is an ever-present aspect of all transactions; and that which constitutes additional commentary on communicative transactions. In this appendix we will discuss the functions each of these two types of metacommunication serve in everyday interaction and the special role of metacommunication in psychopathology and psychological health.

Metacommunication which inevitably accompanies all communication

Those who have pointed out that metacommunication is always present in human interaction maintain that when we communicate we always communicate at two levels, one of which is metacom-

---

[1]This paper was presented in slightly revised form by C. Rossiter at the annual conference of the International Communication Association, New Orleans, 1974.

municative. Ruesch and Bateson (1968) discuss these as the "report" and "command" aspects of messages. The "report" level is that which we typically consider the information of the message. The "command" level consists of metacommunication which tells how the report is to be interpreted. Satir (1967) referred to these two levels as "denotative" and "metacommunicative" and says that since both are always present, one must look to both in order to "get the message" completely.

Ruesch's definition of this kind of metacommunication is fairly succinct and complete. He says the term "metacommunication":

> indicates the interpretive devices used in the exchange of messages; explicit instructions, implicit instructions contained in role assumption, reference to context of the situation, rules, sequences, patterning (Ruesch, 1956, p. 47).

Ruesch's comments highlight one of the functions of this type of metacommunication—**it tells others how to interpret messages.** Metacommunications of this type often consist of nonverbal cues which are generated along with verbal messages (Condon, 1966). Giffin and Patton refer to these cues as "qualifiers or interpretational signals about the verbal message—[which indicate] what is really meant or how it is to be understood" (Giffin and Patton, 1971, p. 7). By way of example, the tone of voice used when one says "get out of my office" gives the person being addressed information about how to interpret the words being uttered. It tells him whether the speaker is joking or serious. In this way, paralinguistic factors are often metacommunicative.

In comparing mathematical and human communication theory, Berne (1953) said that in the mathematical view of communication, it is "noise" and not "information" which tells the state of the machine, be it a computer or an electronic telephone system. Likewise, that which is not a part of the "information" in human communication is sometimes called "noise." This is a misnomer, however, because "noise" in human communication indicates something about the state of the person and therefore should best be considered metacommunication. Berne concluded that in interpersonal communication " 'noise' is of more value than 'information' since . . . it is of more value to the communicants to know about each other's states than to give 'information' to each other"

(Berne, 1953, p. 197). Thus a second function of metacommunication is **to indicate something about the psychological state of persons.** Watzlawick **et al.** (1967) refer to the two levels of communication as "content" and "relationship" which points to a third function of this type of metacommunication. It serves to **tell others how we see ourselves, them, and relationships with them.** To give an order to another person in such a way as to convey that it is expected he will carry out the order not only conveys the message that we wish him to do something but also indicates that we believe the relationship to be such that we may expect him to carry out our orders.

Metacommunication has also been discussed in relation to actions. According to Blumer, George Herbert Mead suggested that there is a "triadic nature of meaning" in that any gesture signifies: (1) what the person to whom it is directed is to do; (2) what the person who is making it plans to do; and (3) the joint action that is to arise by the articulation of the acts of both (Blumer, 1972). Thus a fourth function of this type of metacommunication is that of **indicating intentions and expectations about our own and others' actions.**

These four functions are inextricably interrelated. How we see ourselves in relation to others is in part determined by the messages they send us; and we interpret those messages in terms of how we see ourselves in relation to them. Similarly we act with regard to others in terms of how we interpret their messages and how we see ourselves in relation to them. All of these factors are influenced by perceptions of the emotional state of the other.

Other communications about communication

In addition to metacommunication which inevitably occurs as part of all communicative transactions, there exists a second type which consists of all other communications about communication. Technically, of course, this book as well as all other messages about communication are metacommunications. However, in this discussion we will not be concerned with metacommunication which deals primarily with communication in general as do books and articles. Instead the focus will be metacommunication which is concerned

with communicative transactions between or among specific people.

Usually metacommunication of this type is verbal and spoken. It
may or may not be generated by participants in the transaction. It
may refer to a transaction that is happening at the time or about
communication that occurred further in the past. Rossiter (1974)
has outlined the following functions of oral verbal metacommunication which is about face-to-face interpersonal communication that
is in process.

The most important function of metacommunication is that it
focuses conscious attention on the process of interaction. This allows
the participants in the process the opportunity to step back from
their own interaction and look at it. They then have the opportunity
for discussing the process if they wish, and of exploring how the
communication system they have created is functioning. Because of
this focusing on the process several other advantages accrue to those
who metacommunicate and who follow up the metacommunication of
others.

By focusing on the process, interactants can find explanations for
what is going on. For instance, if a group has made very little or very
much progress toward its objectives, metacommunication about the
interaction that has occurred might lead the members to discover
what they have been doing that has fostered or hindered the accom-
plishment of the group goals.

Metacommunication can also help clarify vague feelings about
what is going on. It is predominantly process factors that influence
emotional responses to interaction. Therefore, by knowing more
about the process that is going on, participants are more likely to
understand the feelings they have which accompany that process. By
commenting on some factor that has influenced how the interactants
got where they are, metacommunication can suggest explanations for
why the group is as it is. In this way metacommunication may help
persons to discover why they find the others so enjoyable or unenjoy-
able to work with, why they are somewhat anxious, or why they have
any other particular feeling.

Another function of metacommunication is that it allows the opportunity to check with others to determine if perceptions of what is
happening coincide. In metacommunicating perceptions are made
explicit and public, thus allowing others to know them and to respond
to them.

The last function that metacommunication serves is that of providing direct feedback. In metacommunicating a person tells others how he sees them and their communication behavior and they in turn may tell him how they see him and his communication behavior. This provides the opportunity for focusing attention on the communication behavior and for evaluating and trying to improve it. In this way metacommunication can help increase one's knowledge about how he communicates and relates to others.

The various functions of metacommunication do not exist in isolation from one another but are closely related. Any single metacommunication usually serves several of the functions. Take the following example. A group discussing ways to solve the parking problem on campus is at an impasse, the problem has been defined to everyone's satisfaction but in attempting to reach a group decision about the best solution the group becomes stuck. Two factions have developed with each convinced that its proposed solution is best. For the last fifteen minutes each has repeatedly advocated that the group adopt **its** solution. Finally someone says: "It seems to me we've been repeating the same arguments and conclusions for the last fifteen minutes and I'm starting to feel like we're not getting anywhere. Is there anything else we might do to reach a decision?" This metacommunication about the group's behavior may seem extremely simple, almost superfluous, but in the heat of discussion such a statement can have profound influences on the subsequent course of interaction. Such a statement is likely to perform several of the functions noted above: it provides direct feedback to the group about its behavior; suggests that the group focus its attention temporarily on its own process rather than on the problem it has been formed to solve; and lastly, provides an opportunity for participants to discuss the process that is going on and their perceptions, ideas, and feelings regarding that process.

This particular instance of metacommunication also exemplifies several characteristics which work to enhance the chances that positive outcomes will result for the interactants and that the information made available by the metacommunicator will be pursued. The statement is clear and direct. It is a report of a specific perception of the metacommunicator, and it is descriptive rather than judgmental. Of course, regardless of how well one metacommunicates, there is no guarantee that others in an interaction situation will respond positively to comments or be willing to pursue them to reach a better understanding of communication processes. Responses to metacommunications are as important as the original statements if the statements are to serve the functions outlined above.

Metacommunication, psychopathology, and psychological health

If a strong relationship between the capacity to relate satisfyingly with others is accepted as a correlate of psychological health, then it must be conceded that metacommunication has great potential for fostering therapeutic effects. These effects are realized when metacommunication results in greater awareness and understanding about how one's communication behavior influences one's relationships with others.

The same kinds of therapeutic effects that accrue to those who experience metacommunication about face-to-face communication that is in process may also be derived from metacommunication about communication behaviors and patterns that occurred sometime in the more distant past. Some see this as a primary goal of formal therapy. In fact, Ruesch has said that the feature which characterizes planned therapy is "the setting apart of a period of time when people convene **for the purpose of communicating about communicating** (Ruesch, 1973, p. 33, boldface added). The same may be said of other activities aimed at improving general functioning and capacities to relate meaningfully. Larson has said that "the rationale underlying T-group training is that by observing and analyzing a group in which he is actually participating a [person] becomes more aware and capable of acting upon the enabling and disabling factors in group life" (Larson, 1964, p. 178).

The relationship of metacommunication to psychopathology and psychological health may further be elaborated by considering three key concepts: validation; flexibility; and congruence.

In earlier chapters we explained the importance of validation to psychological health. To reiterate briefly, the person who is not validated with some minimal degree of consistency comes to lose faith in himself as a person. He becomes less sure of himself and his perceptions of what is going on around him. In the extreme he may exhibit bizarre behavior and be diagnosed as mentally ill. Satir provides the link with metacommunication. According to her (Satir, 1967), all messages, when viewed at the highest level of abstraction carry with them the metamessage "validate me." Thus, every message can be seen as carrying a request for validation to which others respond. The response to this request is usually at the metacommunicative level. Watzlawick **et al.** (1967) say that responses to requests for validation can be either confirming (validating), disconfirming, or rejecting and that these responses are at the metacommunicational level. Thus, most validation is based on perceptions of metacommunications of others.

In Chapter 8 we established the capacity to be flexible in relationships with others as an important characteristic of a psychologically healthy person. Metacommunication provides the medium through which we let others know how we see our relationship with them and how we would like our relationship with them to be. Leary (1955) pointed out that we train others to respond to us in certain ways by our implicit messages. This means that one's capacities to metacommunicate with others in different ways, thus inviting different kinds of relationships, can be seen as a correlate of psychological health. Ruesch (1973) in discussing disturbances of communication pointed out that a common problem of those who are mentally distressed is an incapacity to accurately interpret metacommunication from others or to generate appropriate metacommunications. Such persons are incapable of: generating and/or interpreting metacommunicational instructions for message interpretation; understanding messages in terms of the context within which they are generated; considering the social role the other is assuming when interpreting messages from the other.

A congruent communication is one where "two or more messages are sent via different levels but none of these messages seriously contradicts any other" (Satir, 1967, p. 82). To communicate congruently the denotative and metacommunicative levels must generally say the same thing.

Psychologically healthy persons are generally more congruent in their communications and disturbed individuals are generally less capable of generating congruent messages (Rogers, 1961; Satir, 1967). What's more, those who generate incongruent messages sometimes have devastating psychological effects on those with whom they interact. The most direct example of this is known as the "double-bind." Bateson **et al.** have suggested the necessary ingredients for a double-bind situation: Though they refer specifically to the parent-child relationship, persons involved in double-bind situations may be any two or more persons who are significant for one another. The ingredients are:

1. **Two or more persons.** Of these we designate one for purposes of our definition as the "victim." We do not assume that the double-bind is inflicted by the mother alone, but that it may be done either by the mother alone or by some combination of mother, father, and/ or siblings.

2. **Repeated experience.** We assume that the double-bind is a recurrent theme in the experience of the victim. Our hypothesis does not invoke a single traumatic experience, but such repeated experience that the double bind structure comes to be a habitual expectation.

3. **A primary negative injunction.** This may have either of two forms: (a) "Do not do so and so, or I will punish you," or (b) "If you do not do so and so, I will punish you." Here we select a context of learning based on avoidance of punishment rather than a context of reward seeking. There is perhaps no formal reason for this selection. We assume that the punishment may be either the withdrawal of love or the expression of hate or anger—or most devastating—the kind of abandonment that results from the parent's expression of extreme helplessness.

4. **A secondary injunction conflicting with the first at a more abstract level, and like the first enforced by punishments or signals which threaten survival.** This secondary injunction is more difficult to describe than the primary for two reasons. First the secondary injunction is commonly communicated to the child by nonverbal means. Posture, gesture, tone of voice, meaningful action, and the implications concealed in verbal comment may all be used to convey this more abstract message. Second, the secondary injunction may impinge on any element of the primary prohibition. Verbalization of the secondary injunction may, therefore, include a wide variety of forms; for example, "Do not see this as punishment"; "Do not see me as the punishing agent"; "Do not submit to my prohibitions"; "Do not think of what you must not do"; "Do not question my love of which the primary prohibition is (or is not) an example"; and so on. Other examples become possible when the double-bind is inflicted not by one individual but by two. For example, one parent may negate at a more abstract level the injunctions of the other.

5. **The tertiary negative injunction prohibiting the victim from escaping from the field.** In a formal sense it is perhaps unnecessary to list this injunction as a separate item since the reinforcement at the other two levels involves a threat to survival and if the double-binds are imposed during infancy, escape is naturally impossible. However, it seems that in some cases the escape from the field is made impossible by certain devices which are not purely negative, e.g., capricious promises of love, and the like.

6. Finally, the complete set of ingredients is no longer necessary when the victim has learned to perceive his universe in a double-bind pattern. Almost any part of a double-bind sequence may then be sufficient to precipitate panic or rage. The pattern of conflicting injunctions may even be taken over by hallucinatory voices (Bateson **et al.,** 1956, pp.253–54).

Continually experiencing double-bind situations can result in extreme forms of mental disturbance. Receiving conflicting messages at the denotative and the "more abstract" metacommunicative level, the victim does not know what to believe. Either way he chooses to interpret the incongruent messages he will be told he has misunderstood and done wrong. It is common for the victim to solve this issue by deciding to interpret **all** messages as if they expressed the same intent on the part of others. He may decide always to be suspicious of others, reacting as if there are hidden meanings in all that is conveyed to him and as if these hidden meanings bode him ill. Such response in the extreme is generally diagnosed as paranoia. He may decide to consider all messages unimportant rather than trying to sort them out. Should he do this and decide to respond to all communications from others by merely laughing at them his behavior will fit the description of those exhibiting the pathology known as hebephrenia. Finally, the victim may choose to withdraw from the anxiety producing the double-binding situation. Should he do so in the extreme he will be exhibiting the characteristics of catatonia.

The alternative responses to double-bind situations which can "save" the victim are two: he can (usually with the help of someone else) leave the field; and he can (usually with the help of someone else) discuss the double messages he is getting. In this way the capacity for **metacommunicating** about incongruent, double-binding messages can help the victim from experiencing the negative effects of being double bound.

Implications

To learn more about the role of interpersonal communication in human relationships and in relation to psychopathology and psychological health it is imperative to learn more about metacommunication. Future studies are needed which focus on how metacommunicational cues are generated and perceived and how metacommunication functions in specific instances and situations. Knapp **et al.**'s (1973) study of the verbal and nonverbal cues associated with leave-taking represents an example of this kind of research.

Research about metacommunication would benefit from the adoption of the more holistic transactive approach. This would allow for more complete analyses by researchers who attempt to look simultaneously at all messages being generated at both the denotative and metacommunicational levels.

Finally, the effects of direct verbal spoken comments about communication behaviors and patterns merit further exploration as do the effects of training at this kind of metacommunication (Rossiter, 1974).

References

Bateson, Gregory, **et al.** 1956. "Toward a Theory of Schizophrenia," **Behavioral Science,** 1:251–64.

Berne, Eric. 1964. **Games People Play.** New York: Grove Press.

_____. "Concerning the Nature of Communication," **Psychiatric Quarterly,** 27:185–93.

Blumer, Herbert. 1972. "Symbolic Interaction: An Approach to Human Communication," in **Approaches to Human Communication,** New York: Spartan Books. Richard W. Budd and Brent D. Ruben, eds., 401–19.

Condon, John C. 1966. **Semantics and Communication.** New York: Macmillan.

Giffin, Kim, and Bobby R. Patton. 1971. **Fundamentals of Interpersonal Communication.** New York: Harper and Row.

Knapp, Mark L., Roderick P. Hart, Gustav W. Friedrich, and Gary M. Schulman. 1973. "The Rhetoric of Goodbye: Verbal and Nonverbal Correlates of Human Leave-Taking," **Speech Monographs,** 40: 182–98.

Larson, Carl. 1964. "Some Recent Developments in T-Group Training," **Central States Speech Journal,** 15:177–82.

Leary, Timothy. 1955. "The Theory and Measurement Methodology of Interpersonal Communication," **Psychiatry,** 18:147–61.

Rogers, Carl. 1961. **On Becoming a Person.** Boston: Houghton Mifflin.

Rossiter, Charles M., Jr. 1974. "Instruction in Metacommunication," **Central States Speech Journal,** 25:36–42.

Ruesch, Jurgen. 1973. **Therapeutic Communication.** New York: W.W. Norton. (Originally published: 1961.)

_____ and Gregory Bateson. 1968. **Communication: The Social Matrix of Psychiatry.** New York: W.W. Norton. (Originally published 1951.)

_____. 1956. "The Observer and the Observed: Human Communication Theory," in **Toward a Unified Theory of Human Behavior,** New York: Basic Books. Roy R. Grinker, ed., 36–54.

Satir, Virginia. 1967. **Conjoint Family Therapy.** Palo Alto, California: Science and Behavior Books.

Watzlawick, Paul, Janet Beavin, and Don D. Jackson. 1967. **Pragmatics of Human Communication.** New York: W.W. Norton.

Notes and ideas about methodology for studying Communication as a transactive process

This appendix summarizes various notes and ideas from our explorations in the area of methodology. There is much work yet to be done if research is to come closer to reflecting communication as the complex phenomenon that it is. Our hope is that the information presented here will stimulate interested others to join our pursuit of better methodologies for the study of communication as a transactive process.

Communication as a transactive process

1. According to Scheidel, a process model of communication implies three critical attributes: "(1) **ongoingness,** a sequential, changing, developing activity, (2) **complexity,** a multi-variable, multi-faceted activity, and (3) **interrelatedness,** a coherence and interaction among the many dynamic variables in the activity" (Scheidel, 1971, p. 2). After "dissecting" the idea of process, Arundale (1973) noted that the following characteristics are generally attributed to things labeled as processes: change over time; irreversibility; continuity; interrelatedness; relativity; equifinality

(or multicausality); interaction; emergence; and complexity. He agreed with Scheidel that the most important characteristics of processes are change over time, interrelatedness, and complexity.
2. The essential fundamental notions underlying a transactional process view of communication have been outlined as follows:

I. Communication is a complex, dynamic process.
II. All communication transactions are contextual and, therefore, are unique, irreversible and unrepeatable.
III. Since communication is an uninterrupted sequence, it has no beginning or end. To designate some participants as "senders" and others as "receivers" is, therefore, an arbitrary decision and should be recognized as such.
IV. Each participant in a transaction affects and is affected by the other participants—none will ever be the same again.
V. Each participant in a transaction is **simultaneously** encoding and decoding (Wilmot and Wenburg, 1973, p. 8)

Some process-oriented research

3. Over the years there have been some efforts to do research that is somewhat process-oriented. Becker (1965) summarized five general types of procedures that have been employed in "reaction profile" studies to obtain profiles of audience reactions to messages **as they are presented.** They are: continuous overt responding by audience members who turn a knob or pull a switch in one direction when they are interested or like what is being said and turn or pull in another direction when they are not interested or dislike what is being said; intermittent recording of these same kinds of responses by "cueing" audience members to respond at specified time intervals such as every thirty seconds or every minute; unobtrusive data collection by using infra-red photography to photograph audience reactions as a message is presented with reaction profiles constructed afterward from an analysis of facial expressions and other nonverbal cues; gross bodily movement used in the same way to infer interest; and finally, physiological data such as skin-conductivity which has been found to correlate with emotional activity and attention has been used to infer audience interest and involvement (Becker, 1965, p. 188).
4. Brooks and Scheidel (1968) attempted to study the process

of attitude change by having subjects respond intermittently during a tape-recorded speech by Malcolm X. Based on their analysis, they concluded that this method seemed promising for the study of communication as process. However, Tucker and Mack (1971) replicated the original study and in addition conducted four other studies in an attempt to determine the effects of experimental design on the outcomes of this type of experiment. They concluded that repeated testing of the same subjects produced different results than when different groups were used who responded only to pretests and then responded to post tests which were administered at different points during the message. They suggested that the "between subjects" design produced more accurate results since it eliminated the potential effects of repeatedly being tested.

5. Recently, Arundale (1972) has summarized statistical techniques which may be used in the analysis of process data. Arundale cites the following techniques as applicable for reduction of data from process designs:

Pattern Recognition. Techniques for either identifying new patterns or seeking specified patterns in data. Patterns may exist in time or space, with temporal patterns (and data) of special interest here. Actually a broad area containing many techniques, some specifically adapted to certain types or classes of patterns and data. (Uhr, 1966)

Constraint Analysis. Techniques often closely related to pattern recognition techniques, for determining the bounds or constraints present in a given set of data. Again, the data may be temporal, spatial, etc., although temporal data, often termed "protocols," are of special interest here. Individual techniques vary, but are apt to be more generally applicable than many pattern recognition techniques (Ashby, 1963).

Signal Analysis. Techniques for deriving symbolic (mathematical) representations of temporal data or signals. Actually this is a broad area containing many different techniques (Gabor, 1946).

Stochastic Processes. Techniques for deriving a specific class of symbolic representations of data. Data are often temporal, and the representation differs from those above in that it describes the sequence or succession of individual data points (Bartlett, 1966).

Trend Surface Analysis. Techniques for deriving a symbolic representation of a trend or movement in a set of data or form of variation. Data are often spatial, but may be temporal. Actually a broad collection of techniques and may include regression analysis (Chorley and Haggart, 1968).

Arundale also identified the following testing techniques for use with data from process designs:

Analysis of Variance: Analyses and tests of "change" or "time-curve" information by partitioning of variance (Gaito and Wiley, 1967; Bock, 1967).

Trend Analysis: Analyses and tests of the shape of the relation between two variables. Closely related to analysis of variance procedures (McNemar, 1962, esp. ch. 17).

Goodness of Fit: Analyses and tests of the "fit" between two series of data (often the predicted and the observed) (Carroll and Farace, 1968, pp. 71–72).

Time Series Analysis: Analyses and tests of serial correlation (autocorrelation), correlation, partial correlation, and regression between time series (Holtzman, 1967).

Sequential Analyses: Analyses and tests where the number of observations required by the statistical procedure is not determined in advance (Wald, 1947).

Sensitivity Testing: A general approach to testing models in which parameters or relationships are systematically varied over successive "runs" of the model. The resulting differences in outcomes are compared to determine the sensitivity or "strength" of the model. Techniques are basically non-analytic (Carroll and Farace, 1968, pp. 73–74).

Response Analysis: A collection of mathematical techniques for manipulating models to examine characteristics of their operation. Includes analyses of stability or controllability as well as examination of outputs given specified inputs. Techniques are basically analytic (Carroll and Farace, 1968, pp. 53–60).

6. Both the reaction profile studies and the approach to communication as process suggested by Arundale emphasize but one characteristic of process, **ongoingness.** While this is desirable, both are limited by lack of acknowledgment of other important aspects of the **transactional** elements of communication.

The systems approach

7. Hall and Fagan define a system as "a set of objects together with relationships between the objects and between their attributes" (Hall and Fagan, 1956, p. 18). Objects are the components of the system and are limitless in kind. Attributes are properties of the objects. All systems except the largest (the universe) have

environments. For any system, the environment is "the set of all objects a change in whose attributes affect the system and also those objects whose attributes are changed by the behavior of the system" (Hall and Fagan, 1956, p. 20). The purpose or problem at hand usually determines whether a particular object will be considered a part of a system or a part of the environment. Another judgment which must be made when studying any particular system is the determination of the boundaries of the system's environment. This is another subjective judgment that is made differently depending upon the purposes for examining the system. Most organic systems are **open** which means that "they exchange materials, energies or information with their environments" (Hall and Fagan, 1956, p. 23). This means that human systems and communication systems are open to the extent that they influence and are influenced by their environments.

8. Systems may be studied macroscopically by looking at the whole system or microscopically by taking a detailed look at the behavior of the smallest of subsystems. Macroscopically a system may be examined to determine its wholeness, or coherence among its parts. As yet, systems theorists have devised no specific way to measure this. Over time, systems tend to change by moving away from wholeness (progressive segregation) or toward wholeness with a strengthening of relations among parts and the creation of new relationships among parts (progressive systematization).

9. Miller (1955) contributed the notion of "general behavior systems" as the subcategory of systems dealing with living systems, the most important characteristic of which is their openness. Miller believes that: "All behavior can be conceived of as energy exchange within an open system or from one such system to another" (Miller, 1955, p. 514).

10. The similarity between notions of communication as transactive process and open systems has been noted. Arundale (1973) has referred to "process" as a general systems concept; and in discussing his model for communication processes, Hawes (1973) pointed out that some of the propositions of systems theory seem to be "structurally similar" to his perspective of human communication. Thayer has commented that: "the smallest logically indivisible unit of analysis for the systematic and scientific study of communication and intercommunication is the communication system. A communication system is comprised of an organism or the indi-

vidual, together with that which is presently being taken into account, whether some aspect of its environment or another individual or organism" (Thayer, 1972, p. 110). He said that communication systems are characterized by components that are interdependent and historical which means that the elements of particular human communication systems are never the same in different communication systems and are never the same in the same communication systems. Thayer rightfully noted that there has been little exploitation of general systems theory by scholars of communication.

11. More recently Monge (1973) has suggested that the systems paradigm be adopted for the study of communication as process. He claims that the major advantages of this paradigm would be a shift in the set of variables selected for study, an increase in the complexity of analyses, and the ability to integrate research findings into a wider perspective. He says the systems model is "an explanatory model sufficiently complex to account for the complexity of communication" (Monge, 1973, p. 13). Monge compared the systems paradigm with the "covering law" paradigm which is currently in vogue in the social and behavioral sciences. Generally, the covering law paradigm has three major limitations: (1) it is based on the assumption that a generalization can be established that will hold throughout time and space; (2) it assumes a phenomenon will be invariant through time and space; and (3) it is based on a single form of logic which is only one of several forms currently available (Monge, p. 8–9).

When the system paradigm is compared with the covering law paradigm the following differences (advantages of the systems paradigm) are noted:

Systems Paradigm	Covering Law Paradigm
1. system-specific rather than universal generalizations are considered appropriate	1. seeks universal generalizations
2. any given event may be explained without examination of all other similar events. Induction is superfluous	2. universal generalizations are certified by induction from empirical generalizations

3. logical and empirical processes are separated so that whatever logical system is recognized as matching the logic seen in the event being studied can be used

3. logical and empirical processes are combined and thus a logic is imposed on events ... it is stipulated a priori that events be related by the logic of generalization

4. alternative logics are permitted so different explanations may be given for the same phenomenon with the choice made on the basis of the purpose for which the explanation is sought

4. explanations can be articulated without reference to purposes ... the criterion for adequacy is the ability to generate adequate inductive generalizations

5. permits partial explanations

5. deductive explanations give only complete explanations for entire classes of events (Monge, 1973)

Seekers for a humanistic science of man

12. The problems entailed in studying communication so that its complexity as a transactional process is fully acknowledged are very similar to problems which have long been addressed by psychologists and other social scientists who believe that typically employed methods for doing empirical research about man do not do justice to his complexity. They argue that methods which fragment man and mechanistically study isolated variables in search of generalizations about causality are inadequate. Writings which discuss the advantages and limitations of "mechanistic" and "humanistic" sciences of man are therefore pertinent for the communication scholar who is interested in the development of methodologies capable of addressing the full complexity of communication as a transactive process.

13. Summaries and/or critiques of traditional methodologies and their assumptions may be found in Chenault (1965), Matson (1966), and von Bertalanffy (1967). Giorgi (1970) provides a general overview of how these methodologies are related to, and have grown out of, the tradition of nineteenth-century physical

sciences, particularly physics. Hampden-Turner (1971) has written a very readable, brief summary of the limitations of these methods. Both Giorgi (1970) and Maslow (1966) outline their hopes for a more humanistic science of man though they are not specific about methodological procedures.

14. Among the issues pertinent to those interested in a "humanistic" science of man and those concerned with a more adequate study of communication are: fragmentation vs. holism; univariate vs. multivariate; search for understanding as an end vs. the search for the means of control through the discovery of causal relationships; study of the unique vs. the capacity to generalize (idiographic-nomothetic issue); world as static vs. world in process.

Some ideas and implications for methodology

15. The complexity and interrelatedness of all factors involved in communication transactions suggest that traditional ways of doing research about these transactions are inadequate for fully explaining what is occurring.

A. To assume that influences move in only one direction does not adequately account for simultaneous encoding and decoding of messages by all participants. Nor does it recognize the arbitrariness of designating any single participant as the major "influence agent." Watzlawick **et al.** (1967) discuss this problem, pointing out that conclusions about causes and effects can be greatly influenced by the ways in which one chooses to "punctuate" interaction, by arbitrarily designating one participant's behavior as "cause" and the other's as "effect."

B. To assume that single causes can be determined by "isolating" variables does not adequately account for the interrelatedness of all variables in any communication transaction.

C. To isolate a segment of communication, study it, and draw conclusions without reference to events preceeding the beginning of the segment studied or anticipations of events which might follow the end of the segment being studied does not adequately account for the notion that any specific communication transaction is an uninterrupted sequence occurring within a temporal context. This context is made up in part of rememberances of the past and of anticipations for the future. In this way, the past and future are a part of the present and should be somehow taken into account.

16. If research is to account adequately for the full complexity of what occurs during the transactional process of communication, it must differ in specific ways from traditional communication research.

A. Rather than identifying influence agents and presuming that influences go in one direction from these agents to others, research must look at all parties in a transaction as parts of a system, each of whom continually and simultaneously influences himself, others and the environment in which the transaction occurs.

B. The search for single causes might be abandoned in favor of multivariate approaches which acknowledge that variables do not exert the same kinds of influences in different contexts and that different contexts are created by the presence, to greater and lesser degrees, of other significant variables.

C. The arbitrariness of selecting a segment of communicative transaction from an unending sequence must be acknowledged and aspects of the past and future which influence the present must be taken into account when rendering explanations.

17. To accept the twentieth-century view of process also entails accepting that "reality is **created** rather than **discovered** and that each creation is limited by the perspective of its creator" (Smith, 1972, p. 179). Several scholars have addressed this issue, each pointing out that the knower and the known cannot be separated, with each being a part of the other. They therefore maintain that all knowledge is "personal" (Dewey and Bentley, 1949; Polanyi, 1962, 1966). A fairly simple introduction to this notion is provided by Maslow (1966).

18. The idea that all knowledge is personal and influenced by the viewpoint of the knower leads to a need for a reevaluation of "objectivity" as a criterion for the evaluation of research. Smith (1972) suggested four implications for researchers as a result of accepting the twentieth century notion of process and the idea that all knowledge is personal: (1) objectivity (at least as typically defined) is no longer relevant as a criterion for evaluating research; (2) researchers should make the nature and limitations of their perspectives explicit when they report their research; (3) different explanations of the same phenomenon can be accepted simultaneously if they emanate from persons with different perspectives; (4) instead of objectivity, "carefulness" should be used as a criterion

for evaluating research. Reports of research can be evaluated to determine if the scholar has been sufficiently careful in avoiding errors of logic and inference, in generalizing, and in specifying the personal dimensions of the research.

19. If less emphasis is placed on a deterministic, cause-effect approach to the study of communication then the use of different techniques and methods becomes more appropriate. Among those which seem more appropriate are: correlational analyses, factor analyses to discover trends and categories; exploratory research without hypotheses; and subject self-reports (Smith, 1972).

20. Several research methods and approaches to human interaction already in existence and of proven value have not been used much by empirically oriented communication scholars. Methods which allow a more thorough examination of all relevant variables as they interact in communication transactions seem particularly useful and merit further exploration.

21. Case studies, save historical analyses, seldom appear. Yet Dukes (1965) surveyed the literature and concluded that despite problems of generalization, in some instances the case study might not only provide greater insight into the phenomenon studied, but might also be the most powerful and efficient design available. He said studies of single subjects are particularly desirable when: (1) the uniqueness of the subject is such that he exhausts the population; (2) (at the other extreme) inter-subject variability is so low that to study any one subject is as good as studying any or all other members of the population; (3) the goal is the intensive study of an "ideal" type; (4) findings of the study disconfirm a generalization previously thought to be universal; (5) opportunities to observe are limited by the situation or the rarity of the phenomenon of interest; and (6) the primary goal is to focus on a problem. According to Dukes, problem-centered research on only one subject may be valuable in clarifying questions, defining variables, and indicating promising approaches for future research.

22. The viewpoints of symbolic interactionists and the closely related ethnomethodologists are pertinent for their view of human interaction is close to the conceptualization of communication as a transactive process. Symbolic interaction is based on three premises: (1) humans act on things based on the meanings they have for those things; (2) meanings are derived from social interaction

with others; (3) meanings are handled and developed by an inter-pretive process through which the individual indicates to himself the things toward which he is acting and their meanings (Blumer, 1972). From the symbolic interactionist's viewpoint, meanings are constantly being revised. Each instance of social interaction is viewed as a new situation in which meanings must be established and developed. It is recognized, however, that each new situation has arisen out of past actions of the participants and, therefore, occurs in a context made up, in part, of those past actions. Mi-crosociologically oriented ethnomethodologists represent an out-growth of symbolic interactionism. Ethnomethodologists focus on communication as the basic social action of everyday life. As Dreit-zel puts it, the focus is the "meaning of social action . . . ethnosoci-ologists try to analyze just how people go about finding a meaning in their mutual action; doing interpretation, i.e., the procedure of understanding the other, is the phenomenon under investigation" (Dreitzel, 1970, p. x)

23. Field observation is a methodology employed by some eth-nomethodologists in their efforts to describe and analyse interper-sonal communication in everyday life. Many studies such as **Street Corner Society** (Whyte, 1937), **The Midwest and Its Children** (Barker and Wright, 1957), and **Ecological Psychology** (Barker, 1968) have productively used this methodology. Studies in which the observer is a participant (at least partially) constitute a specific kind of field observation known as participant observation. This method is said to be especially promising for unearthing hypothe-ses and exploring areas in which little is known (Lofland, 1971). According to Lofland this methodology is particularly useful for capturing the "richness" and "fullness" of reality as it unfolds. **Asylums** (Goffman, 1961) and **Talley's Corner** (Liebow, 1967) are but two examples of what can be accomplished with this method.

24. It is not necessary or even desirable to abandon completely research about communication which approaches the subject by seeking causal relationships among variables which are studied in specific communication situations. The best way to come to the most thorough knowledge of understanding is to do both the tradi-tional research **and** the more process oriented research that has been the focus of this appendix (Pearce, 1973). It is important to

recognize, however, that either approach includes the tacit acceptance of some assumptions about how communication can be viewed and influences the kinds of questions which can be asked and answered.

25. It is possible to arrive at transactionally oriented conclusions about communication by synthesizing research done from the linear, cause-effect approach. Throughout much of **Communicating Personally** that is what we have tried to do. One way in which this can be seen particularly well, we think, is in the Lieberman **et al.** research on encounter groups reported at length in chapter 8. This research consisted of many research studies all conducted at the same time and focusing on the same events—encounter group experiences. By synthesizing all of the various kinds of data that were collected, it was possible to arrive by informed inference at an understanding of the ways in which the different variables interacted in producing the final outcomes which the subjects experienced. In this way the combining and synthesizing of nontransactionally oriented research can result in conclusions which are transactional in nature.

References

Arundale, Robert B. 1972. "Learning to Deal with **Process** in the Study of Communication: A Guide to Information," paper presented at the annual conference of the International Communication Association, Atlanta, Georgia.

————. 1973. "Dissecting the 'Idea of Process': Some Implications for Theory and Research on Communication," paper presented at the annual conference of the International Communication Association, Montreal, Canada.

Ashby, W.R. 1963. **An Introduction to Cybernetics.** New York: Wiley.

Barker, R., and H. Wright. 1957. **Midwest and its Children.** Lawrence, Kansas: University of Kansas Press.

Bartlett, M.S. 1966. **An Introduction to Stochastic Processes.** Cambridge, England: Cambridge University Press.

Becker, Samuel L. 1965. "Methodological Analysis in Communication Research," **The Quarterly Journal of Speech,** 51: 382–91.

Blumer, Herbert. 1972. "Symbolic Interaction: An Approach to Human Communication," in **Approaches to Human Communication.** New York: Spartan. Richard W. Budd and Brent D. Ruben, eds., 401–19.

Bock, R.E. 1967. "Multivariate Analysis of Variance of Repeated Measurement," **Problems in Measuring Change.** Madison, Wisconsin: University of Wisconsin Press. C.W. Harris, ed., 85–121.

Brooks, Robert D., and Thomas M. Scheidel. 1968. "Speech as Process: A Case Study," **Speech Monographs,** 35:1–7.

Carroll, T.W., and R.V. Farace. 1968. "Systems Analysis, Computer Simulation, and Survey Research: Application to Social Research in Developing Countries," unpublished manuscript, Department of Communication, Michigan State University.

Chenault, J. 1965. "Research and the Monolithic Tradition," **Personnel and Guidance Journal,** 44:6–10.

Chorley, R.J., and P. Haggart. 1968. "Trend-Surface Mapping in Geographical Research," in **Spatial Analysis.** Englewood Cliffs, N.J.: Prentice-Hall. B.J.L. Berry and D.F. Marble, eds., 195–217.

Dewey, John, and Arthur F. Bentley. 1949. **Knowing and the Known.** Boston: Beacon Press.

Dreitzel, Hans P. 1970. "Introduction: Patterns of Communicative Behavior," in **Recent Sociology No. 2.** Hans P. Dreitzel, ed., vii-xxii.

Dukes, William F. 1965. "N = 1," **Psychological Bulletin,** 64:74–79.

Gabor, D. 1946. "Theory of Communication," **Journal of the Institution of Electrical Engineers,** 93:429–41.

Gaito, J., and D.E. Wiley. 1967. "Univariate Analysis of Variance Procedures in the Measurement of Change," in **Problems in Measuring Change.** Madison, Wisconsin: University of Wisconsin Press. C.W. Harris, ed., 60–84.

Giorgi, Amadeo. 1970. **Psychology as a Human Science.** New York: Harper and Row.

Goffman, Erving. 1961. **Asylums.** Garden City, N.Y.: Anchor Doubleday.

Hall, A.D. and R.E. Fagan. 1956. "Definition of System," **General Systems: Yearbook of the Society for the Advancement of General Systems Theory,** 1:18–28.

Hampden-Turner, Charles. 1971. "The Borrowed Toolbox and Conservative Man," in **Radical Man.** Garden City, N.Y.: Doubleday, 1–22.

Hawes, Leonard C. 1973. "Elements of a Model for Communication Processes," **The Quarterly Journal of Speech,** 59:11–21.

Holtzman, W.H. 1967. "Statistical Models for the Study of Change in the Single Case," in **Problems in Measuring Change.** Madison, Wisconsin: University of Wisconsin Press. C.W. Harris, ed., 199–211.

Laszlo, Erwin. 1972. "Introduction: The Origins of General Systems Theory in the Work of von Bertalanffy," in **The Relevance of General Systems Theory: Papers Presented to Ludwig von Bertalanffy on His Seventieth Birthday.** New York: Braziller. Erwin Laszlo, ed., 1–11.

Liebow, Elliot. 1967. **Talley's Corner.** Boston: Little, Brown and Co.

Lofland, John. 1971. **Analyzing Social Settings.** Belmont, California: Wadsworth.

Maslow, Abraham. 1966. **The Psychology of Science.** Chicago: Henry Regnery.

Matson, Floyd. 1966. **The Broken Image.** Garden City, N.Y.: Doubleday.

McNemar, Q. 1962. **Psychological Statistics.** New York: Wiley.

Miller, James G. 1955. "Toward a General Theory for the Behavioral Sciences," **American Psychologist,** 10:513–31.

Monge, Peter R. 1973. "Theory Construction in the Study of Communication: The System Paradigm," **Journal of Communication,** 23:5–16.

Pearce, W. Barnett. 1973. "Interpersonal Communication Behavior and Communication Process: An Analysis of Perspectives and Concepts," paper presented at the annual conference of the Western Speech Communication Association, Albuquerque, New Mexico.

Polanyi, Michael. 1962. **Personal Knowledge.** Rev. ed. Chicago: University of Chicago Press.

———. 1966. **The Tacit Dimension.** Garden City, N.Y.: Anchor Doubleday.

Rossiter, Charles M., Jr. 1973. "The Search for a Humanistic Methodology," paper presented to the annual conference of the Association for Humanistic Psychology, Montreal, Canada.

Scheidel, Thomas M. 1971. "The Behavioral Scientist and the Speech Communication Process," paper presented at the annual conference of the Speech Communication Association, San Francisco.

Smith, David H. 1972. "Communication Research and the Idea of Process," **Speech Monographs,** 39:174–82.

Thayer, Lee. 1972. "Communication Systems," in **The Relevance of General Systems Theory: Papers Presented to Ludwig von Bertalanffy on His Seventieth Birthday.** New York: Braziller. Erwin Laszlo, ed., 93–121.

Tucker, Raymond K., and Herschel L. Mack. 1971. "Speech as Process: Effects of Experimental Design." **Speech Monographs,** 38:341–49.

Uhr, L. 1966. "Pattern Recognition," in **Pattern Recognition.** New York: Wiley. L. Uhr, ed., 365–81.

von Bertalanffy, Ludwig. 1967. **Robots, Men and Minds.** New York: Braziller.

Wald, A. 1947. **Sequential Analysis.** New York: Wiley.

Watzlawick, Paul, Janet H. Beavin, and Don D. Jackson. 1967. **Pragmatics of Human Communication.** New York: W.W. Norton.

Whyte, W.F. 1937. **Street Corner Society.** Chicago: University of Chicago Press.

Wilmot, William W., and John R. Wenburg. 1973. "Communication as Transaction," paper presented at the annual conference of the International Communication Association, Montreal, Canada.

For additional reading

Chapter Two

Barnlund, Dean. 1968. **Interpersonal Communication: Survey and Studies.** Boston: Houghton Mifflin.

Borden, George A., Richard B. Gregg, and Theodore G. Grove. 1969. **Speech Behavior and Human Interaction.** Englewood Cliffs, New Jersey: Prentice-Hall.

Carson, Robert C. 1969. **Interaction Concepts of Personality.** Chicago: Aldine.

Haney, William V. 1967. **Communication and Organizational Behavior: Text and Cases.** Homewood, Illinois: Richard D. Irwin. Rev. ed.

Johnson, Craig F., and George B. Klare. 1961. "General Models of Communication Research: A Survey of the Development of a Decade," **Journal of Communication,** 2:13–26.

Mortensen, C. David. 1972. **Communication: The Study of Human Interaction.** New York: McGraw-Hill.

Smith, David H. 1972. "Communication Research and the Idea of Process," **Speech Monographs,** 39:174–82.

Watzlawick, Paul, Janet Beavin, and Don Jackson. 1967. **Pragmatics of Human Communication.** New York: Norton.

Weaver, Carl H. 1972. **Human Listening: Processes and Behavior.** Indianapolis: Bobbs-Merrill.

Chapter Three

Brown, Charles T., and Paul W. Keller. 1973. **Monologue to Dialogue: An Exploration of Interpersonal Communication.** Englewood Cliffs, New Jersey: Prentice-Hall.

Carkhuff, Robert. 1969. **Helping and Human Relationships: A Primer for Lay and Professional Helpers.** New York: Holt, Rinehart and Winston.

Combs, Arthur W., Donald L. Avila, and William W. Purkey. 1971. **Helping Relationships: Basic Concepts for the Helping Professions.** Boston: Allyn and Bacon.

Giffin, Kim, and Bobby R. Patton, eds. 1971. **Basic Reading in Interpersonal Communication.** New York: Harper and Row.

Johannesen, Richard L. 1971. "The Emerging Concept of Communication as Dialogue," **The Quarterly Journal of Speech,** 57:373–82.

Matson, Floyd M., and Asley Montagu. 1967. **The Human Dialogue.** New York: Free Press.

Mayeroff, Milton. 1971. **On Caring.** New York: Harper and Row Perennial Library.

Rogers, Carl R. 1961. **On Becoming a Person.** Boston: Houghton Mifflin.

Chapter Four

Cozby, Paul C. 1973. "Self-Disclosure: A Literature Review," **Psychological Bulletin,** 79:73–91.

Culbert, Samuel A., 1968. **The Interpersonal Process of Self-Disclosure: It Takes Two to See One.** New York: Renaissance Editions, Inc.

Goffman, Erving. 1959. **The Presentation of Self in Everyday Life.** Garden City, New York: Doubleday. Anchor Books Edition.

Jourard, Sidney M. 1971. **Self-Disclosure: An Experimental Analysis of the Transparent Self.** New York: Wiley-Interscience.

————. 1971. **The Transparent Self.** New York: Van Nostrand Reinhold. Rev. ed.

Rogers, Carl R. 1961. **On Becoming a Person.** Boston: Houghton Mifflin. Chapters 17 and 18.

Appendix A of this book.

Chapter Five

Laing, R. D. 1967. **The Politics of Experience.** New York: Ballantine.
————, and A. Esterson. 1970. **Sanity, Madness and the Family.** Baltimore: Pelican.
Watzlawick, Paul, Janet H. Beavin, and Don D. Jackson. 1967. **Pragmatics of Human Communication.** New York: W. W. Norton.

Chapter Six

Deutsch, Morton. 1962. "Cooperation and Trust: Some Theoretical Notes," in **Nebraska Symposium on Motivation.** Lincoln: University of Nebraska Press, 275–319. (M.R. Jones, ed.)
Gibb, Jack. 1964. "Climate for Trust Formation," in **T-Group Theory and Laboratory Method New York:** Wiley, 279–309. (L. Bradford, J. Gibb and K. Benne, eds.)
Giffin, Kim, and Bobby Patton. 1971. "Personal Trust in Human Interaction" in **Basic Readings in Interpersonal Communication.** New York: Harper and Row, 375–91. (Kim Giffin and Bobby Patton, eds.)
Appendix B of this book.

Chapter Seven

Josephson, Eric, and Mary Josephson, eds. 1962. **Man Alone.** New York: Dell.
Laing, Ronald D., and A. Esterson. 1970. **Sanity, Madness, and the Family.** Baltimore: Penguin. 2nd ed.
Barrett, William, 1964. **What is Existentialism?** New York: Grove Press.
Fromm, Erich. 1968. **The Revolution of Hope: Toward a Humanized Technology.** New York: Bantam.
Moustakas, Clark. 1961. **Loneliness.** Englewood Cliffs, New Jersey: Prentice-Hall.
Schacht, Richard. 1971. **Alienation.** Garden City, New York: Anchor Doubleday.
Wilson, Colin. 1956. **The Outsider.** New York: Delta.

Chapter Eight

Axline, Virginia. 1967. **Dibs: In Search of Self.** New York: Ballantine.

Hall, Calvin S., and Gardner Lindzey. 1970. **Theories of Personality.** New York: John Wiley and Sons. 2nd ed.

Hampden-Turner, Charles. 1971. **Radical Man.** Garden City, New York: Anchor Doubleday.

Harris, Thomas. 1967. **I'm OK, You're OK.** New York: Harper and Row.

Maslow, Abraham. 1968. **Toward a Psychology of Being.** New York: Van Nostrand. Rev. 2nd ed.

Ruesch, Jurgen. 1973. **Therapeutic Communication,** New York: W.W. Norton. 2nd ed.

Wilson, Colin. 1972. **New Pathways in Psychology: Maslow and the Post-Freudian Revolution.** New York: Taplinger.

Index